Why the Soviets Violate Arms Control Treaties

Pergamon Titles of Related Interest

Bittman THE KGB & SOVIET DISINFORMATION

Borawski FROM THE ATLANTIC TO THE URALS: NEGOTIATING ARMS CONTROL AT THE STOCKHOLM CONFERENCE

Collins U.S.–SOVIET MILITARY BALANCE, 1980–1985

Davis ASYMMETRIES IN U.S. & SOVIET STRATEGIC DEFENSE PROGRAMS

Gareev M.V. FRUNZE, MILITARY THEORIST

Lin NEW WEAPON TECHNOLOGIES AND THE ABM TREATY

Mikheyev THE SOVIET PERSPECTIVE ON THE STRATEGIC DEFENSE INITIATIVE

Perry & Pfaltzgraff SELLING THE ROPE TO HANG CAPITALISM?: THE DEBATE ON WEST–EAST TRADE AND TECHNOLOGY TRANSFER

Schelling & Halperin STRATEGY & ARMS CONTROL

Shultz & Godson DEZINFORMATSIA: ACTIVE MEASURES IN SOVIET STRATEGY, Second Edition, Revised

Tsipis et al. ARMS CONTROL VERIFICATION

Weeks BRASSEY'S SOVIET AND COMMUNIST QUOTATIONS

Related Journal
(Free specimen copy available on request)
Defense Analysis

Why the Soviets Violate Arms Control Treaties

Joseph D. Douglass, Jr.

Published with the cooperation of the
Institute for Foreign Policy Analysis, Inc.,
Cambridge, Mass., and Washington, D.C.

PERGAMON-BRASSEY'S
International Defense Publishers, Inc.

WASHINGTON · NEW YORK · LONDON · OXFORD · BEIJING
FRANKFURT · SAO PAULO · SYDNEY · TOKYO · TORONTO

U.S.A. (Editorial)	Pergamon-Brassey's International Defense Publishers, 8000 Westpark Drive, Fourth Floor, McLean, Virginia 22102, U.S.A.
(Orders)	Pergamon Press, Maxwell House, Fairview Park, Elmsford, New York 10523, U.S.A.
U.K. (Editorial)	Brassey's Defence Publishers, 24 Gray's Inn Road, London WC1X 8HR
(Orders)	Brassey's Defence Publishers, Headington Hill Hall, Oxford OX3 0BW, England
PEOPLE'S REPUBLIC OF CHINA	Pergamon Press, Room 4037, Qianmen Hotel, Beijing, People's Republic of China
FEDERAL REPUBLIC OF GERMANY	Pergamon Press, Hammerweg 6, D-6242 Kronberg, Federal Republic of Germany
BRAZIL	Pergamon Editora, Rua Eça de Queiros, 346, CEP 04011, Paraiso, São Paulo, Brazil
AUSTRALIA	Pergamon-Brassey's Defence Publishers, P.O. Box 544, Potts Point, N.S.W. 2011, Australia
JAPAN	Pergamon Press, 8th Floor, Matsuoka Central Building, 1–7–1 Nishishinjuku, Shinjuku-ku, Tokyo 160, Japan
CANADA	Pergamon Press Canada, Suite No. 271, 253 College Street, Toronto, Ontario, Canada M5T 1R5

Copyright © 1988 Pergamon-Brassey's International
Defense Publishers, Inc.

All Rights Reserved. No part of this publication may be reproduced, stored in a retrieval system or transmitted in any form or by any means; electronic, electrostatic, magnetic tape, mechanical, photocopying, recording, or otherwise, without permission in writing from the publishers.

First edition 1988

Library of Congress Cataloging in Publication Data
Douglass, Joseph D.
Why the Soviets violate arms control treaties.
Includes index.
1. Nuclear arms control—Soviet Union. 2. Nuclear arms control—United States. 3. Soviet Union—Military policy.
4. Communist strategy. I. Title.
JX1974.7.D79   1988   327.1'74'0947   87-25703

British Library Cataloguing in Publication Data
Douglass, Joseph D.
Why the Soviets violate arms control treaties.
1. Arms control 2. Soviet Union—Foreign relations—1945-
I. Title
327.1'74   JX1974

ISBN 0-08-035960-4

Printed in Great Britain by A. Wheaton & Co. Ltd., Exeter

Contents

Preface	vii
Introduction	xi

1. The U.S. View of Soviet Policy — 1
  The Essence of Soviet Policy — 1
  The U.S. View — 2

2. Marxist-Leninist Ideology — 13
  Different Dimensions of the Ideology — 15
  Law and Morality — 22
  Armaments and War — 23

3. Political Strategy — 27
  Soviet Strategy: Marxism-Leninism or Big Power Politics? — 27
  Superiority as a Main Objective of Soviet Political Strategy — 31
  Prospects for Change — 33

4. Arms Control in Soviet Strategy — 38
  Soviet Disarmament Strategy — 38
  Nuclear Disarmament and Peaceful Coexistence — 40
  The Emergence of Arms Control as a Strategic Operation — 44
  Arms Control Goals and Objectives — 48

5. The Soviet View of the United States   54

Imperialism: The Source of All War   54
Effect of U.S. Efforts to Improve Relations with the USSR   57

6. Cheating and Deception   63

The Planning and Decision Process   64
Soviet Strategy for Responding to Cheating Charges   70
Soviet Instructions on Cheating and Deception   73
The Use of "Learned Professionals"   76
The Problems of Language   79

7. Risk Assessment   83

Probable Dominant Risks   87

8. Conclusions   94

APPENDICES

A   The Soviet Approach to Arms Control, by Zdzislaw M. Rurarz   97

B   Arms Control and Soviet Strategy, by Jan Sejna   121

C   Linguistic Deception and U.S.-Soviet Arms Control Treaties, by Igor Lukes   138

D   Summary of U.S. Reports on Soviet Violations, compiled by William R. Harris   155

E   A Soviet View of Arms Control: Lessons from the Past, by William F. Scott and Harriet Fast Scott   162

BIBLIOGRAPHY   185

INDEX   191

ABOUT THE AUTHOR   203

Preface

In November 1982 President Reagan asked his General Advisory Committee on Arms Control and Disarmament to conduct a detailed review of Soviet compliance with arms control treaties. As stated in the Committee's report, submitted one year later, this was the first concerted effort to examine arms control compliance since the start of the arms control process twenty-five years earlier. This review was followed by a series of five interagency studies conducted under the auspices of the National Security Council and reported to Congress in 1984–1985.

The results of these detailed examinations were, at best, discouraging. The Soviets were judged guilty of deliberate and serious violations, circumventions, and related transgressions that implicitly brought into question the entire arms control process. The violations were not just scattered or isolated cases, but rather were directed against nearly all major treaties and agreements.* In all cases, the U.S. government has raised its concern with the proper Soviet authorities who have responded with silence, with answers that clearly belie the facts, or with simple "nyets."

The only evident conclusion at this juncture is that there exists a serious, and probably unresolvable, difference between the objectives of the USSR and those of the United States in negotiating arms control "agreements." The heart of the problem, and crucial to the future of arms control, is the Soviet decision to "cheat"—to deliberately violate the agreements.

The purpose of this study is to gain an understanding of how the Soviets view cheating and what calculus, if any, enters into their assessment of risks when they decide to cheat. Because of the frequently erroneous

---

*A summary of the U.S. reports on violations, prepared by Dr. William R. Harris, is included as Appendix D.

interpretations in the West of Soviet interests and objectives, this study analyzes the Soviet decision process and policies as reflected in past Soviet practices and as understood by individuals who have lived and operated within the communist system, whose firsthand experience qualifies them as experts on selected facets of the Soviet decisionmaking system. The violations themselves, which have already been thoroughly scrutinized elsewhere, are not addressed here. The focus is on the questions: Why do the Soviets cheat, and what goes through their minds when they decide to cheat?

While the use of firsthand sources has many benefits, especially in light of the problems in analyzing data produced by a nation renowned for its tight censorship and deception/disinformation practices, the associated problems are equally obvious: finding sources with sufficiently high-level access to qualify as experts or true insiders; conducting thorough debriefings; and documenting, or otherwise confirming, important findings. Very few high-level officials in the Soviet Union or Eastern Europe have sought political asylum in the West, and none of those are former Soviet citizens who have had any direct access to the arms control decision process. Most importantly, there is a traditional reluctance in the West to accept such testimony as valid source material, especially when the message conveyed does not support the desired policy options.

The principal sources who have contributed to this study are Zdzislaw M. Rurarz and Jan Sejna, former high-level officials from Poland and Czechoslovakia, respectively. Zdzislaw M. Rurarz, Ph.D., had 25 years of experience in Polish military intelligence and was a former Professor of Economics at the Central School of Planning and Statistics in Warsaw. Dr. Rurarz participated in numerous international conferences and high-level meetings with Soviet counterparts, and served as economic advisor to the Ministry of Foreign Trade, the Ministry of Foreign Affairs, the Central Committee, and the First Secretary of the Communist Party of Poland, Edward Gierek. He also served for several years as division chief in the Ministry of Foreign Trade, as Deputy Ambassador to the United Nations, and as Special Advisor to the Secretary-General of the United Nations Conference on Trade and Development. He was appointed Ambassador to Japan in February 1981 and subsequently received a concurrent appointment to the Philippines. Dr. Rurarz left Poland and sought asylum in the United States in December 1981.

Jan Sejna, a political officer or commissar in the Czechoslovak Army, held a variety of high-level positions between 1956 and 1968. He was a member of the Central Committee and National Assembly, was on the Presidium of the National Assembly, and was a member of the Presidium Party Group. He was a member of the Main Political Administration, where he also served on the Bureau. At the Ministry of Defense, Sejna was First Secretary of the Party, Chief of the Minister's Cabinet, and a member of the Kolegium. He was a member of the Military Section of the Administration Department. His most important position was Secretary of the Defense Council. Jan Sejna left Czechoslovakia and sought asylum in the United States in February 1968.

Statements on Soviet behavior and policy, especially those made by the highest Soviet authorities from Lenin to Gorbachev, together with official statements of the Communist Party of the Soviet Union (CPSU), have been used to confirm and extend the analyses provided by Rurarz and Sejna. (See Appendices A and B.)

Other lower-level former officials who have contributed to this study are Tomas D. Schuman (formerly Yuri Bezmenov), Aleksandr A. Ushakov, and Anatoliy Golitsyn. Tomas D. Schuman, a linguist and journalist, was first employed by the KGB as an interpreter and was then assigned as a KGB officer to Novosti Press, which had been set up as a disinformation agency to serve the CPSU International Department and the KGB. He worked for the International Department and directly for the KGB in active measures operations prior to his leaving in 1970. Aleksandr A. Ushakov, Ph.D., was an Associate Professor in the Department of Philosophy at the Odessa Higher Maritime and Engineering Institute, where he taught courses on Marxism-Leninism and conducted research on methodology for officer selection and training prior to his leaving in May 1984. Anatoliy Golitsyn, a former KGB officer, provided a synopsis of his views and made available his lengthy manuscript on the evolution of Soviet political strategy in the 1950s. Golitsyn was trained in counterespionage and schooled at the KGB Academy. He served as a senior analyst in the NATO Section of the Information Department of the Soviet intelligence service and was posted to Finland, where, under cover as vice-consul, he worked in counterintelligence until December 1961, when he left and sought asylum in the United States.

Drawing on both firsthand knowledge and internal Soviet and East European materials, this study describes the Soviet decision process with respect to arms control in order to establish a basis for deducing what role arms control plays in Soviet strategy and how risk analysis enters into the Soviet decision process. Both Soviet and East European literature has been used wherever possible to provide confirmatory documentation or elaboration of the important points made by former communist officials. In general, specific details and recollections related to the arms control process—in some cases dating back 15 to 20 years—have been included in this report. These data are believed to be highly pertinent today because (1) they describe the manner in which the arms control process was initially established in the Soviet Union, and (2) Soviet strategic and arms control planning is a long-term process. The actions of Soviet leaders in the late 1950s and 1960s are directly relevant to the arms control treaties of the 1970s.

Dr. William F. Scott and Harriet Fast Scott have provided invaluable advice and assistance throughout the course of the study. They have reviewed official Soviet writings and unofficial statements, memoirs, and analyses to furnish background analyses of Soviet behavior (See Appendix E), insight into Soviet ideology and political strategy, and a better understanding of the role of arms control in Soviet strategy.

Because of the importance of language in Soviet strategy and a concern that this element of Soviet strategy is not widely appreciated, Dr. Igor Lukes was asked to examine the treaties from his perspective as a linguist and international relations specialist. He has reviewed the Russian and English versions of the more important arms control treaties and prepared an analysis (Appendix C) of the problems that result from the linguistic deceptions inherent in the Soviet use of language.

The assimilated material also has been subjected to critical review by several Western scholars with specialties in Soviet foreign policy and U.S. national security. Special thanks are extended to Dr. Alvin Z. Rubinstein, Dr. Paul Seabury, Mr. Brian Crozier, Dr. William R. Harris, Dr. William R. Van Cleave, Mr. Dmitry Mikheyev, Mr. Brian Dailey, and Colonel Raymond S. Sleeper (USAF, ret.), for their many comments and valuable suggestions. I also want to thank Dr. Uri Ra'anan and Dr. Richard H. Shultz for permission to refer to selected portions of their oral history interview project at the Fletcher School of Law and Diplomacy, Tufts University; Dr. William R. Harris for permission to use his summary tables of U.S. reports on Soviet violations; and Dr. Albert Weeks and Dr. Charles T. Baroch for their help in tracking down important supporting data.

Introduction

The Soviet Union's quest for world dominance is inherent in its Marxist-Leninist ideology. Marxism-Leninism provides a coherent world outlook and operating philosophy; it formalizes and legitimizes absolute totalitarian control of the state and the so-called world revolutionary movement. Understanding this ideology is an essential step in assessing Soviet objectives and in estimating realistically what can be accomplished through arms control.

The United States is not about to change the Soviet ideology, its goals, or its methods. Nor can the Soviet Union afford to change. Changes that do occur are, more often than not, mainly cosmetic or transitory, sometimes reflecting a shift in tactics and, occasionally, strategy. But the goals do not change, nor do the principles that govern the operation of the communist system. Even changes in strategy and tactics seem to be more a case of modernizing and assigning new names and trappings to methods and techniques that have proven successful in the past. Where changes are introduced, they are almost always designed to strengthen the ideology and the process by which the state seeks to achieve its goals. They are not changes to improve relations with the West—except those deceptively undertaken as a temporary expedient to enhance the Soviet Union's ability to triumph over the West.

In Soviet political strategy, arms control is a strategic military and intelligence tool that is used to help achieve the strategic goals of the state. Arms control is used to confirm intelligence on Western weapons systems, technologies, and plans. It is used in a counterintelligence role to test U.S. intelligence and to evaluate Soviet *maskirovka* and deception practices. Militarily, it is used to affect adversely U.S. defense programs, and, politically, it is used to split the bourgeoisie within Western nations and between nations. An especially important role of arms control is in promoting continued Western trade with, and financial assistance to, Soviet bloc countries. Conversely, arms control must not allow the West to gain accurate knowledge about Soviet weapons and technologies or lead to an adverse change in the balance of power.

While the Soviet preference is to structure treaties so that only the adversary is constrained, the Soviets will violate—or otherwise cheat on—any treaty when that is determined to further their interests. Cheating is an important tool used to advance state interests. Cheating, deception, disinformation, and misleading the enemy are vital functions of both party and government organizations because they help protect socialism, blind the enemy to the nature of the main strategic goals, and cover the methods used to achieve those goals. Accordingly, these activities are considered to be the preeminent responsibilities of the highest party and government officials. Failure to take advantage of an opportunity to serve state interests through cheating and deception would be regarded as a crime.

Normally, how and when cheating will be organized is decided before the treaty is signed. Moreover, at the same time, the response to be employed by the Soviets should the enemy detect cheating and raise the issue is also initially planned. As a general principle, such responses are to be "offensive denial," which means to deny any wrongdoing while simultaneously placing the blame on the enemy.

In deciding whether to cheat, the Soviets consider both positive and negative aspects. The positive aspects can be inferred from the basic arms control goals set forth above. The negative aspects are believed to be the risk that cheating would lead to: (1) a heightened political or military awareness in the West; (2) an adverse impact on the image of the Soviets as peaceloving, strictly defense-oriented, and the defender of all oppressed people, which might cause the Soviet Union to lose support among progressive movements and "realistic-thinking" politicians; and (3) an adverse impact on the flow of Western trade and financial assistance, the increase of which is one of the two major goals of the Soviet peaceful coexistence strategy—the other being an irreversible shift in the military balance of power in favor of the Soviet Union.

The Soviet Union is unlikely to be concerned about a possible U.S. defense response to violations; based on past experience, a U.S. "response" would likely result in a beneficial (from Moscow's perspective) delay in weapons systems development, as happened with the MX, Trident D-5, and B-1 programs. Further, the Soviets are likely to reason that a meaningful U.S. response is unlikely in light of the many anti-defense pressures in the United States that have been artfully cultivated by the Soviets over the past thirty years. The Soviets are more likely to be concerned that effective publicity of their cheating could damage their image among "progressive" and anti-defense organizations in the United States. However, the manner in which violations over the past five years have been surfaced and given publicity in the West has not generated any significant negative impact. The Soviets have good reason to have confidence in the long-term ability of their propaganda apparatus to overcome any such difficulties, should they arise.

The most serious Soviet concern would appear to be that their cheating might lead to a dampening of detente—which continues, albeit without publicity—and the related loss of trade and financial assistance. It might also lead to an increase in the types of restrictions the United States instituted following the Soviet invasion of Afghanistan and imposition of martial law in Poland. But it has become clear over the past three years, as trade and credits have expanded in synchronization with the public unfolding of a wide array of Soviet cheating, that this risk, while perhaps the most serious from the Soviet perspective, is also the least likely to occur.

In general, the Kremlin incurs little risk, because there has been no U.S. response other than mildly critical rhetoric. Actually, the situation is worse, because the main American response appears—as most evident in the chemical and biological case—to be to excuse or ignore Soviet behavior and place the burden on the United States itself to negotiate a "better treaty." Nevertheless, the Soviets have been careful to monitor U.S. complaints. In one case they actually stopped employment of chemical agents in Kampuchea following their signing of the 1925 Geneva Protocol in 1975 and the 1972 Biological and Toxin Weapons Convention treaties in March 1983. They are careful not to cheat where incontrovertible evidence could be collected by the enemy.

At the present time, a logical strategy for Soviet leaders is to bask in the warmth of very successful arms control results over the past twenty-five years and to conclude that during the remainder of the Reagan Administration they might as well simply prolong negotiations, rely on political pressures to constrain U.S. defense efforts, and continue to violate arms control treaties whenever they consider it advantageous to do so. Considering current U.S. practice, which essentially grants the Soviets all the benefits that accompany the spirit of arms control without imposing any penalties for cheating, the Soviets have little to risk by continuing their present policies of negotiating while cheating.

1
THE U.S. VIEW OF SOVIET POLICY

Widespread concern over Soviet violations of arms control treaties suggests that something is wrong. The treaties were not supposed to have been violated, or even circumvented. They were believed to have been based on "a mutual willingness to curb arms competition,"[1] and to have represented "a decisive turn away from the confrontations of the past quarter-century."[2]

By now, most observers recognize that the true situation was, and remains, quite different. The Soviets did not view arms control as U.S. decisionmakers thought they did. Accordingly, U.S. concern over Soviet violations and circumventions may really signal the presence of significant errors in the image of the Soviet Union that has dominated U.S. foreign and military policy for over twenty-five years.

THE ESSENCE OF SOVIET POLICY

Reduced to its simplest terms, Soviet policy is based on Marxist-Leninist ideology blended with traditional Russian imperialism. Marxism-Leninism defines the main strategic goals, sets forth the strategy and tactics that are used to achieve the goals, and provides the principles of organization and control that are used to maintain direction and discipline.

The Soviet goal or strategic aim is the victory of the working class over the capitalists, the establishment of dictatorships of the proletariat, the destruction of the bourgeoisie and of the entire capitalist system, and subsequent rule according to the principle of international proletarianism.[3]

The control center, the leading force in the process, is the Communist Party of the Soviet Union (CPSU). The party is all important in the Soviet system. The party, along with its instruments of control and power, is the State. It monitors policy direction and ensures that the policy and strategy are based on the firm foundation of Marxist-Leninist principles. The party is responsible for establishing and assuring adherence to the main strategic goals. The party determines the strategy, approves the plans for implementing the strategy, and introduces corrections when appropriate.

This is the essence of Soviet policy as described by former high-level communist officials: Marxism-Leninism; Russian tradition; the party; strategic goals; and the principles, strategy, tactics, and planning used to achieve the goals. Official Soviet documentation also repeatedly emphasizes that these elements—except for the Russian tradition—are of paramount importance. Yet it is precisely this essence of Soviet policy and goals that is missing from the image of the Soviet Union held by so many Americans, including our policymakers. As a result, the U.S. image of the Soviet Union diverges sharply from the image of the Soviet Union that is projected by Soviet literature, by Soviet behavior, and by former high-level communist officials.

THE U.S. VIEW

In what has become common practice in the West, the importance of communist ideology is first stressed and then immediately ignored. A good example of this process is U.S. policy leading to the various arms accords of 1972. In 1970, President Nixon wrote to Congress:

> We will deal with the Communist countries on the basis of a precise understanding of what they are about in the world, and thus of what we can reasonably expect of them and ourselves. Let us make no mistake about it, leaders of the Communist nations are serious and determined. Because we do take them seriously, we will not underestimate the depth of ideological disagreement or the disparity between their interests and ours. . . . We will regard our Communist adversaries first and foremost as nations pursuing their own interests as *they* perceive these interests, just as we follow our own interests as we see them.[4] (Emphasis in original.)

While this approach is described as the basis of the U.S. policy on arms control negotiations with the Soviet Union, the subsequent dialogue and actions of the United States present a far different picture. For the most part, Soviet ideology and strategy—both political and military strategy—simply do not appear to have entered into the U.S. policymaking or negotiations process. Sometimes these factors are ignored, sometimes they are misunderstood, and sometimes they are just not accepted. Whatever the situation, Soviet ideology and strategy are not an important influence on U.S. policy. This is the heart of the Soviet violations problem. For example, a fundamental error of U.S. decisionmakers is their characterization of Soviet ideology as Marxism.[5] According to former high-level communist officials, this is a very significant error, because the ideology of the Soviet Union is Marxism-Leninism, not Marxism. Marxism is a *theory* of spontaneous workers' revolt. In contrast, Marxism-Leninism is a *tool* used to pursue Soviet state interests. Marxism is used in Marxism-Leninism to lend an aura of respectability, a deceptive cover, to what really is a strategy for world conquest.

The difference between Marxism and Marxism-Leninism is most apparent in four important aspects: (1) Proletarian internationalism is one of the primary linchpins of Marxism-Leninism. Proletarian internationalism is the principle that the Soviet Union is the supreme authority over the affairs of other socialist nations. But there is nothing in Marxism that cedes this authority to the Soviets or suggests that any loyalty is due the Soviet Union. Instead, this is a fundamental tenet of Marxism-Leninism. (2) In Marxism, the workers' revolution is a spontaneous, self-generated movement. There is nothing that suggests the movement is to be orchestrated by or directed from Moscow, which is another tenet of Marxism-Leninism. (3) Nothing in Marxism places a duty on the working class or communist movement to combat anti-Sovietism. (4) In Marxism-Leninism, the very concept of revolution is a deception. What is really meant is the takeover and exploitation of the people, not a revolution and freeing of the people from oppression, as Marx envisioned.

As described by Brian Crozier,

> Leninism added two main ingredients to Marxism: a successful technique for seizing power, and a range of techniques for extending the ideology of Marxism-Leninism all over the world. But note one other point: as the original home of the "first workers' revolution," the Soviet Union itself decides, or claims the right to decide, just what constitutes Marxist-Leninist orthodoxy. In practice, therefore, it is not just the ideology that is exported, but Soviet power.[6]

Perhaps the best indication of the strong difference between Marxism and Marxism-Leninism, as described by former communist officials, is the actual dislike for Marx that is prevalent within the Soviet state apparatus. Marx understood the Russians too well, and he even advised Engels that communism would be doomed if it were first established in Russia. "Russia's policy is changeless," he wrote. "Its methods, its tactics, its maneuvers may change, but the Pole Star of its policy—world domination—is a fixed star."[7] Marxism was merely adopted by Lenin as a cover to conceal his own political strategy and, in so doing, deceive the masses.

While acknowledging the importance of understanding Soviet ideology and interests, U.S. policymakers in practice seem to ignore or downgrade these elements of Soviet policy. Thus, *U.S. Foreign Policy for the 1970s* states, as a basic premise of U.S. policy, that "the Marxist dream of international Communist unity has disintegrated."[8] Unquestionably, international communism has suffered setbacks, most notably the breaking away of China from Soviet domination. But to conclude that the Soviet dream of a world socialist republic has been shattered or has disintegrated, or that Marxism-Leninism is any less important, or that Soviet leaders are any less determined, is risky and unwarranted.

In approaching the arms control negotiation process, the United States decided that "It was no longer realistic to allow Soviet-American relations to be predetermined by ideology"[9]; ideology does not "preclude serious consideration of disputed issues"[10]; and "both sides had to recognize that in this continuing competition there would be no permanent victor, and equally important, that to focus one's own policy on attempts to gain advantages at the other's expense, could only aggravate tensions and precipitate counteractions."[11] These interpretations are contrary to the tenets of Marxism-Leninism, which admit no compromises in its ideology, hold that its goal of complete and permanent victory is not only realistic but preordained, and actually sponsor a policy that is organized to introduce and deal with tension. While there have been Western counteractions to Soviet challenges, more often than not these have been ineffective, and in the case of arms control, almost nonexistent.

In U.S. policy it is rare to find statements of Soviet goals or aims, of which the most important are to replace competing forms of government with dictatorships of the proletariat and to destroy totally the bourgeoisie and its entire state apparatus. Where Soviet goals are mentioned, as in the case of ideology, they are usually dismissed as not relevant. Rather than recognize that Soviet Marxist-Leninist goals and strategy exist, which is an essential step in devising an effective U.S. counterstrategy, the approach of U.S. policymakers has been to see the Soviet Union as opportunistic or pragmatic. As an example, we can use Dr. Henry Kissinger's background discussion on the development of President Nixon's foreign policy:

> The question is continually asked: What are the Soviet Union's ultimate aims? What are the Soviet leaders' real intentions? It may be the wrong question. It seems to imply that the answer lies in the secret recesses of the minds of the Soviet leaders, as if Brezhnev might divulge it if awakened in the middle of the night or caught in an unguarded moment. Focusing on the question of ultimate aims is bound to leave the democracies uncertain and hesitant at each new Soviet geopolitical move, as they try to analyze and debate among themselves whether the intrinsic value of the area at stake is of any "strategic importance," or whether it heralds a turn to a hard line. . . . It seems to me more useful, therefore, to view Soviet strategy as essentially one of ruthless opportunism.[12]

In characterizing the Soviets as "opportunistic," the implication is that no strategy guides Soviet actions. This avoids the need to come to grips with the reality of Soviet strategic planning (discussed below). This "opportunistic" view also serves to justify the general lack of strategy and strategic planning in the United States. To a certain extent, the Soviets are opportunistic. If opportunities arise that enable the Soviets to achieve their goals more quickly or easily, they will exploit those opportunities—when they fit into overall Soviet strategy. But as such, they are not isolated cases as the term "opportunistic" suggests. They are part of Soviet strategy and operations plans. Soviet policy is Marxist-Leninist, and it turns "opportunistic" only when opportunities can be incorporated into Soviet strategy.

While the Soviets may appear to be constantly probing for weakness, this image draws attention away from the decades of preparation that normally have preceded the probing. This is particularly evident in U.S. complaints of Soviet takeover activity in the 1970s, actions that were contrary to U.S. concepts of linkage that the Soviets were supposed to have "accepted" as part of the SALT process.[13] These complaints only reflect the failure of the Administration and many commentators to recognize the longstanding and not-about-to-be-abandoned Soviet strategy of conquest through subversion and "revolutionary wars"—a process that was intensified under Khrushchev in 1957 and again in 1961, and by Brezhnev in 1968—or the Soviet strategy of using "peace" campaigns and arms control as a cover for such activities. Of course, if one is to disparage their ideology, then it is only natural to place little credence in their goals. Similarly, when Soviet policy is characterized as "pragmatic," the implication is that Soviet policy is governed by reason (reason consistent with Western logic) and not unduly influenced by theories or ideas, that is, by Marxism-Leninism.

The failure of the United States to take into account Soviet ideology and political strategy is embarrassingly evident in the Declaration on Basic Principles of Relations that was signed, along with the ABM Treaty and Interim Agreement to Limit Strategic Arms, in Moscow in May 1972. This declaration has received major emphasis in Soviet literature. In contrast, it receives but scant attention in the United States, even though it represents a major victory for Soviet political strategy. The declaration stands as official U.S. acceptance of Soviet peaceful coexistence strategy as a basis for mutual relations. The opening statement in the treaty reads: "They [the U.S. and USSR] will proceed from the common determination that in the nuclear age there is no alternative to conducting their mutual relations on the basis of peaceful coexistence."

Peaceful coexistence was introduced in the early 1920s by G.V. Chicherin, Lenin's Commissar for Foreign Affairs, and then developed by Lenin.[14] It was given new life by Khrushchev and made the centerpiece of contemporary Marxist-Leninist strategy. Since 1955, a major goal of Soviet policy has been to force the United States to accept peaceful coexistence as the only alternative to nuclear war. The role of peaceful coexistence, one of the fundamental deceptions of Marxism-Leninism in practice, is stated very clearly in the fifth (1986) edition of *Soviet Military Power*, which correctly refers to peaceful coexistence as "the furtherance of socialist revolution and class struggle with industrialized nations by means short of major war."[15] That is, under peaceful coexistence, the West is not to use military power to change the status quo of the Soviet empire or to oppose its further expansion. Moreover, an integral part of peaceful coexistence calls for the United States to provide economic and trade assistance to the Soviet Union so that it can more quickly and easily destroy the nonsocialist nations, most importantly, the United States.

Peaceful coexistence "is subordinate to the aims and requirements of the world revolutionary process and the struggle against imperialism. It cannot be interpreted or applied in isolation from the fundamental Leninist propositions on the ways and forms of the world revolutionary movement."[16] Peaceful coexistence does not relate to peace, but rather is a form of the class struggle. Indeed, as stated in the final communique of the 1960 World Communist Conference, peaceful coexistence implies the *intensification* of the international class struggle.[17]

The former Canadian Ambassador to the Soviet Union, Robert A.D. Ford, had this to say about the 1972 Declaration on Basic Principles of Relations:

> The Soviets never concealed what they meant by peaceful coexistence and must have been delighted if not somewhat mystified when President Nixon and Mr. Kissinger accepted the use of the phrase in the official American-Soviet documents signed in Moscow in 1972. Indeed, it is baffling that this was done. The Canadian Prime Minister, Pierre Trudeau, the year before, politely rejected its inclusion in the Canadian-Soviet declarations.[18]

The semantics of Soviet political strategy and Marxist-Leninist ideology are found throughout this treaty: for example, equality; noninterference in internal affairs; peace and security; general and complete disarmament; sovereign equality; legislative bodies; and the renunciation of claims to special privileges by either country in any region, which the United States "interpreted as a denial of the Brezhnev Doctrine."[19]

It is also clear from Kissinger's description of the negotiations that led to the declaration on basic principles that President Nixon and he were uncertain why the Soviets appeared so interested in statements of "principles" unless it was just a Soviet "device to create the impression that major progress is taking place in bilateral relations."[20] This is another problem with the "pragmatic and opportunist" view of the Soviet Union in U.S. policy: It leads American officials to the erroneous conclusion that the principles—of organization, control, military conflict, strategy and tactics, foreign policy, and so forth—which dominate Soviet official literature and are repeatedly emphasized by former high-level communist officials, have no real function or importance.

The picture that emerges is a U.S. image of the Soviet Union that is, for the most part and in the most important areas, determined by a combination of Western concepts and value judgments (mirror-imaging) and by either a reluctance to face the reality of Soviet goals or by a desire to mold the image so that it supports an acceptable or desirable course of action—that is, the image is molded to fit the policy. Moreover, when the implementing details of Soviet policy are also considered, it becomes clear that the U.S. image of the Soviet Union is distorted by an extensive Soviet strategic deception program that is designed to promote exactly such distortions of the Soviet Union while "misleading the enemy [i.e., the United States] concerning the basic questions of State policy."[21]

When U.S. decisionmakers downgrade the importance of Marxist-Leninist ideology, they also downgrade the importance of the CPSU, which has the leading role in ensuring adherence to the Leninist line and goals. For example, "The Soviet system is unstable politically; it has no mechanism for succession. . . . It is one of the ironies of elaborated Communist states that *the Communist Party has no real function* even though it permeates every aspect of society."[22] (Emphasis added.) Or, "The Party apparatus duplicates every existing hierarchy without performing any function. It members are watchdogs lacking criteria. . . ."[23] It is difficult to conceive of an image that is more at odds with the situation as described by former high-level communist officials.

Closely coupled with ideology, goals, and the role of the party is Soviet strategy and long-range planning. Like the former, the concept of Soviet long-range strategic planning is another of the very important dimensions of Soviet policy that is lacking in the U.S. image of the Soviet Union. Kissinger explains the view in the U.S. policy community quite accurately: "Nothing could be more mistaken than to fall in with the myth of an inexorable Soviet advance carefully orchestrated by some super-planners."[24] This was his belief and one that he conveyed quite clearly to President Nixon: "I sent the President an analysis of Soviet policy at the end of 1969, which I prepared with the help of Hal Sonnenfeldt and Bill Hyland of my staff. It began by rejecting the proposition that Soviet policy necessarily followed a master plan. . . . My analysis concluded: 'In sum, there does not seem to be any single unifying thread to Soviet policy.'"[25]

The lack of attention in intelligence analyses to Soviet strategic planning or grand strategy was described by Richard Pipes in congressional hearings in 1980:

> The fundamental problem is that the people drafting these [national intelligence] estimates do not believe that there is such a thing as a Russian or Soviet grand strategy, for which reason they deal with each aspect of Soviet

behavior separately. They deal with politics and military affairs separately, economic, propaganda and ideology separately, and then within each of these categories, with each item, such as each weapons system, separately. There isn't some kind of an overview which operates on the assumption that there is an overall Soviet strategy of which these weapons and so on are expressions.[26]

Additional insight is provided by the official debriefing of Jan Sejna in 1968–1969. During his debriefing, he told U.S. officials that in his opinion the most important information he possessed was his detailed knowledge of the "Long-Range Plan for the Next Ten to Fifteen Years and Beyond," which was the Soviet political strategy given to the East European satellites for coordinated planning in 1967, but that he would not discuss it until the decision to grant him political asylum had been reached. After that decision was made, he was never debriefed on the plan, not even after an interview discussing the plan was published by Lord Chalfont in the United Kingdom in 1975 and after Walter Hahn subsequently drew attention to Chalfont's articles and Sejna's knowledge in *Strategic Review*.[27]

Notwithstanding numerous statements on Soviet strategy and long-range planning by former communist officials, and the importance that is attributed to such activity in official Soviet documents, the U.S. image of the Soviet Union denies the existence of a "master plan" or "orchestration." Actually, the situation is worse than this, as there appears not to be the slightest concept of what a master plan might look like or of what orchestration is possible. This neglect lies at the heart of the arms control problem: It results in a widespread failure to recognize the existence of Soviet strategy and the role of arms control in that strategy.

Complementing the set of perceptions, or misperceptions, of Soviet policy in general is a similar set on Soviet military and armaments policy. The crux of these perceptions that have dominated U.S. arms control policy is that the Soviets view the utility of nuclear weapons and nuclear war in the same manner as U.S. decisionmakers view them: namely, there can be no victor in nuclear war; both sides want to stop the arms race; and the Soviet Union is interested in the stability associated with strategic balance and will be satisfied when parity is achieved.[28] For example:

> Each of us had the power single-handedly to destroy most of mankind. Paradoxically, this very fact, and the global interests of both sides, created a certain common outlook, a kind of interdependence for survival. Although we competed, our conflict did not admit of resolution by victory in the classical sense. We seemed compelled to coexist. We had an inescapable joint obligation to build a structure for peace. Recognition of this reality has been the keystone of United States policy since 1969.[29]

"Both sides have recognized a vital mutual interest in halting the dangerous momentum of the nuclear arms race."[30] And, "The more nearly equal strategic balance between the United States and the Soviet Union suggested that conditions might be optimal for reaching agreement to limit strategic competition."[31]

In line with these perceptions, in his May 1973 U.S. foreign policy statement, following the signing of the interim agreement and the declaration of basic principles, the President reported to Congress: "For the first time two nations agreed to limit the strategic weapons that are the heart of their national survival."[32] Within less than three months following the signing of these agreements, U.S. intelligence had received clear indications that the Soviet view was quite different from the American and that the agreements signed would not affect Soviet plans. This data was reinforced in 1973 by a British intelligence report on Brezhnev's view of detente and the arms control process. The contents of this report were first made public by the *New York Times* in September 1973.[33] Brezhnev had explained to his East European comrades that arms control and detente were being pursued as a tactical shift designed to assist the Soviet Union in strengthening its military and economic power so that by 1985 "a decisive shift in the correlation of forces" would enable the Soviets to "exert our will whenever we need to."

This speech, as reported by William Beecher in 1977, was presented at a secret meeting of East European Communist Party leaders in Prague. This meeting was called to assuage fears that Brezhnev was ready to sacrifice East European interests at the altar of detente. Brezhnev's message was that detente was designed to serve their interests, not compromise them. "We are achieving with detente what our predecessors have been unable to achieve using the mailed fist."[34]

The Soviet detente strategy also had been brought to the attention of U.S. officials in the summer of 1970 during the debriefings of the former Novosti-KGB propaganda specialist, Tomas D. Schuman. He stated that the first time he had encountered the word "detente" was in a classified teleprinter dispatch from the Moscow Novosti headquarters in 1968. Subsequently, in the fall of 1969, Nikolai Agayantz, a KGB officer and member of the CPSU's International Department, explained to a small gathering of Novosti-KGB staff members in Ambassador Pegov's office at the USSR embassy in India that a new project, "detente," would "bring the policy of the Party to the knowledge of the masses and facilitate the national liberation and anti-colonial struggle." (Nikolai Agayantz was the son of General-Major Ivan Agayantz, the head of the KGB disinformation Department D.) Following Agayantz's briefing, Schuman returned to the Novosti offices, where his senior colleagues, Valery Neyev and Alexander (Sasha) Gornov, explained that "detente" was not just a newly coined propaganda cliché; rather, it was part of a new strategy, based on the theory and practice of the ideological offensive as formulated in various texts, such as *The Art of War* by Sun Tzu. As Schuman recalls, the only reaction of U.S. officials to his recounting the episode was, "Don't you think you're being too paranoid?"

It was not until 1975 that an accurate appraisal of detente emerged from the intelligence community—in the form of an unclassified Defense Intelligence Agency report, *Detente in Soviet Strategy*.[35] The report spelled out Soviet objectives through detente, including the breakup of Western alliances; freer access to Western trade, credit, and technology; establishment of Soviet political, military, technological, and economic superiority worldwide; and cancellation of U.S. nuclear superiority without provoking extensive Western counterefforts.[36] Publication of this report was met with anger by the State Department and White House. It was the "last straw" that led to the dismissal of Secretary of Defense James Schlesinger.

In attempting to understand why the Soviets violate arms control agreements, the place to begin is by recognizing that little attention is given in the United States to Soviet ideology, political and military strategy, and tactics. These factors, as they relate to arms control, are examined in the following chapters. Because of the importance of Soviet ideology and the clear failure in the West to understand its role in the arms control dialogue, the analysis begins with a brief survey of Marxism-Leninism and how it functions in the Soviet system, according to former high-level communist officials. Perhaps the most important insight is that there need be no mystery regarding Soviet ideology, strategy, or tactics, or surprise over Soviet violations. The data on Soviet ideology and behavior are abundant and clear. The only mystery is why the West refuses to face the facts.

NOTES

1. *U.S. Foreign Policy for the 1970s: A Report to the Congress by Richard Nixon*, February 9, 1972 (Washington, D.C.: U.S. Government Printing Office, 1972), p. 171. (Hereinafter cited as *U.S. Foreign Policy for the 1970s*, with the appropriate year.)
2. Ibid., 1973, p. 26.
3. See, for example, *Fundamentals of Marxism-Leninism* (Moscow: Foreign Languages Publishing House, 1961); *Leninist Strategy and Tactics* (Moscow: Novosti Press Agency Publishing House, 1969); and *The Fundamentals of Marxist-Leninist Philosophy* (Moscow: Progress Publishers, 1974).
4. *U.S. Foreign Policy for the 1970s*, 1970, op. cit., pp. 134–135.
5. Ibid., 1970, pp. 3, 133, 136. See also Henry Kissinger, *White House Years* (Boston, Mass.: Little, Brown, 1979), pp. 119, 525; and Alexander M. Haig, Jr., *Caveat* (New York: Macmillan, 1984), pp. 28–30, 98.
6. Brian Crozier, *Strategy of Survival* (New Rochelle, N.Y.: Arlington House, 1978), p. 128.

7. Paul W. Blackstock and Bert F. Hoselitz, editors, *The Russian Menace to Europe by Karl Marx and Fredrick Engels* (Glencoe, Ill.: The Free Press, 1952), p. 106; cited in Dr. Albert L. Weeks, "The Kremlin's Russian Superiority Complex," *Military Intelligence*, January–March 1986.
8. *U.S. Foreign Policy for the 1970s*, 1970, op. cit., p. 3.
9. Ibid., 1973, p. 27.
10. Ibid.
11. Ibid.
12. Kissinger, *White House Years*, op. cit., pp. 118–119.
13. Richard M. Nixon, *The Memoirs of Richard Nixon* (New York: Grosset & Dunlap, 1978), p. 346.
14. Crozier, *Strategy of Survival*, op. cit., pp. 24, 132. See also V. Trukhanovsky, "Proletarian Internationalism and Peaceful Coexistence—Foundation of the Leninist Foreign Policy," in *Principles of Lenin's Foreign Policy* (Moscow: Novosti Press Agency Publishing House, 1970).
15. Department of Defense, *Soviet Military Power* (Washington, D.C.: U.S. Government Printing Office, 5th edition, March 1986), p. 7.
16. K. Kapchenko, "The Leninist Theory and Practice of Socialist Foreign Policy," in *Principles of Lenin's Foreign Policy*, op. cit., p. 21.
17. Crozier, *Strategy of Survival*, op. cit., p. 133.
18. Robert A.D. Ford, "The Soviet Union: The Next Decade," *Foreign Affairs*, Summer 1984, p. 1141.
19. Kissinger, *White House Years*, op. cit., p. 1250.
20. Ibid., p. 1132.
21. KGB training manual, quoted in the CIA study, *Soviet Covert Action and Propaganda*, Deputy Director for Operations, CIA; in U.S. Congress, House, *Soviet Covert Action (The Forgery Offensive)*, Hearings before the Subcommittee on Oversight of the Permanent Select Committee on Intelligence (Washington, D.C.: U.S. Government Printing Office, 1980), p. 63.
22. Kissinger, *White House Years*, op. cit., pp. 119–120.
23. Henry Kissinger, *Years of Upheaval* (Boston, Mass.: Little, Brown, 1982), p. 244.
24. Kissinger, *White House Years*, op. cit., p. 120.
25. Ibid., pp. 161–162.
26. U.S. Congress, House, *Soviet Strategic Forces*, Hearings before the Subcommittee on Oversight of the Permanent Select Committee on Intelligence, February 7 and 20, 1980 (Washington, D.C.: U.S. Government Printing Office, 1980), p. 34. See also Richard Pipes, *Survival Is Not Enough* (New York: Simon & Schuster, 1984).
27. Walter Hahn, "A Soviet Game-Plan?," *Strategic Review*, Spring 1983. Lord Chalfont's articles in *The Times* (London) were: "Moscow's Brutal Reality" (July 28, 1975); "How Israel Fits into the Jigsaw of Soviet Power" (August 4, 1975); and "How Britain's Economic Difficulties Help the Soviet Grand Strategy" (September 1, 1975).
28. A detailed analysis of distortions in U.S. perceptions of Soviet military strategy is presented in William C. Green, *U.S. Interpretations of Soviet Publications on the Nuclear Weapons Policy of the USSR 1950–1980*, Ph.D. Thesis, University of Southern California, May 1986.

29. *U.S. Foreign Policy for the 1970s*, 1973, op. cit., p. 36.
30. Ibid., 1970, p. 3.
31. Ibid., 1973, p. 27.
32. Ibid., 1973, p. 11.
33. John W. Finney, "Brezhnev Said to Assure East Europe that Accords with West are a Tactic," *New York Times*, September 17, 1973.
34. William Beecher, "Brezhnev Termed Detente a Ruse, 1973 Report Said," *Boston Globe*, February 11, 1977. This report is confirmed in Wynfred Joshua, *Detente in Soviet Strategy*, Defense Intelligence Agency, September 2, 1975, p. 6; Crozier, *Strategy of Survival*, op. cit., p. 76; Winston Churchill II, *Defending the West* (Westport, Conn.: Arlington House Publishers, 1981); and Charles T. Baroch, *Freedom Under Communist Siege: A Primer On Marxism-Leninism*, Republican Study Committee, Washington, D.C., October 28, 1985.
35. Joshua, op. cit.
36. For a broader discussion of detente in the context of Soviet strategy, see Crozier, *Strategy of Survival*, op. cit., pp. 72–100.

2

MARXIST-LENINIST IDEOLOGY

The common tendency in the West is to disparage Marxist-Leninist ideology. For example, as described by the conservative columnist George Will:

> The Soviet elite subscribes to a "science" utterly insulated from evidence. The Soviet regime, armed to its iron teeth and ignorant as a stump, is lurching around on the world stage preening itself on its "science" while subscribing to the superstitions of a 19th-century German who sat scribbling in the British Museum, imagining the future.... Marxism-Leninism sits like a squat rock unmarked by the waves of evidence that it is nonsense.[1]

Many commentators, defectors, and Sovietologists claim that communist ideology is dead. This and the preceding example pose a delicate question: If the ideology is just gibberish, ancient incantations, dead or dying, then how can it be as important as former high-level communist officials insist it is?

The confusion that exists was readily apparent in the news reports on the Reagan-Gorbachev summit in the fall of 1985. Reporters expressed their surprise that Gorbachev sounded like a *Pravda* editorial. They were disturbed by his image of the United States, an image that corresponded closely with traditional Marxist-Leninist views of the United States as a corrupt society controlled by capitalists, in which average citizens are exploited by the ruling class and government policy is made to protect the vested interests of the rich. A *New York Times* article reported, "There may be an element of posturing and calculated propaganda, but all the evidence suggests that the man sincerely believes these things."[2]

There are several different ways to explain what Soviet ideology is and why it is important. The simplest is that the Soviet people have been immersed in Marxism-Leninism daily since their first days in grade school.

Those who resist the concepts drop out or are kicked out of the system. Those who remain learn that (1) in order to advance, they must abide by the ideology and employ it in everyday life, and (2) how far they advance depends on how well they learn what the ideology really is and requires. Whether or not they believe the ideology is valid is unimportant. That is the main point. Whether you believe the ideology is nonsense or dead is irrelevant, because it is an active and effective force, and in this sense it is very much alive.

A good example of how the ideology operates is provided by Michael Voslensky, who describes conditions in the Soviet Union:

> It is in fact practically impossible to find a convinced Communist in the Soviet Union. They are to be found only in nonsocialist countries. Nowadays nomenklaturist propaganda does not even take the trouble to try to make people believe what it says. Its aim is a different one, namely to make Soviet citizens understand that they must use a definite phraseology. . . . If anyone dares to cast doubt on a propagandist claim or actually deny it, the nomenklatura does not try to reason with or instruct him, but punishes him. The labor camp and the firing squad are not the only penalties available; the security agencies have almost unlimited powers and have full authority to make the punishment fit the "crime."[3]

The staying power of the ideology is explained another way by Brian Crozier, a noted British authority on communism and Soviet strategy:

> Even when events disprove the assumptions of Marxism-Leninism (as has been the case in many areas), not only is the dogma not rejected, but it is reaffirmed. The dogma, in fact, *can't* be abandoned (though it can be and is modified from time to time) for it is the *only* claim to legitimacy of the ruling party in the Soviet Union and of ruling Communist Parties wherever they may be (including countries hostile to Moscow, such as China). The pressures for world revolution go on relentlessly, and if at any time they appear to have abated, the abatement is purely tactical because conditions are judged temporarily unfavorable. *Communists never give up.*[4] (Emphasis in original.)

At the same time, there also appears to be considerable evidence of varying degrees of belief in the ideology. Consider, for example, the Nobel Laureate and human rights activist, Andrei Sakharov. In an article he wrote shortly after being exiled to Gorky, he examines the varying reasons why many people promote Soviet goals:

> Some of them are motivated by ideas that at least merit discussion. After all, in the Soviet Union, the ideological epicenter, and in China as well, communist ideology is not a complete fraud, not a total delusion. It arose from a striving for truth and justice, like other religious, ethical and philosophical systems. Its weakness, its failure and its degradation—evident from the very beginning—represent a complex historical, scientific and psychological phenomenon that requires separate analysis.[5]

It is not unusual for people from many walks of life to attribute the weaknesses and failures of the ideology to normal human frailties, or officially to the capitalists, their universal scapegoat, rather than to the internal structure of the ideology. Indeed, this is one of the operating principles of Marxist-Leninist politics: the problems lie with individuals and with government ministries, not with the party—which is responsible for successes, not failures.

Still a different example of belief in the ideology is provided by Anatoliy Golitsyn. In analyzing the events of the decade of the 1950s, he wrote that toward the end of Stalin's life "ideology was dead and propaganda ineffective." The reasons Golitsyn listed in support of his conclusion were numerous: the classless society had given rise to a two-class society, the new social elite versus the proletariat and peasants. The salaries of the elite had risen and their privileges had expanded. Corruption was widespread and the most "democratic" constitution in the world denied all rights and freedoms to its citizens. He then explained that following Stalin's death there were efforts from many quarters to restructure and reform, led by people such as Beria, Khrushchev, and Malenkov, to mention a few. Reforms proceeded immediately in intelligence affairs, military and foreign policy, and internal domestic policy, all of which were ideologically aligned and designed to steer the communist ship back on course. "By 1958 the crisis of the communist regime had been stemmed but not dispelled. The communist party apparatus, tired of the power struggle, longed for consistent policy and higher motivation than the personal interests of their leaders. They wanted to resume the traditional role of the party as the builder of a new society and organizer of its victories."[6] Thus, the ideology was in no sense dead, nor were people merely responding to the dictates of the state.

DIFFERENT DIMENSIONS OF THE IDEOLOGY

Marxism-Leninism is not a simple subject to study or describe. The verbiage tends to be obtuse, pedantic, dogmatic, and, as stressed by George Will, detached from reality. Notwithstanding these negative characteristics, it has been extremely effective insofar as the Soviet Union is concerned. The Soviet Union now claims that more than one-third of mankind has embraced Marxism-Leninism. Over the past thirty years, the USSR has overtaken the United States in most categories of military power. Its economy, notwithstanding its critical shortcomings, has never been stronger.

Marxism-Leninism was described by Yuri Andropov, just prior to his promotion to General Secretary, as a "textbook for revolution." Jan Sejna, a former high-ranking Czechoslovak political officer, describes it as a tool that is employed by the hierarchy to enforce discipline, maintain direction, and provide the framework within which the decision process operates.

It is useful to approach Marxism-Leninism from several different directions: its idealistic goals, its theoretical constructs, and its practical side—the instructions or "blueprints" for action, and the manner in which the ideology is used. Marxism-Leninism has a variety of internal mechanisms that perform different functions. In some cases, these are clearly and straightforwardly expressed. In most cases, however, there are major differences between what is said (or left unsaid) and what is meant. Marxism-Leninism is a masterpiece of deception and these deceptions are essential to its operation.

The *idealistic goals* are the most widely appreciated element of Marxism-Leninism. These goals are the proletarian revolution, the workers' revolt, the end of exploitation by the ruling class, the development of a classless society, and the withering away of the state. These are the ideals that have been so effective in attracting people to Marxism-Leninism. They are all false goals, bearing little resemblance to the real objectives of Marxism-Leninism. They may be more accurately described as "ideological snake oil," or a deceptive cloak used to hide the true imperialistic goals of the Soviet Union and to entrap the unwary, especially the masses. There is no proletarian revolution; rather, the goal is to establish dictatorships of the proletariat. The word *proletariat* is a deception. It does not represent the working class but rather a new elite that has seized the reins of power. The ballyhooed ideals, the ultimate goals, are not dead; rather, they are deliberate deceptions used to entrap, and they are still used with effect against those who are still free and vulnerable.

The *theoretical* basis of Marxism provides the ideology's justification and long-term prognosis. This is the "history is on our side" portion of the ideology. The twin pillars upon which the Marxist-Leninist philosophy rests are dialectical and historical materialism. *Dialectical materialism* sets forth the "laws" of social development, which are said to be as reliable as the laws of physics. They reveal how and why capitalism must and will give way to socialism, which will then evolve into communism. One might as well ask water to run uphill as to challenge the inevitability of the transition from capitalism to socialism, that is, from a "democracy of the minority" to a "democracy of the people," as the Soviets would say. *Historical materialism* is the methodology for obtaining knowledge through study of the laws of history. Historical materialism enables people to understand what role the people as well as specific individuals play in history, how classes and the class struggle arose, how the state appeared, why social revolutions occur, and what their significance is in the historical process. It enables people to understand the meaning of "real freedom," which is said to be achievable only through socialism, and of "social progress," which is defined as progress toward revolution—which, of course, is not a revolution but rather a communist takeover.

Because of the way in which Marxism-Leninism is constructed, there is no room for compromise or negotiation that would alter the goals or principles. This is fundamental. Compromise and negotiation are used only as a tactic to further the goals. The Marxist-Leninist world is a bipolar world in which all entities—people, ideas, sciences, and so forth—are placed in one of two categories, depending on whether they are viewed as pro or con, good or bad. There are very few neutrals. Entities either support communist goals or oppose them. Thus, there are the bourgeoisie and the proletariat, philosophies that are either materialist or idealist, and people who are either exploiters or the exploited. There are, in the main, two types of governments and societies, capitalist and socialist, and two classes of people, progressive and reactionary. Occasionally other categories are considered for historical purposes or to discuss possible alignments, but most of the ideology is concentrated on the clash between the two different social systems, and the dominant emphasis on how everything relates to one side or the other. Even the core of the ideology derives from the conflict of opposites.

The importance of this approach takes on practical meaning when one adds to the above another dominant precept of Marxism-Leninism: that in all issues and questions, the sole source of knowledge, the whole truth, is the exclusive province of Marxist-Leninists, and that in interpreting this knowledge the judgment of the Soviet Union and specifically the CPSU is supreme. "The Marxist theory of knowledge is based on recognition of the objective world, its objects and phenomena as the *sole source* of human knowledge."[7] There is no divine force or being whose judgment or authority supersedes that of the party. Marxism-Leninism is "the highest stage of the development of world philosophy. It has assimilated all that was best and most progressive in the centuries of development of philosophy."[8] Being a correct, deep reflection of reality, being true and able to reveal the true laws of social development, Marxism-Leninism is able not only to act correctly, but to foresee the future and, in a totally scientific way, to plan activities for many years ahead. In short, "The Soviet Union, the world's first socialist country, is a recognized standard-bearer of social progress."[9] The CPSU is in the driver's seat; the party is the only authority and the party never makes mistakes. Individuals err, government bodies and ministries make mistakes, but not *The Party*.

Another important precept concerns the ability of opposites to coexist. It is fundamental to Marxist-Leninist ideology that "opposite sides cannot coexist peacefully," and that "the contradictory, mutually exclusive character of opposites necessarily causes a *struggle* between them. The old and the new, the emergent and the obsolete, must come into contradiction, must clash. *It is contradiction, the conflict of opposites that is the main source of development of matter and consciousness.*"[10] It is the conflict and its resolution that is manifest in the revolution. This is the core of dialectical materialism and the basis for the laws of social development. Its heart and soul is the contradiction between the bourgeoisie and the proletariat. This is what feeds the class struggle and determines its inevitable outcome.

Unfortunately, this cuts against the grain of Western concepts. The need to be able to coexist is fundamental in the West. As explained by President Nixon to the Soviet leadership, "There must be room in this world for two great nations with different systems to live together and work together."[11] Or, as explained by Henry Kissinger, "A lasting peace depended on the settlement of the political issues that were dividing the two nuclear superpowers."[12] In the Soviet system, the only compromises possible take the form of temporary expedients or tactical maneuvers designed to further the Kremlin's complete victory. As explained by Crozier,

> Very few Western spokesmen or speechmakers have ever faced the fact that Soviet behaviour is built into the Soviet system, and that the system rests on an ideological foundation that makes expansionism obligatory; indeed that communist regimes, starting with the Soviet regime, have no legitimacy other than Marxism-Leninism. In other words, that it is futile to attempt to talk the Soviet leaders out of attempting, as a permanent policy, to impose their system on the rest of the world in the name of "History." Despite the irrefutable evidence, each change of Soviet leadership is greeted with public expressions of hope in Western countries, that changes for the better may be on the way. But the lesson of the inevitable disappointment that follows, sooner or later, is never learnt.[13]

One of the theories that has been popular in Western analyses of East-West relations for over fifty years is the so-called convergence theory, whereby the capitalist and socialist (Soviet) systems are seen to be evolving toward one another. This theory is used to justify arguments in favor of trade and social and scientific intercourse, and most recently, detente. Moreover, it is closely coupled to many Western views on the role and importance of arms control. Unfortunately, in Marxism-Leninism the conflict between the two systems is, without question, irreconcilable. The two systems are described as being qualitatively different, sufficiently so that no amount of quantitative change can bring the two systems together. Only a revolutionary upheaval that succeeds in destroying capitalism and replacing it with a dictatorship of the proletariat can lead to convergence. "The transition to socialism in any country can be effected only through a socialist revolution. Without a qualitative leap, without a revolution, transition to socialism is impossible."[14]

At the same time it is important not to lose sight of the fact that the Soviets will exploit such notions as the convergence theory whenever it would be advantageous for them. This is stated with unusual clarity in a 1970 book, *Present Day Bourgeois Theory About Capitalism and Socialism*, which discusses the convergence theory and why it is bourgeois nonsense. In two critical paragraphs near the end, the text points out the need to identify those countries in which the theory is present and, wherever the notion seems useful to the capitalists, to criticize and denigrate it. Then the authors, a group from the Academy of Sciences, immediately emphasize that at the same time "we have to exploit the theory if we conclude the theory can play a positive role and support the progressive and revolutionary forces."[15]

This is a sampling of the logic and the theoretical basis of Marxism-Leninism as it is taught from grade school within the communist system. While this may seem to be patently absurd to those of us who have not been subjected to such dogma, this is not the case for those raised in a Marxist-Leninist state. It is certainly true that as Soviet citizens mature, they may recognize that the Soviet system disproves its own ideology. Yet, as people begin to appreciate the deceptions, they still have a basic decision to make: whether to participate or risk expulsion. Should they question the ideology, they risk what happened to Aleksandr Ushakov, one of the sources for this study. After he began questioning the ideology, he lost his job, his position in the union, and his party membership—all three in one day. At the time of his expulsion, he held a Ph.D. in Marxist-Leninist philosophy, was an associate professor at the Odessa Higher Maritime and Engineering Institute, and was performing research that had been demonstrated to be very effective in improving the performance of naval officers in operating various combat ships.

The merging of these idealistic goals and theoretical constructs produces Marxism-Leninism *in practice*. Most important, as emphasized throughout texts on Marxist-Leninist philosophy, the ideology is action oriented. The philosophy is not designed for ivory tower theorists or for "the idle reflections of dilettantes."[16] In practice, Marxism-Leninism is really a tool, developed by Lenin and refined by his successors, that is used by the leadership to advance the interests of the state[17] and achieve its strategic goals. As one progresses in the communist system, the real internal structure of the ideology—its deceptions, principles, and instructions—gradually become recognized. As the individual begins to understand, and *decides to participate*, the party "helps" him understand what the ideology really means.

Top Soviet leaders, immersed in Marxism-Leninism since kindergarten, have learned to use the ideology to advantage. They have discovered that it is a tool for the state, a tool one must learn to exploit in order to advance in the system. As a general rule, Soviet leaders do not concern themselves with dialectical or historical materialism, or with the conflict of opposites, or with many of the other window-dressing aspects of the ideology. By the time they are accepted into the *nomenklatura*, these things have become second nature and have faded into the background. What they do concern themselves with are the basic laws governing Leninist takeovers, principles of organization and control,[18] and the strategy and tactics that are the practical essence of Marxism-Leninism.

Consider, for example, the basic Marxist-Leninist rules for takeovers: nationalize the banks and industry, and destroy the bourgeoisie. Nationalization of banks and other large financial institutions is a leading priority because of their power over industries. Nationalization of banks facilitates nationalization of industries. Destruction of the bourgeoisie (i.e., of the entire state structure) is most important. No seeds of capitalism that might germinate in the future are to be spared. As stated in *Law of the Soviet State*:

> The revolution consists in the proletariat's *destroying* the apparatus of government and the *entire* state apparatus, putting in its place a new apparatus, composed of armed workers. . . . The revolution must consist not in the fact that a new class manages with the help of the *old* machinery of state, but in *smashing* the old and commanding and managing with the aid of new machinery.[19] (Emphasis in original.)

The Marxist-Leninist approach to organization and control emphasizes the dictatorship of the proletariat, party unity and discipline, and democratic centralism—all maintained by political organization work.[20] The essence of these organizational and control principles is absolute control of all processes by the "representatives" of the proletariat (i.e., the vanguard, the Communist party). Each principle is deceptively labeled to cover up the reality, which is totalitarianism in its most extreme form.

The tactics of the revolutionary movement include infiltration, subversion, sabotage, takeover, and destruction of all non-Marxist-Leninist aspects of a society's culture, with the entire process conducted under the banner of nationalism and camouflaged by Soviet policies of peace, friendship, and nonintervention. If Marxist-Leninist philosophy and texts on scientific communism are read with the above key to the translation in mind, one can clearly discern the strategy, tactics, and instruments of communist revolutions. Without the key, the reader is easily mislead, confused, and quickly becomes bored with the dialectic.

As indicated earlier, the dual goals of Marxism-Leninism are to place "dictatorships of the proletariat" in every country of the world and to maintain all under the principle of "proletarian internationalism." Neither of these goals originated with Marx. They are pure Lenin. The purpose of

Marxist-Leninist ideology is to maintain an unswerving loyalty to these goals, which is the meaning behind Khrushchev's many statements that the Soviet Union would never renounce the course charted by Lenin. The tactics and strategy to be employed are designed by the leadership to exploit the unfolding situation, always with the objective of leading to an improvement in the correlation of forces. The course is in no sense rigid, but stresses flexibility. As set by Lenin, it stresses "one step forward, two steps back,"[21] which again is misleading unless one recognizes that the step forward is a giant one and the two steps backward are really limited tactical maneuvers designed to deceive the opponent and prepare for the next surge forward.

The importance of ideology in maintaining constant awareness of the goals and in ensuring that the strategy and tactics, while dictated by changing state interests, are developed with constant ideological guidance is evidenced by the leading role played by the Department of Ideology and by the Secretary of the Central Committee, who is in charge of ideology. The Department of Ideology is responsible for developing the philosophy that guides the party program and for explaining and interpreting the party line. While there are strong conflicts between the theorists (ideologists and propagandists) and organizers, the important point is that ideology is at the top of the structure to ensure continued adherence to Marxist-Leninist principles and the proper evolution of Marxist-Leninist logic and tactics.

To many people looking at the Soviet system from the outside, the ideology may appear to be so much nonsense, disconnected from the modern world, or even dead. That external observers might arrive at such interpretation is not surprising, nor would it be unwelcome in the Kremlin. To the contrary, this view of Soviet ideology might well have been promoted deliberately by Moscow through a carefully constructed ideology, designed in part to maintain Soviet security by appearing not to pose a threat abroad.[22] Indeed, its construction follows one of the basic principles of Soviet strategic deception: to hide the goals of the state and the main instruments used to achieve the goals, beginning with Marxism-Leninism. On the other hand, to those who have passed the test, decided to participate, and learned the "hidden portion," as Ushakov refers to it, the ideology is alive and well because those people realize that much of the ideology is false and deceptive, and is exactly that way for a purpose. This knowledge is generally held by those who have become *apparatchiki* in the Central Committee Secretariat, those who are referred to in the West as the *nomenklatura*. Knowing this about Marxism-Leninism is essential if we are to have a clear understanding of the Soviet Union's decisionmaking process and, especially, its interest in arms control.

LAW AND MORALITY

An aspect of the Marxist-Leninist ideology that is especially relevant to Soviet arms control strategy and the philosophy that guides their decisions to violate arms control treaties is Marxist-Leninist law and morality, which bears little resemblance to Western concepts of law and morality. The labels are the same, but the concepts are antithetical.

"In the course of the revolutionary struggle the working class masters Marxist theory, creates its own morality, and its own political, legal and aesthetic views."[23] Thus, Marxism-Leninism is a form of social consciousness, a plan for action, a weapon of the proletariat to use in its struggle against capitalism. This struggle is the essence of Marxism-Leninism. Winning the struggle, creating a dictatorship of the proletariat in all nations of the world, is the driving force and supreme goal, and all elements of social behavior are organized in support of the revolution. That which supports the revolutionary process is moral, and that which opposes it is immoral. This is as true and evident today, for example, as expressed in the 27th Party Congress in February 1986, as it was in the days of Lenin.

In the Soviet view, the two moralities are pitted against each other, communist and bourgeois. "The world's most progressive, humane and noble morality is *communist morality*."[24] From the point of view of communist morality, "that which promotes the movement of society toward communism is moral. *Devotion to the cause of communism, love of the socialist motherland* which blazes for mankind the trail into the communist morrow, *love of all the socialist countries*, is the first, cardinal demand in the moral code of Soviet citizens."[25] (Emphasis in original.)

The same distinction exists with regard to laws:

> Only socialist law expresses the interests of the working people and is the true law of the people. . . . Bourgeois law protects capitalist property and serves to justify exploitation and the suppression of all progressive forces. . . . Socialist law and the legal ideas underlying it radically differ from the law and legal ideas of antagonistic class societies [such as the United States]. They express the interests of the entire people, protect and help to consolidate the economic basis of socialism, socialist property, and teach Soviet people to observe the law and conscientiously do their duty.[26]

Obligation, as a category of law, not a moral principle, was clearly described by Lenin when he said, "The source of law is strength."[27] That is, in consonance with the teachings of Lenin, the Soviets feel obliged from a legal point of view to comply with the terms of treaties only when they fear the consequences or risks associated with not living up to their obligations.

When it comes to any obligation resulting from treaties that interferes with the Kremlin's interpretation of security, the Soviets, following a long Russian tradition, would break any such treaty if they believed it would provide them with a tactical or strategic advantage. This would be done without regard for international law or bilateral obligations.

As explained by Zdzislaw Rurarz, former advisor to the First Secretary of the Polish Communist Party and Ambassador to Japan with over thirty-six years in the communist movement, the Soviet leadership acts fully in accord with its Marxist-Leninist doctrine and does indeed believe that the world order is dictated not by any divine forces but by the laws of nature. Specifically, it is the stronger one who prevails, or, if both contenders are equally strong, then it is the more aggressive one who prevails. This doctrine absolves the Soviet leadership morally when it resorts to force or aggressiveness. The result is that all treaties, especially those of a strategic nature, are turned into a mockery by the Soviets. Encouraged by past successes and hindered by no moral constraints of any sort, the Soviets will honor only those obligations that exclusively serve their goals.

ARMAMENTS AND WAR

"Armaments" and "war" also have meanings in Marxism-Leninism that are quite different from those in the West (especially those dealing with nuclear war), which are essential to understanding Soviet arms control policy and behavior.

Armaments and weapons of war, according to Marxism-Leninism, are a threat only when they are in the hands of the imperialists. When held by the Soviet Union, weapons serve the interests of peace and social progress. Weapons in the hands of the imperialists are used to support reactionary policies and wage unjust wars. Weapons in the hands of the Soviet Union are progressive and employed only for just wars.

In Marxist-Leninist ideology, the capitalists are preparing for war to destroy the most progressive form of society known to mankind—socialism. Accordingly, first priority goes to dealing the capitalists a sound rebuff. War itself, by definition, would be initiated by the capitalists. In such a case, the Soviets intend to "retaliate," if possible, *before* the West has launched its strike.[28] A major war is to be avoided if possible, but if thrust upon the communists it will be a continuation of politics, the ultimate revolutionary war, a "holy war" in which "the masses will have to decide a task of historic importance: the destruction of the entire system of capitalism."[29]

The Soviets are not unmindful of the dangers of nuclear war. At the same time, however, their approach to nuclear war is quite different from that of the United States. In addition to understanding the need to prevent it, they have invested enormous resources in preparing for exactly such a war, even to the extent of working to ensure the continued functioning of the critical segments of the economy during the war. As the Soviets view nuclear war, it would not be the end of the political process. They state this very clearly. For example, "Nuclear war [has not] ceased to be an instrument of politics, as is claimed by the overwhelming majority of representatives of pacifist, antiwar movements in the bourgeois world. This is a subjective judgment. It expresses merely protest against nuclear war."[30]

To the Soviets, nuclear war, because of its decisive character, is the most political of all wars. "The social, class content of nuclear missile war and its aims will be determined by politics. . . . The nuclear missile war will also be a continuation of politics, although some ideologists of imperialism deny this; in fact, it will be even more 'political.'"[31]

One of the clearest Soviet statements is expressed in a 1987 book on the relevance to modern times of the thoughts of Soviet hero M.V. Frunze.

> The Marxist-Leninist understanding of the essence of war and a clear definition of the relationship between politics and war are of great importance under present-day conditions, too. Unfortunately, in recent years not only abroad but at times even in our nation, statements have appeared that, due to the appearance of nuclear weapons, war has now ceased to be a continuation of politics. Some scientists have even gone so far as to say that with the appearance of nuclear weapons wars are almost automatically excluded from the life of mankind. Certain pacifists have asserted that in the event of a nuclear attack by the imperialists, a peace-loving socialist state should not resort to a retaliatory nuclear strike as this would also be an unjust war. [That is, the strike would indiscriminately kill proletariat and bourgeois alike in the capitalist states and hence would be as much an attack on the working class as on the exploiting class, and hence contrary to the precepts of Marxism-Leninism.] In unmasking the fallaciousness of such arguments, Academician P.N. Fedoseyev [one of the highest Soviet authorities on Marxist-Leninist philosophy] has rightly commented that "this is a philosophy not of peace and progress but rather a philosophy of capitulation to the forces of aggression and reaction." . . . The assertion that nuclear war will not be a continuation of politics is completely fallacious.[32]

Impossible as these thoughts sound to Westerners, they are nevertheless constantly repeated themes in Marxist-Leninist teachings. It is what the communists are taught and told to believe. As such, they need to be understood as precepts that determine Soviet views of arms control and of the related decisionmaking process, and should not be dismissed as mere military rhetoric or Stone Age thinking, which so many Westerners are prone to do.

NOTES

1. George F. Will, "Abolishing the 20th Century," *Newsweek*, December 9, 1985, p. 104.
2. Philip Taubman, "Gorbachev's Gloomy America," *New York Times*, November 15, 1985, p. A3.
3. Michael Voslensky, *Nomenklatura: Anatomy of the Soviet Ruling Class*, translated by Eric Mosbacher (London: The Bodley Head, 1984), p. 296.
4. Crozier, *Strategy of Survival*, op. cit., p. 131.
5. Andrei D. Sakharov, "Sakharov Urges Europeans to Join U.S. in Standing up to Soviet Expansionism," *Washington Star*, June 9–11, 1980.
6. Anatoliy Golitsyn, *From the Satellites to the Partners* (forthcoming); see also his *New Lies for Old* (New York: Dodd, Mead & Company, 1984), pp. 23–51.
7. V.G. Afanasyev, *Marxist Philosophy* (Moscow: Progress Publishers, 1980), p. 151.
8. *The Fundamentals of Marxist-Leninist Philosophy*, op. cit., p. 15.
9. Afanasyev, op. cit., p. 116.
10. Ibid., p. 82.
11. Nixon, *Memoirs*, op. cit., p. 611.
12. Kissinger, *White House Years*, op. cit., p. 127.
13. Brian Crozier, "Introduction," in Ion Ratiu, *Moscow Challenges the World* (London: Sherwood Press, 1986), p. 4.
14. Afanasyev, op. cit., p. 105.
15. USSR Academy of Sciences, *Present Day Bourgeois Theory About Capitalism and Socialism* (Moscow, 1970; Slovak edition, 1971), pp. 197–198.
16. Afanasyev, op. cit., p. 14.
17. "State," when used in the Marxist-Leninist context, translates to the party elite and to the power apparatus this elite uses to maintain and extend its control.
18. See Chapter 1 of Jan Sejna and Joseph D. Douglass, Jr., *Decision-Making in Communist Countries: An Inside View* (McLean, Va.: Pergamon-Brassey's, for the Institute for Foreign Policy Analysis, 1986).
19. Andrei Vyshinsky, *The Law of the Soviet State* (New York: Macmillan, 1948), p. 1.
20. See Chapter 1 of Sejna and Douglass, op. cit.
21. V.I. Lenin, *One Step Forward, Two Steps Back* (Moscow: Progress Publishers, sixth printing, 1973).
22. The Soviet party members who play the most important role in spreading this deception are those who interact with Westerners, particularly those from the research institutes and the Academy of Sciences.
23. Afanasyev, op. cit., p. 203.
24. Ibid., p. 376.
25. Ibid., p. 377.
26. Ibid., pp. 372–373.
27. See Appendix A, fn 6.
28. The Soviets always retaliate; they never instigate. However, in the context of their discussion, it is clear that preemption is the intended meaning.

29. *Marxism-Leninism on War and Army* (Moscow: Progress Publishers, 1972), in *Soviet Military Thought*, No. 2 (Washington, D.C.: U.S. Government Printing Office, 1974), pp. 73, 106–107.
30. General-Major A.S. Milovidor, Editor-in-Chief; Colonel V.G. Kozlov, Editor, *The Philosophical Heritage of V.I. Lenin and Problems of Contemporary War* (Moscow: Voyenizdat, 1972), in *Soviet Military Thought*, No. 5, op. cit., 1974, p. 37.
31. *Marxism-Leninism on War and Army*, op. cit., p. 29.
32. Col. Gen. Makhmut Al. Gareev, *M.V. Frunze—Military Theorist* (McLean, Va.: Pergamon-Brassey's International Defense Publishers, Inc., 1987), pp. 94–95.

3
POLITICAL STRATEGY

National political strategy provides the framework that guides arms control policy and is a significant factor in the analysis of a nation's arms control policy and related actions. In reviewing national political strategy in this study, four important conclusions emerged: the Soviet Union has one; it is a Marxist-Leninist policy imbedded in the matrix of traditional Russian imperialism; the United States does not appear to have one[1]; and the United States does not seem to recognize that the Soviets do have one.

The absence of national political strategy in the United States[2] is a topic that has received continuing attention and has led to numerous recommendations regarding the creation of departments of political strategy, national strategy advisory boards, and so forth. Why we have this strategy vacuum is not clear. Perhaps it is merely an unfortunate consequence of a "live and let live" national aim, as described by Ambassador Paul Nitze.[3] On the other hand, the absence of a formal policy allows greater "flexibility"; for example, the bureaucracies are free to establish their own policies, and underlying assumptions are not surfaced and subjected to criticism. Of course, the most critical such assumptions for the United States are those regarding the nature of the Soviet threat.

SOVIET STRATEGY:
MARXISM-LENINISM OR BIG POWER POLITICS?

One of the continuing arguments about Soviet strategy is whether the men in the Politburo are just "power politicians" carrying out the traditional Russian program of expansion under a new guise, or are Marxist-Leninists striving to bring about their rightful destiny, the historical triumph of communism. Not surprisingly, there is a strong correlation between those who believe communist ideology is dead and those who see Kremlin politics merely as traditional big power politics.

Insofar as the communist literature is concerned, the answer is unquestionably clear. The basis of Soviet policy and political strategy is Marxism-Leninism. This is even stated in the Constitution of the USSR. Chapter 1, Article 6, of the Constitution states:

> The leading and guiding force of the Soviet society and the nucleus of the political system of all state organizations and public organizations is the Communist Party of the Soviet Union. The CPSU exists for the people and serves the people. The CPSU, armed with Marxism-Leninism, determines the general perspectives of the development of the society and the course of domestic and foreign policy of the Soviet Union, directs the great constructive work of the Soviet people, and imparts a planned, systematic, theoretically substantiated character to their struggle for the victory of communism.

The 1982 text, *Politics and Socialism*, provides a very clear statement on ideology and its linkage with politics. Politics under Marxism, the text explains, is all encompassing.

> Marxism regards politics as activity which expresses the rivalry or competition of classes for domination, the power to rule, leadership of society, participation in state affairs and control of state activity. This is not, however, limited simply to the relationship between classes. Under Marxism, politics also refers to the activity of social groups trying to attain some degree of political power to influence the formulation of state tasks as well as the means and methods by which the state is to fulfill its functions.[4]

The relationship between ideology and politics is defined as follows:

- Ideology is the intellectual and theoretical basis for political action, which gives political movements and parties their values and directives as to the means used to realize these values;
- Ideology is a factor that unites a political movement by convincing its members that they belong to a group of persons of identical or similar beliefs, and this is what binds together every party and political movement;
- Ideology forms a set of emotional symbols that intensify the actions of individuals, groups, and social classes.[5]

In contrast to the common belief in the West that ideology is dead and that nations such as the United States and the Soviet Union are merely pursuing big power politics, this text explains: "It is wrong for many bourgeois theorists to claim that the 'era of ideology' has ended and that the policy of states is based less on ideology now than on pragmatic concerns."[6] This statement certainly seems to contradict many fundamental assumptions of U.S. policy, as described in the preceding discussion of U.S. views of Soviet policy.

It is also instructive to note the clear statement in this text on the premises of Marxist-Leninist ideology:

> First, capitalism is a historically transient social order, that is, it has outlived itself, is reactionary, and the bourgeoisie is a class which has recently entangled itself in antagonistic conflicts and can neither extricate itself from them nor can it slow down the process of their intensification. Second, the liberation of the working class presupposes that the antagonism between the proletariat and the bourgeoisie may only be solved by socialist revolution, and a dictatorship of the proletariat and the working class can liberate itself only once it frees all of the rest of society from human exploitation.[7]

Shortly before Stalin's death, John Ausland presented an analysis of Soviet tactics and strategy to determine whether it was better to consider Soviet behavior as motivated by power politics or communist revolution. His conclusion was, "In a way, they are both; it all depends on the angle from which you happen to be looking at them. A corollary of this is that the argument about whether they are trying to carry out the world revolution or just advance the interests of the Soviet Union is not necessarily relevant, since the interests of the two may be viewed by them as identical."[8]

Ausland's analysis is still a good assessment of the issue. There are only two qualifications worth adding to his analysis: The first is that it would be more accurate to assert that the alternative to power politics is not a communist revolution, but a Marxist-Leninist revolution in which the driving interests are those of the state, not Marxism or communism. As discussed earlier, Marxism-Leninism is the textbook for revolution. The second is to underscore the word "both" in his conclusion: Soviet strategy is Marxism-Leninism imbedded in a matrix of traditional Russian imperialism.

This point is repeatedly stressed by the principal sources in this study. While Marxism-Leninism is important and an essential part of any understanding of Soviet strategy, without the Russian experience and traditions Soviet leaders would not have the power they have. Conversely, Soviet strategy cannot be explained as just a continuation of Russian imperialism or as pragmatism in operation. Principles are equally important. Marxist-Leninist operating principles have been proven to be incredibly effective tools, almost optimally designed to take advantage of the Russian heritage.

A number of problems arise if one views Soviet behavior as just power politics and ignores the Marxist-Leninist foundation. One problem is that the viewer is placing the Soviets on a par with all other countries, both past and present, that have practiced power politics: Britain, France, Spain, Germany, Holland, Belgium, Portugal, and the United States. Portraying Soviet actions as big power politics is an act of granting them moral equivalency with other forms of government, most notably democracy.[9] This, of course, is an objective of Soviet political strategy and related disinformation activity.

The real danger in portraying Marxist-Leninist politics as merely big power politics is that the two are vastly different and, by focusing on the latter, one only avoids coming to grips with the reality of Marxist-Leninist politics. Attributing Soviet behavior to power politics does not explain the Soviet Union's approach to arms control or its analyses of risk in deciding to violate arms control agreements. It does not explain the revolutionary war movement or the carnage that follows wars of national liberation.[10] It does not explain the extensive Soviet active measures program, of which the propaganda dimension alone costs over $3 billion per year. Further, unlike other nation-states, in the Soviet Union all power—all industry, all military, all intelligence and secret police, all communications, all justice, all education—is concentrated in the hands of a small group of elite power politicians. Moreover, this power is organized to pursue a very definite long-range plan whose objective is the destruction of all other social organizations. This is Marxist-Leninist law. These and other important laws and principles governing Soviet state behavior do not conform to those governing the operation of the international system of power politics. By persisting in a power politics view of Soviet behavior, we will generate an erroneous and misleading understanding of the tactics, strategy, and goals of the Soviet Union, which do not correspond to simple hegemony and the balance of power as many in the West would like to believe.

Soviet political strategy is applied Marxism-Leninism. It is the strategy for the world revolutionary process, which translates into installing a dictatorship of the proletariat in every nation of the world, with each dictatorship obeying the principles of proletarian internationalism. "The Communist Party directs the politics of our state, and the political strategy of the Soviet Union is the party's strategy."[11] Soviet political strategy

> defines the basic direction of the working class's struggle for a prolonged historical period, for a whole strategic stage. The political strategy defines the purpose and goal of every state, the plan of placing the revolutionary forces, which are able to secure the solution of the goal put before the revolutionary movement at every stage, and the duration of the main strike. The political strategy determines the basic ways and methods of implementing the goal of each stage.[12]

The importance and accuracy of this statement have been underscored by all the sources in this study.

SUPERIORITY AS A MAIN OBJECTIVE OF SOVIET POLITICAL STRATEGY

There is no suggestion in Marxism-Leninism that there will be any disarming of any socialist country until peace has been achieved; moreover, peace is not achieved until Soviet-style communism has been extended to all countries of the world without exception. As stated by Lenin, for the proletariat to be victorious over the bourgeoisie, it is essential to disarm it and put an end to wars[13]: "It is only when we have vanquished and completely destroyed the bourgeoisie throughout the world that wars will become futile."[14] The immediate socialist objective is clear superiority, which is required to defeat the capitalists and compel them to accept "disarmament."

The contemporary Soviet drive for superiority began with the reforms introduced by Khrushchev in the mid-1950s. Emerging from the 20th Party Congress in 1956 was a consensus among the top leadership on the need to form a new long-range policy and strategy for the Soviet bloc and communist parties. As explained by Anatoliy Golitsyn, an important contribution to the concept of this policy was Mao's secret speech on the need to change the world balance of power in favor of the communist bloc. This was also the Soviet view, as reported by Jan Sejna, and was one of the main reasons behind the Soviet desire to end the cold war: They wanted to use trade and economic assistance to change the balance of power, with initial priority placed on achieving nuclear superiority.[15]

What the Soviets mean by "ending the cold war" is to end U.S. opposition to Soviet policy and expansionism while the Soviet Union's protracted conflict against the United States and other independent nations is to continue, not only unopposed, but assisted by Western finance and technology transfer.[16]

The Soviet drive for superiority was also one of the principal influencing factors in the development of the new long-range plan and strategy that dominated the Soviet planning process beginning in the fall of 1957 and culminating in the development of the seven-year economic plan and special 21st Party Congress in 1959.

There have been three clear motivations spurring the Soviet effort to gain superiority. The first is to triumph over the United States in the event of war and be overwhelmingly the most powerful survivor. The second is the effect of Soviet superiority on the world revolutionary process through its psychological impact on people in the Third World and in Europe. The third is to stop the United States from interfering in the world revolutionary process, which is also integral to the Soviet policy of peaceful coexistence.

Specifically, Soviet superiority is to be used to stop the United States from "exporting counter-revolution." In a sense, the Soviet statements read almost as though they were a direct response to former Secretary of State John Foster Dulles's threat to use nuclear forces to stop Soviet aggression. A recent example of this Soviet policy was couched in threatening terminology: "It is certain that further growth in the power of world socialism will make still easier any revolutionary changes in the capitalist world."[17] The most explicit statements on the role of military superiority in advancing the world revolutionary movement have appeared more frequently in the Soviet literature since the early 1970s, which corresponds to the time when Western experts began to recognize that the Soviets were about to surpass the United States in overall military strength.[18] This also appears to have been the period when the Soviets stepped up their revolutionary war movement, although the intensification began as early as 1968 and, as indicated earlier, the planning extended back to 1957.[19]

The logic of the Soviet position is also summarized quite effectively by Gareev, who quotes Frunze:

". . . one of the most dependable guarantees for peace is not only our peace-loving policy but also a strong, powerful Red Army. The stronger our Red Army fist is, the more grounds the workers and peasants of our Union will have for confidence that their peaceful labor will not be disturbed, and the fewer the persons who wish to intervene in our internal affairs." The false assertions by bourgeois propaganda of the "excessive armaments of the Soviet Union" and the "Soviet Threat" both then and now are needed by the imperialists to justify the arms race being carried out by them and conceal their aggressive attentions against the USSR and the other socialist countries.[20]

Another pertinent example is the following excerpt from 1977 when detente was still flourishing.

The guarantee of the defense of all socialist countries is the defense might, the nuclear rocket shield of the Soviet Union—the most powerful state in the fraternal family of countries of the socialist community. There is no doubt that imperialism long ago would have tried to carry out its aggressive plans over the whole planet if on its path there had not been an insurmountable barrier—the might of the first socialist country in the world. "There is not an unprejudiced person in the world who would not admit," said Todor Zhivkov, First Secretary of the Bulgarian Communist Party speaking at the 10th Congress of the Bulgarian Communist Party, "that if mankind has not been swallowed up in the flames of a new world war, if imperialism has not been able to rudely force its will on recently liberated countries, if socialist countries are successfully building a new life, that for this we are obliged to the Soviet Union, the Red Giant, standing tall over one-sixth of the earth's surface, strong, peaceloving, generous like a brother, ready to go to the aid of each nation which is struggling for its freedom and independence, for a better life."[21]

PROSPECTS FOR CHANGE

There has been a constant, almost fervent, hope in the West for change in the Soviet Union. After each main event, especially after each change in General Secretary, Western commentators, diplomats, politicians, and businessmen focus their microscopes and look for change: always for change in one direction—a softening of the Soviet ideological line and matching political strategy. But each time, the Soviets toughen their ideological line and intensify the rhetoric—including their emergence from near catastrophic times, such as the collectivization of agriculture, the 1937–1938 purges, and World War II. One would think that these Western observers would soon come to recognize that the communist system is highly resistant to ideological change.

The Soviet Union does pursue a zig-zag policy. There have been numerous shifts in tactics and the ideology has been selectively refined. There are also clear revisions in political strategy that take place: for example, the New Economic Plan (NEP) in the 1920s and Khrushchev's efforts to end the Cold War in the mid-1950s. But the fundamentals of communist ideology, its totalitarian nature, and its drive for a world socialist republic do not change. The main state principles—the leading role of the party, the liquidation of private interests, the dictatorship of the proletariat, the primacy of state power, the role of central planning—do not change. If anything, they grow stronger. All changes that have occurred have been changes to strengthen the basic principles of organization and control. Moreover, those who advocated change or introduced change in opposition to Marxism-Leninism have been ruthlessly destroyed. This is especially true among the satellites and foreign communist parties, which upon occasion have been purged, even totally destroyed, to eliminate growing tendencies toward change. It is very true, as Khrushchev said in 1959, that "In questions of ideology we have firmly stood and will continue to stand like a rock on the basis of Marxism-Leninism."[22] Or, as he stated more graphically in 1955 while visiting India: "We have never renounced and will not renounce our political line chartered for us by Lenin."

There are three reasons why the West continues to misinterpret the prospects for change in the Soviet Union. First, there is an enormous cultural chasm. Westerners tend to think of the Soviet people in terms of a mirror image of their own experiences and desires. People are all alike, they say, and those in the Soviet Union are no different from those in the United States; we all want food, shelter, a better life for our children, and so forth. Thus, the failure of the Soviet economy is seen as a reason to anticipate change, as a reason why the Soviets want to cut back on their expensive military procurement programs. This reasoning, however, ignores Soviet ideology, which is not particularly concerned about the welfare of people, except in extreme situations where a poor standard of living might be judged detrimental to defense efforts and to the furtherance of the world revolutionary movement. One cannot justify the purges and collectivization of agriculture under Stalin, or the subsequent typical Russian nostalgia for the days of Stalin when there was a firm hand at the helm,[23] by reference to Western experiences or traditions. When the Soviet system is examined in terms of Marxist-Leninist goals, one would have to say that it has been remarkably successful and that there is no reason for fundamental change; history is proving the Soviets correct.

The second reason is self-interest. For a wide variety of reasons, we all *want* to see the Soviet Union change. The diplomats want to see change leading to normalized relations that do not present nasty problems. Those concerned about war and the implications of modern technology for war—not only nuclear but conventional and chemical/biological as well—want to see the Soviet Union change and the risk of war diminish. Western capitalists want to see the Soviet Union change and open new vistas for trade and banking.

The third reason is Soviet deception. The Soviets are well aware of Western mirror-imaging, self-interests, and desire for surcease of tension. In the interests of promoting their own "social progress," they make maximum use of deception tailored according to Lenin's reputed guidance to Dzherzinski, "Tell them what they want to believe."

An especially good example of Lenin's "one step forward, two steps back" strategy and associated deception is the New Economic Plan of the 1920s. In 1920, the country was in serious economic and political trouble. The goal of the NEP was to get the country back on its feet and solidify the position of the new government. As explained by Golitsyn,[24] this plan was so successful that the new long-range strategy developed in the late 1950s was in large measure modeled after that plan. The NEP was designed to expand foreign trade, attract foreign capital and expertise, and achieve political recognition from noncommunist countries. In the face of an unfavorable balance of power, it was to change that balance by exploiting contradictions in and between the capitalist countries through an activist diplomacy. It was also designed to neutralize the emigré movement, prepare conditions for building socialism in Soviet Russia, and promote world revolution through the communist movement.

Lenin recognized that in order to strengthen the regime, the party needed to retreat from rigid wartime communism. It had to take two steps back to take one step forward. Internal concessions were temporary, designed to win over or to eliminate particular pockets of resistance. Concessions to foreigners served to gain economic and diplomatic advantage from ideological enemies. The main task was to reestablish trade relations, and to do this, Lenin said, it was necessary to have at least some of the capitalists on their side.

While the NEP was planned as a long-range, ideologically correct policy, designed to increase the effectiveness of the regime, expand its political influence, and strengthen communist ideology, the image presented to the outside world was that of a nationalistic state that had thrown overboard some of its ideological baggage and was pursuing a number of opportunistic policies. "The picture to be presented to the outside world would be consistent with what the outside world wanted to see: a weak, slowly collapsing regime coming to terms with the capitalist system."[25]

Substantial improvements were achieved in the 1920s under the NEP. However, in considering the changes engendered by the assistance provided by the West and the increases in the standard of living in the Soviet Union, it is important not to lose sight of what followed. The system did not "change," it was only strengthened—two steps back, one step forward. The NEP led directly to the collectivization of agriculture and the purges of the 1930s that resulted in the deaths of some twenty to thirty million or more Soviet citizens.[26]

Sejna's description of Khrushchev's strategy in the mid-1950s is almost a carbon copy of Golitsyn's description of the NEP. Both strategies were directed toward improving the stability of Marxist-Leninist ideology and hastening the destruction of the West. Both employed the same deceptive themes and techniques. Both were intended to project a false image of change, which was believed important to realize economic and trade benefits and to cover the true nature of Soviet intentions and strategy. Both were eminently successful.

In an almost comic-opera fashion, while the Soviets are busy projecting a deceptive image of change to open the doors for Western trade and finance, the West seems intent on providing trade and finance as an incentive to promote change. Thus, President Nixon explained the establishment of interrelationships and cooperation as

> the first stage of detente: to involve Soviet interests in ways that would increase their stake in international stability and the status quo. There was no thought that such commercial, technical and scientific relationships could by themselves prevent confrontations or wars, but at least they would have to be counted in a balance sheet of gains and losses whenever the Soviets were tempted to indulge in international adventurism.[27]

There is no reason to expect the Soviet leadership to introduce the types of *positive* changes the West would like to see. There will continue to be shifts in Soviet tactics and strategy. As in the past, these are likely to strengthen the regime, not weaken it or change it into something approaching a normal, modern nation-state. Perhaps the best approach for the West is to recognize that positive change, should it ever come, will be a very long-term process. In 1995 it may be possible to say that a decade earlier the Soviet Union did appear to begin experiencing and reacting to the need for positive change. It is unwise and unfounded to make such prognostications today.

NOTES

1. The closest recent representation of a national political strategy was the Basic National Security Policy that was discarded in favor of an "ad hoc" approach to policy in 1963.
2. As an example of the problem of discerning U.S. policy, Richard Pipes writes: "Inquiries among highly placed officials involved in its [detente] formulation indicated that there exists no official document from that time that spells out the assumptions and objectives of detente. In practice, the doctrine of detente, as adopted in Washington, turned out to be nothing more than a patchwork of commonsensical opinions, loosely stitched together and never subjected to the test of critical analysis." *Survival Is Not Enough* (New York: Simon & Schuster, 1984), p. 221.
3. Paul H. Nitze, "Living With the Soviets," *Foreign Affairs*, Winter 1984–1985. Also, as explained by Henry Kissinger, "Despite lip service to planning, there is a strong bias in favor of making policy in response to cables and in the form of cables." Kissinger, *White House Years*, op. cit., p. 27.
4. Yevgeniy Ambartsumov and Adolf Dobieszewski, *Politics and Socialism*, translated from Polish in JPRS-EPS-85-007-L, June 14, 1985, p. 3.
5. Ibid., p. 4.
6. Ibid.
7. Ibid., p. 7.
8. Diplomaticus (John Ausland), "Stalinist Theory and Soviet Foreign Policy," *The Review of Politics*, Vol. 14, No. 4, October 1952, p. 483.
9. See, for example, Jeane J. Kirkpatrick, "The Myth of Moral Equivalence," *Imprimis*, Hillsdale College, Hillsdale, Michigan, Vol. 15, No. 1, January 1986.
10. Haig, op. cit., p. 29.
11. Gareev, op. cit., p. 128.
12. Professor V.S. Aleksandrov, *The Political Strategy and Tactics of the Communist Party* (Moscow, 1971), p. 9.
13. Gareev, op. cit., p. 70.
14. V.I. Lenin, *Complete Works*, 3rd edition, Vol. 23, p. 67; cited in Brian Crozier, *The Price of Peace* (Washington, D.C.: National Center for Public Policy Research, second revised edition, 1983), p. 22.
15. For a discussion of Khrushchev and de-Stalinization, see Chapter 2 of Jan Sejna, *We Will Bury You* (London: Sidgwick & Jackson, 1982).
16. For a thorough review of the cold war, see Brian Crozier, *This War Called Peace* (New York: Universe Books, 1985), p. 329.
17. Ambartsumov and Dobieszewski, op. cit., p. 329.

18. One of the earliest studies to reach this conclusion was a U.S. Air Force (Foreign Technology Division) study of 1967. Their estimate was that the Soviets would pass the United States in 1969. This data provided the basis for an American Security Council study on the *Changing American Strategic Balance*. In January 1969, Secretary of Defense Clark Clifford said the Soviets would surpass the United States later that year. The changing balance theme was then repeated and given widespread prominence by the National Strategy Information Center and, later, the Committee on the Present Danger.
19. In this regard, a parallel can be drawn between U.S. policy statements just prior to the Korean War and the U.S. signing of the Declaration on Basic Principles in May 1972. As noted by Canadian Ambassador Ford, "It is just possible that the Soviets misunderstood the Nixon gesture and felt the agreements signed in the Kremlin gave them freedom of action to support 'national liberation movements' in Angola, Ethiopia, and Mozambique." Ford, op. cit., p. 1141.
20. Gareev, op. cit., p. 59.
21. D.A. Volkogonov, A.S. Milovidov, and S.A. Tyushkevich, editors, *War and Army*, translation by Harriet Fast Scott (Moscow: Voyenizdat, 1977), p. 366.
22. U.S. Congress, Senate, *Khrushchev's Strategy and Its Meaning for America*, a study presented to the Subcommittee to Investigate the Administration of the Internal Security Act and other Internal Security Laws, Committee on the Judiciary (Washington, D.C.: U.S. Government Printing Office, 1960).
23. See Oleg Penkovskiy, *Penkovskiy Papers* (Garden City, N.Y.: Doubleday, 1965); and Anton Antonov-Ovseyenko, *The Time of Stalin* (New York: Harper & Row, 1981), pp. 339–344.
24. See Golitsyn, *New Lies for Old*, op. cit., for a brief summary of the NEP as a successful Soviet deception. See also John J. Dziak, "Soviet Deception: The Organizational and Operational Tradition," in Brian D. Dailey and Patrick J. Parker, editors, *Soviet Strategic Deception* (Lexington, Mass.: Lexington Books, 1986).
25. Golitsyn, *New Lies for Old*, op. cit., pp. 10–17; see also Golitsyn, *From the Satellites to the Partners*, op. cit.
26. Antonov-Ovseyenko, op. cit., p. vii. Some estimates run in excess of 50 million. See Iosif G. Dyadkin, *Unnatural Deaths in the USSR 1928–1954* (New Brunswick, N.J.: Transaction Books, 1983), who estimates that between 43 and 52 million Soviet lives were lost due to a combination of Soviet state terror and World War II.
27. Nixon, op. cit., p. 618.

4

ARMS CONTROL IN SOVIET STRATEGY

Universal and complete disarmament has been an integral part of Marxist-Leninist strategy since the early 1920s. In contrast, beginning roughly in 1963, arms control emerged as a distinct strategic military and intelligence operation, an integral part of Soviet political-military strategy. While retaining certain links with Soviet disarmament policy and being guided by the same overall political strategy of peaceful coexistence, arms control as a strategic instrument is treated quite differently from disarmament. Thus, it is appropriate to examine arms control both as an element of Soviet disarmament strategy and as an element of broader Soviet strategy.

SOVIET DISARMAMENT STRATEGY

Disarmament is an integral Soviet objective, in much the same way that peace is an avowed objective. In both cases, the meanings of the terms are vastly different from Western concepts. Peace, the Soviets say, can be achieved only after capitalism has been liquidated. In the Soviet world view, when capitalism disappears so does class conflict and the basis for all war. Disarmament is similar to the Soviet concept of peace. It strives for the abolition of all arms used to wage unjust wars, which are wars waged by capitalists. As explained by Col. V.V. Larionov just prior to his promotion to general-major: ". . . the Soviet Union . . . has always resolutely opposed international agreements legalizing *unjust* wars. Our country is consistently struggling for general and complete disarmament. That is, for the destruction of all material means for waging *such* wars."[1] (Emphasis added.) Another explanation of disarmament, one that dates back to Lenin, is that disarmament is the process whereby arms are taken from the bourgeoisie and given to the proletariat. This is what disarmament means in Soviet strategy.

Disarmament, like peace, is a deception used to trap the unwary, the idealists, and those whose attention is focused elsewhere—peasants, workers, bourgeoisie. Disarmament and peace also are weapons used to hide the true nature of communism. As explained by former Novosti propaganda expert Tomas Schuman, arms control and disarmament propaganda is designed to promote the image of the Soviet Union as peaceloving and to place the Soviet Union morally above the Western democracies that are to be portrayed as imperialists, warmongers, and the source of all wars. In no sense is the Soviet view of arms control similar to that of the United States.

Soviet ideology emphasizes the need to recruit—that is, to deceive—the masses. The masses must see Marxism-Leninism as the friend of the people, the champion of the working class and peasants. Accordingly, the desire for peace and disarmament is a major theme in Soviet propaganda and disinformation.

The primary target of Soviet disarmament propaganda is the people. The disarmament weapon, like other propaganda, is viewed by the Soviets as an effective tool because it operates over the heads of governments and is aimed directly at the population. As stated at the 3rd World Congress of the Communist International:

> The disarmament policy of the Soviet government must be utilized for purposes of agitation. However, it must not be utilized as a pretext for advancing similar demands in capitalist countries, but as a means for (1) *recruiting sympathizers* for the Soviet Union—the champion of peace and socialism, and (2) utilizing the results of the Soviet disarmament policy and its exposure of the imperialists in the effort to eradicate all pacifist illusions and carry on propaganda *among the masses* in support of the only way toward disarmament and abolition of war—arming of the proletarian dictatorship.[2] (Emphasis added.)

A good example of this strategy is contained in a recent article by G.A. Arbatov, Director of the Institute of the USA and Canada: "The strength of the Soviet proposals lies precisely in the fact that they present the United States and NATO with a dilemma: either join in the good-neighborly quest for paths to disarmament, or expose yourself in the people's eyes and demonstrate that all your talk about the desire to save mankind from the threat of nuclear confrontation is mere hypocrisy."[3]

In analyzing Soviet disarmament proposals, the critical question most often overlooked is: Who is the target of the Soviet disarmament proposals? Are, for example, proposals sent to the U.S. government directed at the government, as most often implicitly appears to be the case? Or is the government merely being asked to play the role of the unwitting dupe, while the real audience is composed of international "progressive" organizations, the media, unwitting politicians, and the Third World?

An excellent recent example of who the intended audience is comes from Gorbachev's statement of January 15, 1986, which set forth a three-phase nuclear and chemical disarmament proposal. The proposal was patently absurd, a throwback to those of Nikita Khrushchev in the 1950s, with the added feature of requiring the United States to cease all space defense efforts. However, labeling the proposal as "absurd" does it a disservice by failing to recognize that the proposal was not intended as a genuine proposal submitted for consideration by U.S. officials, but rather as a weapon directed toward a worldwide audience, designed to influence people to perceive the USSR as the champion of peace and disarmament. The Soviet rationale is clear. As stated by Boris Ponomarev, one of the top policymakers in the Soviet Union for over a quarter of a century until his removal from office in 1986: "A major factor compelling the U.S. administration to agree to negotiate has been the pressure from the *mass anti-war movement* and the anti-war feeling that has spread even to circles that cannot be called anti-imperialist."[4] (Emphasis added.) It is also obvious that the proposal served as advance public relations for the February 1986 Party Congress, which had been advertised as establishing Soviet political strategy for the remainder of the century.

In analyzing Soviet policies, there is a tendency in the West to overlook the fact that many strategies that appear to be directed at the West are aimed also at other parts of the world. The rest of the world, not the United States, may often be the primary target. This is particularly true in the case of a significant portion of the peace and disarmament propaganda. The Third World is the immediate target for Soviet takeovers; hence, a major portion of Soviet propaganda is designed to mislead these countries in their assessments of what the Soviet Union represents. Achieving the proper image in Third World countries as well as in the industrialized nations is a major task in Soviet revolutionary strategy, and one they work hard to maintain. The ethnocentric tendency[5] in the United States to interpret such propaganda statements as directed primarily against the United States causes many U.S. professionals to miss a significant dimension of Soviet strategy.

NUCLEAR DISARMAMENT AND PEACEFUL COEXISTENCE

Nuclear disarmament and peaceful coexistence are closely related themes that were made major elements of Soviet political strategy by Khrushchev in the mid-1950s. When Stalin died, the Soviet Union was in a state of near crisis. As described by Golitsyn, corruption was rampant; the classless society had become a two-class society of the elite and everyone else; underground nationalist movements had formed in several republics; and the economy was no better off than it had been at the end of World War II. The need for change and reform was widely recognized.

One of the major changes Khrushchev sought was an end to the cold war. As explained by Sejna, his objective was to improve the image of the Soviet Union in the West so that: (1) Western technical and economic assistance would flow into the Soviet-bloc countries; (2) the West would reduce its concern over the spread of communism and lower its guard relative to the revolutionary movement in the Third World (which was to be intensified); and (3) the growth of the U.S. nuclear capability would be slowed, enabling the Soviet Union to catch up and eventually go ahead.

To bring about this major change, as Khrushchev explained to a gathering of high-level Czech communist officials in August 1954, the intellectual middle class in the West had to be convinced that the Soviet Union had instituted reforms. It was necessary to place the blame for the past on the shoulders of the only person who could carry the burden—Stalin. Moreover, Golitsyn adds, de-Stalinization was also believed to be essential as an internal mechanism to correct the theory and practices enforced by Stalin that had produced the condition of internal crisis and to set Marxism-Leninism back on course. De-Stalinization was approved by the party presidium in 1955, setting the stage for the Party Congress in February 1956, at which time Khrushchev would denounce Stalin and reveal a "changed" Soviet Union.[6]

Lenin's deceptive strategy of peaceful coexistence was rejuvenated and introduced in 1955 as the new Soviet policy, as the alternative to the cold war. Peaceful coexistence was, and remains, the Soviet strategy for destroying capitalism in the most efficient manner and without a war that would threaten the survival of the Soviet homeland. The goals of peaceful coexistence were and are to secure technical and economic assistance for the Soviet-bloc nations, to clear the path for stepped-up revolutionary activity in the Third World, to prepare the West for the emergence of antiwar forces that would undermine Western military readiness, and to give the Soviet Union a chance to catch up with the West and eventually gain military superiority.[7]

One of the major propaganda tools incorporated into the new strategy was the threat of nuclear war. The Soviets concluded that the Americans could not stand up to the rigors of the nuclear threat. Accordingly, the threat of nuclear war became an important weapon in the Soviet campaign to convince "realistic thinking" people in the West to unite against their "reactionary" governing elites and to convince the West to accept peaceful coexistence as the *only* acceptable alternative to nuclear war. The threats of nuclear war and arms control were two sides of the same sword.

The Soviet objective of splitting the West through this and other techniques was one of the main agenda items at a meeting of the CPSU Central Committee on July 4–12, 1955. This meeting was an important turning point in the post-Stalin struggle for power in the Soviet Union and in the formation of contemporary Soviet political strategy in the war against capitalism. While the importance of this meeting is not readily apparent from the agenda published in *Pravda*, it can be discerned in a Czechoslovak reference book, *World History in Facts*, where the agenda is shown to have included a discussion on "How to exploit disharmonies between the bourgeoisie in different states."[8]

In the mid-1950s, the image of peaceful coexistence and nuclear disarmament emerged as the central theme of Soviet political strategy. The primary targets of the deception were scientists and the intellectual middle class in the West. The deception was enormously successful. In fact, it was so successful that Suslov, the top ideologist in the Soviet Union and deputy to Brezhnev (who was then a member of the presidium and Secretary of the Central Committee) in the strategic planning effort undertaken in the fall of 1956 to bring the Soviet Union into the nuclear age, remarked to Sejna that the effectiveness of this tactic had encouraged them to greatly expand the effort.[9]

Particularly relevant in this context is the analysis by Golitsyn on the reorganization of the KGB that took place in the late 1950s under Alexander Shelepin, who, according to Sejna, headed the intelligence panel on the Brezhnev study. Shelepin was a friend of Mironov (a friend of Brezhnev), who was to become head of the Administrative Organs Department. Mironov (who would be in charge of arms control by 1963) and Shelepin argued that the KGB should be transformed from the political secret police force it had become under Stalin into a flexible political organ able to play an active external role in implementing state policy. This suggestion was adopted by Khrushchev, and Shelepin was placed in charge of the KGB. In its new form, vastly increased emphasis was placed on disinformation and deception.

Shelepin, with Khrushchev's full concurrence, created a disinformation Department D within the First Chief Directorate of the KGB.[10] To assist in this disinformation operation and other KGB active measures undertaken in implementing state policy, the Novosti Press Agency was formed in 1961. As explained by Tomas Schuman, formerly Yuri Bezmenov, Novosti was run by the KGB disinformation department under the direction of the International Department of the Communist Party.

The International Department is the direct successor to the Communist International (Comintern) that had directed the world communist movement from 1919 until 1943, when Stalin "abolished" it to convey the impression to his wartime allies that the Soviets no longer were trying to orchestrate revolutions around the globe. It was "reestablished" as the Information Bureau in 1947. This bureau, which reported to a numbered department of the Central Committee, is also referred to in different writings as the Inform Bureau and as the Cominform, short for Communist Information Bureau. In 1956 Khrushchev "abolished" this bureau, as Stalin had done, to show the world the Soviet Union had reformed once again. This was just another of the tactical moves that made up the strategic "peaceful coexistence" deception. Other accompanying propaganda themes that were part of this deception were: (1) socialism can be established without weapons; (2) there could be independent paths to socialism, even parliamentary ones; (3) the newly coined "wars of national liberation," a euphemism for revolutionary wars; and (4) as socialism spreads, so do the friends of socialism.

In 1958 the International Department and Headquarters of Peace and Socialism emerged as the successors to the Information Bureau. The Headquarters of Peace and Socialism, which had been located in Bucharest, was moved to Prague, where, from an ideological perspective, it directed the communist movement.[11] It reported to the Soviet International Department just as the Information Bureau had reported to a numbered department. Indeed, the two likely were one and the same. Novosti was set up in the old Inform Bureau offices in Moscow as an adjunct KGB operation.

Department D activity is believed to have been further increased in 1968, coincident with the change in foreign operations of Novosti. Assignments to Novosti posts, previously short term, were made long term, with major emphasis placed on developing close ties to influential citizens and recruiting them to the Soviet cause. New Novosti departments of research and counterpropaganda were formed to carry on this infiltration and sabotage. Prior to his leaving in 1970, Schuman was deputy director of the newly established Novosti Research and Counterpropaganda Department in India. One of his tasks was to develop profile analyses of Indian citizens to identify those who could be used in support of Soviet policy and those who were reactionaries. One of the factors leading to his decision to defect was the realization that the latter list of names he was developing was in actuality a death list that would be used to cleanse the subcontinent of state enemies and possible troublemakers in the event of war and/or takeover.

The expansion and increased professionalism of the Novosti operation are likely the early fruits of a major operation to upgrade the communist world press influence operation initiated in 1963. A still further increase in the role of the KGB disinformation and deception apparatus took place in 1971, when Department D was elevated in importance and made a

"Service." All of this suggests strongly that the role of deception, disinformation, and other active measures in advancing Soviet views, given fresh emphasis in the mid-1950s, has been increasingly important and that this operation has been assessed as quite effective from the Soviet point of view.

THE EMERGENCE OF ARMS CONTROL AS A STRATEGIC OPERATION

In the early 1960s, the Soviets came to realize that arms control could serve other purposes beyond propaganda. As described by Sejna, this recognition originated with the military and the Administrative Organs Department, both of which lobbied to have the process placed under their control.[12] The Administrative Organs Department is one of the most important departments of the CPSU Central Committee. It has cognizance over military affairs, internal security and intelligence (KGB), and justice. The basic uses for arms control envisioned by the Administrative Organs Department and the military were to delay or disrupt U.S. military programs and help shift the balance of power in favor of the Soviet Union; to confirm Soviet knowledge of U.S. capabilities and plans; to influence U.S. perceptions of Soviet capabilities and intentions; and to help split Western societies. To achieve these objectives, the Soviet military and the Administrative Organs Department argued that the West must be forced to get "serious" about arms reduction, and that the best way to accomplish this was to show the West that the Soviet military was involved. Further, it was necessary to shift the discussions from general disarmament to specific arms reduction measures. Because military leaders alone were qualified to discuss such specifics, they argued that they should be placed in charge of the process.[13] By 1964 the arms control process had been placed under the Administrative Organs Department. This transition of arms control from a propaganda weapon to a strategic military and intelligence operation in 1961–1963 is particularly significant because 1963 seems to be the year when the Soviet adoption of an offensive strategy toward the West, begun in 1955, entered its final phase.

In 1955, Soviet political strategy went on the offensive with the adoption of peaceful coexistence, which was designed to enable the Soviets to leap forward with Western assistance. The main strategic guidelines were formulated by a strategic planning effort headed by Leonid Brezhnev that began in the fall of 1956 and finished in the spring of 1957. His deputy in this strategic planning effort was Mikhail Suslov, the ranking ideologist. The guidelines that emerged were approved in May 1957. The impact of the guidelines was so extensive that an immediate effort to revise the five-year plan that had just been approved was initiated, again under the leadership of Brezhnev. This effort led to the unusual seven-year plan and special Party Congress in February 1959. The main activities in this new offensive were the military buildup, adoption of a nuclear doctrine, and an intensified Third World offensive undertaken under the guise of wars of national liberation. Coincident with the formulation of the new strategy, plans to restructure the KGB and turn it into an active instrument of state policy were developed and implemented. In the latter half of the 1950s, an intelligence offensive against the West was launched in support of the political and diplomatic measures adopted in the mid-1950s.

The effect of the new strategy of Soviet military organization became apparent in December 1959 with the formation of the Strategic Rocket Troops. The formal announcement of the new military doctrine was made at the Fourth Session of the Supreme Soviet in January 1960. Particularly noteworthy were the talks by Khrushchev on "Disarmament for Durable Peace and Friendship," and by Marshal Rodion Ya. Malinovskiy, Minister of Defense. According to Soviet spokesmen writing years after the event, these speeches laid out the new Soviet military doctrine, which was an offensive nuclear doctrine.[14] The unveiling continued through the fall of 1960. As described by Golitsyn, the new long-range policy was approved at the Congress of Communist Parties in November 1960, and was reflected in a statement published in *Pravda* in December, referred to as a "Manifesto," and a report by Khrushchev, "For New Victories for the World Communist Movement," delivered to a meeting of the party organization in the Higher Party School, the Academy of Social Sciences, and the Institute of Marxism-Leninism of the Central Committee.[15]

By 1963, the actions to shift the military balance of power had been sufficiently successful that the Soviets decided to shift from what had been a defensive military strategy to an offensive military strategy. This shift was extended to include all East European satellites. The decision was announced to the Czechoslovak military leadership by Marshal Malinovskiy at a meeting of the Kolegium of the Ministry of Defense in Prague in May 1963. Also in 1963 intelligence and disinformation operations against the West were integrated and intensified.[16]

Concurrently in 1963, the Soviets began a concerted effort to exploit the press in support of Soviet policies. The Kremlin had concluded that the press was a far more effective tool to use than politicians in obtaining support for Soviet policy, and that Soviet efforts in this direction had to be improved. The press was divided into three categories: communist, neutral, and right wing. The first effort was to improve the ability of the communist press to influence the Western press and public opinion. Soviet leaders decided that they needed to "qualitatively improve the service of the journalists," that is, to educate them better so that they could interact more effectively with the Western press corps. In addition, the KGB and GRU were given free rein to infiltrate Western and Third World press institutions, except that they were prohibited in the process from penetrating the communist press, for example, *Pravda* or *The Daily Worker*, without Suslov's permission.

Instructions on intelligence objectives for operations against the Western press were given to Czechoslovakia in September 1963. There were roughly twenty-five tasks that were discussed. Four of the more important tasks were to use the neutral press to: (1) convince the readers of the benefits of peaceful coexistence; (2) promote and exploit disharmonies within Western society and between Western nations; (3) change Western perceptions about the Soviet Union and communism; and (4) create the belief that it is hopeless to fight the Soviet Union and that it is senseless to make any important decision without consulting the Soviet Union.

Thus, 1963 was the year when the modern Soviet offensive strategy was in place and operational in all its main dimensions. An article in *Voyennaya Vestnik* in March 1964 explained the situation as follows:

> If we analyze the military fight, Lenin thought the decisive role would be played by the attack. Attack must be very active until the enemy is completely destroyed. The strikes must be very fast, decisive and the troops must exploit the most important moment to attack the most important targets. In military strategy, attack is most important and failure to recognize that is worse than idiocy, it is criminal.[17]

The article went on to say that Lenin's remarks were more important now than ever before.

Given this new Soviet offensive strategy, the emergence of arms control as a strategic military and intelligence operation was a logical step, fully in keeping with the modern Soviet political, intelligence, diplomatic, and military initiatives that grew out of the basic post-Stalin Soviet strategy formulated in the mid-1950s.

In its new form, arms control was placed directly under the General Secretary's deputy. Initially, while Khrushchev was General Secretary, Brezhnev was in charge of arms control. Following Brezhnev's promotion to General Secretary in 1964, Kirilenko took charge. The head of the Administrative Organs Department, commonly called the Administration Department, ran the arms control operation as the deputy to the Deputy General Secretary. This gave him higher authority and enabled him to carry out the task of coordinating the activities of the different departments of the Central Committee that were involved, including the International Department and the Propaganda Department, and such particularly sensitive agencies as the KGB, GRU, and Operations Main Administration of the General Staff. The head of the Leningrad KGB, N.R. Mironov, was appointed chief of the Administrative Organs Department in 1958.

Mironov, who was regarded by Sejna as especially tough and a master of deception, had headed the effort to bring arms control under the military and make it a strategic operation. Until his death in 1964, he was in charge of arms control as Brezhnev's deputy. Subsequently, General-Major Nikolai Savinkin, who took Mironov's position as head of the Administrative Organs Department in 1964, ran the operation as Kirilenko's deputy.

The main responsibility for preparation of the arms control process within the military was assigned to the Chief of the General Staff, but the individual who really did the work was the head of the Operations Main Administration. Within that organization, the people who dominated the initial staffing process came from the Operations Administration, the very sensitive General Staff agency responsible for the Operations Plan and for developing the requirements of that plan, which would then be incorporated into the plans of all other agencies. This administration is also the source of requirements for weapons systems research, development, and acquisition, all of which are determined by the needs of the Operations Plan.

The initial task in the Operations Administration was to review Soviet weapons development and acquisition plans, and determine how far the Soviets could go in negotiating arms control agreements: what might be acceptable or proposed, and so forth. At this stage, primary participants, in addition to the Operations Administration, were the GRU, especially the deputy in charge of strategic intelligence; the Main Administration for Material and Technical Supply, which was responsible for the production and supply of weapons; and the Science and Technology Main Administration, which was responsible for development.

When this task was completed, the package went to the Administration of Special State Interests, which was responsible for deception within the Operations Main Administration. In putting together the basic package, estimates had been made on those weapons the Soviets would be able to deploy in the future and those that would be in the development stage. The arms control package proposed measures that the Soviet Union could live with, and, in each case, indicated what weapons developments would have to be hidden in the process. The Administration of Special State Interests had the task of determining how to do that. In developing the arms control package, it had the last word before the package was ready for submission to the Defense Council for decision. As the process operated in the beginning, when the decisions had been prepared the head of the Administration Department, together with the heads of the other concerned agencies, presented their plan to the Deputy General Secretary for approval prior to its submission to the Defense Council for decision.

Organizations outside the national security apparatus, for example, the Politburo, International Department, and Foreign Ministry, were not main parties to the preparations. Their duties came afterward, when they were instructed on the roles they were to play in the process, the foremost of which was to provide a diplomatic cover for an operation that was essentially a strategic military operation. This was a good example of what Khrushchev meant when he explained that the essence of Soviet strategy was to have a Soviet marshal behind each diplomat.

ARMS CONTROL GOALS AND OBJECTIVES

Arms control differs sharply from disarmament in Soviet political strategy, although the two are closely connected. Disarmament is mainly a propaganda weapon of political strategy, and, as such, falls under the purview of the International and Propaganda departments. Arms control is a strategic military operation with its goals, objectives, and analyses formulated mainly within the Administrative Organs Department and General Staff, and with important input provided by the KGB. Except as specifically directed by the Defense Council, such bodies as the Politburo, Council of Ministers, Foreign Ministry, International Department, and so forth, could not be privy to the development of strategy or any of the discussions, analyses, or decisions in this process. Their main role would be as tools in the associated deception and disinformation plan that would be formulated as an integral part of the development of the arms control strategy, which ultimately would be approved and supervised by the Defense Council. In the current situation where the General Secretary has had limited experience in these matters, his primary advisors likely would be the heads of the primary organizations, the Administrative Organs Department, the KGB, and the General Staff.

Zdzislaw Rurarz reasons that the Soviet arms control process has the following objectives: (1) to seek strategic superiority over the adversary at minimum risk to the Soviet military posture by structuring treaties in such a way that only the adversary would be obliged to follow their stipulations; and (2) to gather as much information as possible on the adversary's strength and determination to use force, while at the same time lowering his vigilance through all available means of disinformation and deception and striving to confuse him.

Thus, for the Soviets, arms control is a mechanism to be exploited for slowing down U.S. military programs and as an instrument of military reconnaissance and deception. Sejna points out that an additional objective of considerable importance is the political use of arms control to split the Western alliance and exacerbate internal disharmonies in Western societies. Thus, while arms control would serve to facilitate the accomplishment of longstanding disarmament goals—indeed, it became a far more effective tool than disarmament propaganda in the accomplishment of these goals—its real goals were of quite a different character: military, political, intelligence, and counterintelligence.

The Soviet military approach to arms control agreements was explained by the Commander-in-Chief of the Warsaw Pact forces, Marshal Grechko, to the Soviet-bloc defense ministers and chiefs of the general staffs in September 1966. Sejna, who was present at this meeting, reported that Grechko said, first, that arms control agreements must never enable the United States and NATO to develop an accurate picture of Soviet military technology and weapons. Second, Soviet-bloc pressure for arms control and other treaties must be used against the military-industrial complex in the United States and Western Europe. Third, treaties must help in recruiting nonmilitary industries in the West to the Soviet cause and help drive a wedge between the military and nonmilitary industries. Fourth, they must help in influencing Third World countries to adopt policies favorable to the Soviet bloc. Fifth, they must be used to increase Soviet knowledge about Western developments in military technology and weapons and to provide information that can help speed up Soviet advances in military technology and weapons.

In 1967 an effort was initiated to coordinate the long-range plans of East European countries with the Soviet "Long-Range Plan for the Next Ten to Fifteen Years and Beyond." As an official of the Administrative Organs Department, First Secretary at the Ministry of Defense, and Secretary of the Defense Council in Czechoslovakia, Sejna had the task of ensuring that Czechoslovak military responses were fully in accord with the demands of the plan. Soviet analyses of the arms control process were incorporated into the long-range plan. The Soviets viewed arms control as a long-term process—fifteen years and beyond. They did not believe it would be a straight line process; rather, they anticipated the process would follow a zigzag course with many starts, stops, setbacks, and successes. Nevertheless, the long-term process was expected to move forward and fit into the general schedule that had been set forth in the long-range plan—with the last and most dangerous phase, Global Democratic Peace, projected to begin around 1985.[18]

Two major questions addressed in the plan were how to force the United States and NATO to agree to eliminate or reduce severely their strategic weapons, and what the Soviet Union and Warsaw Pact countries would do to ensure that, if there were an agreement, it would serve to strengthen their hand. To put it another way, it was envisioned that an agreement with the West would not lead to a reduction of Warsaw Pact or Soviet weapons commensurate with reductions imposed on the NATO countries. Concepts and instructions were developed by the Special State Interests (deception) Administration of the Operations Main Administration of the Soviet

General Staff on how to hide current weapons, what to "show" in maneuvers, and what weapons should be developed in secrecy. Even the sales of technology to Third World countries were discussed and coordinated with East European satellites from this perspective of deception.

As early as 1963, and explicitly in the long-range plan, the Soviets expressed a belief that it might be possible to prohibit nuclear weapons. They knew this would be a long process, but one day it might happen and the need to prepare for that eventuality was an important task. It was important to prepare in advance so that the Soviets would be made even stronger vis-a-vis the West when nuclear weapons were scrapped. The issue was finding a substitute for nuclear weapons. The solution was chemical and biological weapons, along with control of space. At the same time, prohibiting nuclear weapons did not mean the Soviets would actually eliminate their stockpiles. On the contrary, the issue was how to hide and maintain nuclear capabilities that were to be eliminated, and how to maintain military alliances themselves, if they also were disbanded. (The Soviets had developed a mechanism for running the Warsaw Pact as a military alliance through COMECON so that the Warsaw Pact could be "dissolved" without altering capabilities. Rurarz also points out that CMEA, the Council for Mutual Economic Assistance, has twenty-three standing branch commissions, but only twenty-two are officially listed. The twenty-third, a military commission, is strictly secret.)

In a similar vein, the long-range plan addressed the matter of how to diminish U.S. and West European capabilities to develop new high-technology weapons and, conversely, at the same time how to hide the Soviet development of new weapons and technology within the "civilian" sector—for example, within the Academy of Sciences and other agencies with nonmilitary titles. The Academy of Sciences, as will be discussed later, is far more than an association of academicians. It was given a major role in deception operations run against Western academics and scientists as part of the restructuring of the KGB in the mid- to late-1950s. The academy is also responsible for roughly 75 percent of military research and development in response to directions from the Operations Administration and relevant material and technology administrations.

The Soviets consider the negotiations process to be very important. They believe it must be staged to show the imperialists naked, make them appear guilty of preparing for war, and it must be used to recruit and mobilize the masses to pressure Western governments to reach agreements acceptable to Moscow. This belief can be seen today in Gorbachev's statement before the 27th Party Congress:

> That is why it is not easy at all, in the current circumstances, to predict the future of the relations between the socialist and the capitalist countries, the USSR, and the United States. The decisive factors here will be the

correlation of forces on the world scene, the growth and activity of the peace potential, and its capability of effectively repulsing the threat of nuclear war.[19]

This excerpt also illustrates why the path to arms control is expected to be a zigzag course, and why Gorbachev says they must use "tactical flexibility" in the negotiations and use influence in every aspect, including religion. Schuman adds that Novosti efforts to promote the Soviet image of peace and the image of the United States as warmonger were undertaken around the world and coordinated with related East European efforts. In the Third World, and elsewhere, the objective was to build support for Soviet arms control initiatives.

The long-range plan also spelled out the use of arms control to split the United States from its allies in Western Europe—an objective reflected in the Gorbachev statement before the 27th Party Congress:

> For the first time, governments of some West European countries, the Social Democratic and Liberal parties, and the public at large have begun to openly discuss whether present U.S. policy coincides with Western Europe's notions about its own security and whether the United States is going too far in its claims to leadership. The partners of the United States have had more than one occasion to see that someone else's spectacles cannot substitute for one's own eyes.[20]

Additional important objectives set forth for arms control in the long-range plan were to mobilize the masses; to influence other governments through subversion and deception to criticize and distance themselves from the United States; and to use the process to create a more revolutionary situation within the United States. The basis for this latter objective was the Soviet belief that unemployment would accompany a cutback in the U.S. defense efforts, which in turn would create serious disturbances and economic dislocations. Again, this objective can be seen in Gorbachev's 1986 Party Congress speech: "For them [the groups tied most to the military-industrial complex] disarmament means a loss in profits, a political risk. For us it means good in all respects: economic, political, moral."[21]

NOTES

1. V.V. Larionov, "The Relaxation of Tension and the Principle of Equal Security," *Krasnaya Zvezda*, July 18, 1974; translated by U.S. Air Force, *Soviet Press Selected Translations*, No. 74-77, July 31, 1974, p. 33.
2. Cited in Raymond S. Sleeper, editor, *A Lexicon of Marxist-Leninist Semantics* (Alexandria, Va.: Western Goals, 1983), p. 95.
3. "Arbatov Views CPSU Congress Stand on Disarmament," Moscow, *Komsomolskaya Pravda*; in FBIS, *USSR International Affairs*, March 12, 1986, p. AA2.

4. Boris Ponomarev, "The Communists and Our Day's Pressing Issues," *World Marxist Review*, February 1985, p. 9.
5. See Ken Booth, *Strategy and Ethnocentrism* (New York: Holmes & Meier, 1979), pp. 41–50.
6. Khrushchev's "secret speech" denouncing Stalin was authenticated by the CIA, and obtaining a copy of it has been widely advertised as a major CIA coup. The view that the speech was really a successful deception foisted on the West is presented in Joseph D. Douglass, Jr., "Soviet Strategic Deception," *Defense Science 2002+*, August 1984, pp. 88–91.
7. See Crozier, *Strategy of Survival*, op. cit., and Joshua, op. cit.
8. *World History in Facts, Part III, USSR and European Socialist States* (Prague: Political Literature Publishing Company, 1964).
9. The use of "learned professionals" in this deception operation continues to this day to have great effect. It is described in greater detail toward the end of Chapter 6.
10. Dziak, op. cit., p. 13.
11. The first meeting of the Inform Bureau was on October 5, 1947. *Problems of Peace and Socialism* (also called *World Marxist Review*) was first published on August 8, 1958.
12. As discussed in Chapter 6, Soviet party and government officials are especially important instruments of deception. In creating false images of the Soviet Union in the United States, the most important Soviet instruments include officials such as Dobrynin, Gromyko, Arbatov, and so forth. A good example is Ambassador Dobrynin's description of the interests of the Soviet military in the arms control process: "The Soviet Ministry of Defense, according to Dobrynin, did not have much use for SALT. It consistently put its most unimaginative and unenterprising general on the SALT delegation, he said, with instructions to block any initiative put forward by the Foreign Ministry, which was technically in charge of the negotiations." Kissinger, *Years of Upheaval*, op. cit., p. 269. Dobrynin's account is inconsistent in all particulars with the descriptions of the SALT process provided by the former high-level officials interviewed for this study.
13. Arkady Shevchenko also stated that the Soviet leadership believed that the United States was much more likely to get serious about concrete arms limitation initiatives than general disarmament discussions. Uri Ra'anan and Richard H. Shultz, "Methodologies for Assessing and Projecting Soviet Strategic Defense and Arms Control Policy," Conference on Emerging Doctrines and Technologies: Implications for Global and Regional Political-Military Balances, Fletcher School of Law and Diplomacy, April 16–18, 1986.
14. Harriet Fast Scott and William F. Scott, editors, *The Soviet Art of War* (Boulder, Colo.: Westview Press, 1982), pp. 162–167.
15. U.S. Congress, Senate, *Analysis of the Khrushchev Speech of January 6, 1961*, Testimony of Dr. Stefan T. Possony, Hearing before the Subcommittee to Investigate the Administration of the Internal Security Act and Internal Security Laws, Committee on the Judiciary, June 16, 1961 (Washington, D.C.: U.S. Government Printing Office, 1961).

16. The formal culmination of this process was a meeting of the East European intelligence chiefs (minus Romania) in Moscow in October 1964.
17. E. Beobyeb, *Voyennaya Vestnik*, No. 3, 1964.
18. The phases and contents of the plan are set forth in Sejna and Douglass, op. cit., pp. 48–50.
19. See FBIS, *Party Congresses*, February 26, 1985, p. 5.
20. Information Bureau, *27th Congress of the Communist Party of the Soviet Union*, First Issue 9(553), Vol. 24, 1986; *Peace and Socialism* (Prague: International Publishers, 1986?), pp. 20–21; FBIS, *Party Congresses*, February 26, 1986, pp. O=6–7.
21. Ibid. (*Peace and Socialism*, p. 86; FBIS, p. O=30).

5

THE SOVIET VIEW OF THE UNITED STATES

Lenin set forth a clear view of the United States that remains in force today. The United States, he said, because of its basic economic characteristics, distinguishes itself as the least peace-loving and freedom-loving social system. "There was an epoch of relatively 'peaceful' capitalism. . . . This epoch is gone for good, it has given way to an epoch which is relatively much more violent, spasmodic, disastrous and conflicting, an epoch which for the mass of the population is typified not so much by a 'horror without end' as by a 'horrible end.'"[1]

IMPERIALISM: THE SOURCE OF ALL WAR

The essence of the Soviet view of the United States is encapsulated in Lenin's assertion that "As long as imperialism exists there cannot be peace on earth." Alternatively, as stated in the new Party Program developed for the 1986 Party Congress, "The citadel of international reaction is U.S. imperialism. It is from here, above all, that the threat of war emanates."[2]

A good example of the Soviet view can be gleaned from the report on the interview President Reagan gave to four Soviet journalists in October 1985. The report was published in the November 1985 issue of the (KGB-sponsored) *New Times*. The views expressed by the Soviet journalists, including the brazen *ad hominem* attacks on President Reagan, undoubtedly were sanctioned by the highest Soviet authorities. They ridiculed all U.S. arms control proposals and called all U.S. information on the level of Soviet nuclear forces an outright lie. They reproached the

United States for having the worst intentions toward the USSR and accused the United States of planning atomic attacks against the USSR as far back as 1945. They excoriated the United States for its bases surrounding the USSR and for the 550,000 U.S. servicemen stationed at those bases. No mention was made about the cause for U.S. concern or of the failure of the USSR to demobilize after World War II in parallel with the United States.[3]

Does the Soviet leadership truly believe its own propaganda about the United States? Rurarz's view is that the Soviet leadership may believe its own pronouncements on hostile U.S. intentions toward the USSR. He points out that few "true" Soviet civilians, that is, those who are not connected with either the KGB or the military, have an independent expert knowledge of complex international issues, such as the balance of forces, much less of genuine U.S. intentions. What knowledge civilians possess is based almost exclusively on what the party determines the civilians should know or believe.

As an example of beliefs held within the upper echelons of the Soviet military, Rurarz cites an interview with Col. Yu. Yashin, First Deputy Commander-in-Chief of the Strategic Rocket Force, on November 19, 1985, on the issue of the U.S. Strategic Defense Initiative (SDI). Yashin leaves no doubt that he believes the United States is actually deploying "space strike arms," and that the United States intends to turn space into a "possible theater of military actions."

This image is even projected by Soviets who have lived in the United States. As explained by Rurarz, Soviet Ambassador Dobrynin, despite his twenty-five years in the United States, seems not only to believe the Soviet image of the United States, but has been personally instrumental in advancing the image. This is considerably at variance with the image of Dobrynin that is projected in Kissinger's and Nixon's memoirs, and is further testimony to Dobrynin's effectiveness as a disinformation agent. Dobrynin is a very important case because he has now been appointed head of the International Department, a post previously held by the very durable Ponomarev. The International Department, which is in charge of foreign policy, is one of the four most important CPSU Central Committee departments. Along with the Administrative Organs Department, it has the main role and responsibility in the development and implementation of global deception operations.[4] But whether Dobrynin does believe the Soviet image of the United States, or merely reports what is acceptable to report, is, in a sense, irrelevant because the effect is the same. The image of the United States that has been conjured up by Soviet leaders is extremely distorted; it is designed to support Marxist-Leninist ideology. What the United States is or does is irrelevant because it is the ideology that counts, and any deviation from the ideological line is grounds for being dismissed from the party and losing all professional stature and privileges, including one's job.

Nor is this image inconsistent with the one projected by General Secretary Gorbachev on the eve of the summit meeting—an image which appears to have shocked U.S. reporters. As reported in the *New York Times*, "Gorbachev's America is a land controlled by wealthy capitalists and conservative business interests. Right-wing forces dictate government policy and would never permit a lasting improvement in relations with the Soviet Union." Gorbachev's image of America, as described by Western diplomats, "corresponds closely to traditional Marxist-Leninist views of the United States as a corrupt society controlled by capitalists in which average citizens are exploited by the ruling class and government policy is made to protect the vested interests of the rich."[5]

The vast majority of Soviet Party functionaries, at the middle and lower levels, has very limited contact with the outside world, especially with the United States. They only know what they are taught or what they read in the carefully censored newspapers. The official image of the United States is corruption, warmongering, exploitation, imperialism, and so forth. Needless to say, there is ample material in the U.S. press that can be used to support this view and make it appear credible.

At the same time, Sejna cautions, this distorted image of the United States is less likely to be held by the highest-level functionaries, who often have access to special newspapers. One such paper that Sejna had access to was the *Monitor*, which was published in two editions, a white and a yellow one. The main distinction between the white and yellow copies was that nothing that would compromise the top party leadership was contained in the white edition. In Czechoslovakia, the white edition was available to members of the Central Committee and selected leaders in various agencies and ministries. In the Ministry of Defense, roughly six copies were provided to select individuals. The totally unexpurgated yellow edition went only to the members of the Politburo, the Secretaries of the Central Committee, the heads of the Administrative Organs Department and chiefs of its military and intelligence sections, the heads of the International Department and the Ideology and Propaganda Department, and the Minister of Interior. It did not go to the Minister of Defense or the Chief of the General Staff. The *Monitor* provided an accurate recapitulation of world events as reported by radio, television, and newspapers. Thus, the top leadership in general was very well informed about what was happening. Because of this and the extensive educational briefings held each Monday and Friday on recent events of importance in the West (in both cases, normally three or four hours long), they were extremely cognizant of reality, of deliberate ideological distortions, and of the reasons for these distortions.

However erroneous and unfavorable the image of the United States is as presented in the Soviet Union, what is far worse are the massive efforts throughout the entire communist system to teach its peoples to hate the West. From the litany of the 1960s, we have this example: "Socialist internationalism and respect for the peoples of capitalist countries should not weaken the burning hatred of the imperialists, whose goal it is to destroy by war the achievements of socialism and to enslave the peoples of the socialist countries."[6] There has been no let-up today. A 1984 article in *Krasnaya Zvezda* advised:

> Conducting offensive counterpropaganda means not confining yourself to rebuffing certain specific acts by bourgeois propaganda. It means being generally active in exposing imperialism, its bloodthirsty history, its ideology and policy, and its reactionary nature. It is necessary to extensively criticize the bourgeois way of life and the misanthropic nature of American imperialism as the real focus of all the evils and vices of the present-day bourgeois society and to show the true face of the American Army and its personnel—those hired butchers and suppressors of freedom. We must arm our servicemen with concrete knowledge about the class enemy and educate them in the spirit of devout hatred of the enemies of the motherland and of the cause of peace, freedom, and progress.[7]

The United States is portrayed as the essence of evil, as a disease to be eradicated. Capitalists, especially those located in the citadel of capitalism, the United States, are only interested in exploiting all peoples for their own selfish and materialistic interests. American imperialism is described as the source of all wars and not to be trusted. In the arms control process, the United States is only playing a political game, using the cause of peace as a cover for legalizing spying and hiding its war preparations.

In this regard, Sejna explains, the Soviets reinforce their doctrinal image by engaging in extensive mirror-imaging. The Soviet system is based on lies and deceptions and, in analyzing the actions and intentions of others, they attribute similar behavior to the enemy. Consequently, as they assess the United States, the Soviets regularly read cheating and deception into all U.S. actions, proposals, and statements.

THE EFFECT OF U.S. EFFORTS TO IMPROVE RELATIONS WITH THE USSR

The Soviet image of the United States is independent of, or even inversely affected by, U.S. behavior. There appears to be no perceptible difference in the nature of Soviet statements on U.S. intentions between the cold war era and the heyday of detente. Each year *Communist of the Armed Forces* carries detailed orders for political instructors to follow during the new year in political indoctrination courses for the four million or more soldiers and sailors of the Soviet armed forces. The themes stress the increased aggressiveness of imperialism and the need for further strengthening of the defense capability of the country. All the alleged evils of the United States are spelled out, including details of its militaristic policies and its ideological and psychological war efforts. As pointed out by Harriet Fast Scott, the themes are venomous toward the United States and, in providing guidance for 1986, differ little from the articles that have launched the study year for the past twenty-five years. Whether the Soviet leader is Khrushchev, Brezhnev, Andropov, Chernenko, or Gorbachev, or whether the U.S. leader is Eisenhower, Kennedy, Johnson, Nixon, Ford, Carter, or Reagan is irrelevant.

The subsequent themes in individual issues of *Communist of the Armed Forces* elaborate the basic guidance established at the beginning of the year. These articles should not be dismissed as mere military rhetoric. Their justification is taken directly from the CPSU Party Program:

> The aggressive, reactionary direction of imperialism's policy is thoroughly pointed out in the draft new edition of the Program of the CPSU. It states in this document that "The more strongly the course of historical development erodes the position of imperialism, the more hostile the policies of its more reactionary forces are to the interests of the people. Imperialism offers bitter resistance to social progress, makes attempts to stop the course of history, undermines the position of socialism, and exacts social revenge on a universal scale." Imperialist powers are trying to coordinate their economic, political and ideological strategy, trying to create a common front of struggle against socialism, against all revolutionary, liberating movements.[8]

The Soviet Union's view of the United States is an integral part of its ideology. Where U.S. actions are useful to explain or justify Soviet views, they are readily used. In many cases they are simply invented. For example, the Soviets allege that the United States used the atomic bombing of Japan as a mailed fist against the Soviet Union. Or, the Soviets claim that the United States, Britain, France, and other capitalist countries "encouraged the Nazi aggressors to unleash war in Eastern Europe and to undertake a 'crusade' against the USSR."[9] The United States is not responsible for the way it is viewed by the Soviet Union; Marxist-Leninist ideology and the demands of state policy determine the view. This is another reason why understanding the ideology and state policy of the Soviet Union is so critical to understanding what is taking place in the arms control process.

As a practical example, in 1967, Czechoslovakia proposed a plan that would cut its defense expenditures. The reasoning of Czechoslovak leaders was that, after careful analysis, they had concluded that the United States was not about to attack. The Czechoslovak officials were soon summoned to Moscow and sternly lectured by Marshal Matvei V. Zakharov, Chief of the Soviet General Staff (and formerly Chief of the GRU), on the imperialist enemies. Then Army General Alexei A. Yepishev, head of the Main Political Administration, stated quite bluntly, "If we accept your theory, where is the base of our ideology and propaganda?" The parting volley was strong advice to the Czechoslovak leaders to rid their ranks of the enemies of the state who would propose such traitorous theories.

Moreover, whenever the United States chooses accommodation rather than confrontation when faced with perceived Soviet paranoia or defensive concerns, the Soviet response, Rurarz explains, is to interpret such moves as those of a fool and as a weakness to be exploited in accordance with the old Russian proverb, *"duraka y v tserkvi b'yut"* ("a fool is roughed up even in church"). That is, anyone who is naive and can be cheated should be cheated, and there is nothing immoral in that. Insofar as the Soviets are concerned, in dealing with the West, especially the United States, they are dealing with the devil, with the main enemy that is to be destroyed. Any opportunity to hasten or facilitate this destruction is to be seized. Thus, as will be described in greater detail in Chapter 6, cheating is not only honorable, it is something that should be done whenever profitable opportunities arise.

A good example of a typical Soviet response to host country hospitality is provided by Schuman. His first assignment to India was in 1963 with a Soviet economic aid group (GKES, State Committee for Economic Co-operation), building oil refineries in Gujarat and Bihar states. There were many discussions about "peaceful coexistence" and the expansion of the Soviet military presence in India and Pakistan, he explained. At the same time that Soviet propaganda was raving hysterically against "aggressive U.S. military bases encircling the Socialist camp," the Soviet Union brought groups of Soviet military experts to India to build Soviet MiGs, train Indian pilots to fly them, and prepare Indian seaports in Visaghapatnam and Bombay for Soviet nuclear submarines.

Next to the Soviet residence in Baroda, Schuman reports, there was a spacious bungalow densely populated by a detachment of Soviet air force advisors, who were presented to the media and public as a Soviet "football team." The Indian bureaucracy was well aware of their "presence," especially the local bank, which paid salaries to the "football players." The director of this bank in Baroda revealed to Schuman that, according to the Soviet-Indian agreement, India paid 6,000 to 10,000 rupees to the Soviet embassy for each Soviet "expert" working in India. The "footballers" actually received only 500 rupees. The difference was "deducted" by the Soviet embassy in New Delhi and, as Schuman learned later, was used to finance subversive "active measures" against the host country, India, and against U.S. interests in that country.

The dominance of ideology in shaping Soviet views of the United States and other enemies also shapes the response of Soviet leaders to U.S. actions designed to allay Soviet suspicions—such as the enormous assistance provided to the Soviet Union in the 1920s and in World War II, the increase in trade and technological transfer in the 1970s, the unilateral cutback in armaments and adherence to arms control treaties in the 1970s. The Soviet response to such overtures is one of deprecation, of viewing U.S. leaders as decadent fools. The idea that increased trade and economic relations with the USSR will lead to better relations is false; if anything, exactly the opposite is true. While arms control as a political-military strategy is serious business to the Soviets, Schuman explains that informally it is regarded as a huge joke on the United States. Whenever the topic arose in casual discussions he had with important Soviet officials (his father was a General Staff officer and, hence, Schuman had many contacts with these officers as well as with KGB and International Department officials), the United States was always regarded as the fool in these (and many other) matters.

One of the more insightful descriptions of the Soviet approach is revealed in informal notes written by Lenin to the Central Committee in 1921 providing guidance on dealing with Westerners. The notes were copied by the painter Annenkov, who had been given access to the Lenin files to obtain background prior to painting Lenin's portrait in 1924. His notes were subsequently published in an article in an emigré paper, *The New Review*. Lenin advised his colleagues:

> As a result of my direct observation in the years of my emigration I must admit that the so-called cultured classes of Western Europe and America are not able to understand the present situation of things nor the real relationship of forces; these classes should be considered as deaf and dumb and should be treated on this basis.

Lenin then wrote that it was necessary to convince the West that the Soviet government is separate from the Communist Party and the Comintern (which, of course, was not and is not the case), and that diplomatic and trade relations with Soviet Russia were desirable and safe.

> Capitalists of the whole world and their governments in the race to win Soviet markets will close their eyes to the actuality indicated above and turn deaf and dumb. They will give credit which will serve us with the materials and equipment we lack, they will restore our military industry, which is necessary for our future victorious attack against our suppliers. In other words, they will work on preparing their own suicide.[10]

This was written in 1921 at the time the New Economic Plan (NEP) was being launched. The logic is precisely that which was applied with great effectiveness in the NEP and analyzed with care in the mid-1950s by KGB scholars and strategists during the course of their research to support the reformulation of long-range strategy, as described by Golitsyn. The effectiveness of this strategy in application is revealed in Antony Sutton's three-volume history of technology transfer.[11] Further, an especially interesting account of the connection between the Kremlin and America's most powerful businessmen—Armand Hammer, Averell Harriman, Cyrus Eaton, David Rockefeller, Donald Kendall, and others—is presented in Joseph Finder's *The Red Carpet*.[12]

Sejna also provides numerous examples of Soviet strategy and intent in obtaining trade and economic assistance. In one example, after speaking on the need for peaceful coexistence, Khrushchev was congratulated by an inebriated Czechoslovak composer, who was also a member of the Czechoslovak Central Committee, on Khrushchev's introducing an era of world peace. Sejna reports that Khrushchev turned on him abruptly and told him to shut up. He said that by peaceful coexistence he did not mean pacifism but a policy that would destroy imperialism and make the Soviet Union and her allies the strongest economic and military power in the world. He said that this new diplomacy would be successful only as long as there was a Soviet marshal behind every diplomat. Peaceful coexistence was not "class peace"; it would be impossible to establish global peace while one imperialist lived.

NOTES

1. Lenin, *Works*, Vol. 22, p. 104.
2. *Pravda*, March 8, 1986.
3. After World War II the Soviets remained on a war footing until Stalin's death. Army General S.M. Shtemenko, *The General Staff During the War* (Moscow, second edition, 1981), p. 179.
4. Sejna and Douglass, op. cit., p. 20.
5. Philip Taubman, "Gorbachev's Gloomy America," *New York Times*, November 15, 1985.
6. Marshal V.D. Sokolovskiy, *Soviet Military Strategy*, edited with commentary by Harriet Fast Scott (New York: Crane Russak, 1974), p. 330.
7. Major General N. Shapalin, "Ideological Work: Experience, Opinions," *Krasnaya Zvezda*; translated by FBIS, *USSR National Affairs, Military Developments*, Vol. 2, July 31, 1984.
8. Col. G. Arzumanov, "The Armies and Military-Political Blocks of Imperialist States," *Communist of the Armed Forces*, No. 1, January 1986; translation by Harriet Fast Scott.
9. Marshal N.V. Ogarkov, *History Teaches Vigilance* (Moscow: Voyenizdat, 1985); translation in JPRS-UMS-85-021-L, August 30, 1985, p. 55.
10. Professor Albert Parry, "Lenin's Rope," *Novoye Russkoye Slovo*, June 25, 1978; translation by Harriet Fast Scott. Annenkov's story was translated by

Charles T. Baroch, who talked to Annenkov in Paris in 1964 about the incident. Annenkov showed Baroch his original notes. Baroch's translation of Annenkov's description was published in the *Bulletin of the Institute for the Study of the USSR*, which was affiliated with Radio Liberty. The Institute's funding was canceled in 1972 as part of the U.S. detente policy, and the Institute was dissolved. The article is also available in the *Congressional Record-Appendix*, November 21, 1966, p. A-5929.

11. Antony C. Sutton, *Western Technology and Soviet Economic Development, 1917-1965*, 3 volumes (Stanford, Calif.: Hoover Institution Press, 1968).
12. Joseph Finder, *The Red Carpet* (New York: Holt, Rinehart and Winston, 1983).

6

CHEATING AND DECEPTION

Cheating and deception are two sides of the same coin: Cheating is usually accompanied by deception, and deception is itself a form of cheating.

Cheating and deception, when used in support of Soviet strategy, are entirely moral activities from the Soviet perspective. Indeed, it would be immoral not to cheat and deceive the class enemy. At the same time, this does not imply cheating just for the sake of cheating. Cheating is a serious activity that is in the main reserved for tasks that advance state interests.

While cheating is fully justified in Marxism-Leninism—indeed the ideology itself is an ideal example of ingrained and integrated deception—its roots are to be found in the Russian tradition, where deception is as natural a national characteristic as is freedom in the United States.[1] The fact that the use of cheating and deception has become second nature, almost a necessity for survival in the Soviet Union, has been described by visitors both in recent years—for example, Hedrick Smith in *The Russians*[2]—and many years ago—for example, by the Marquis de Custine in *Journey for Our Time*.[3] The descriptions, notwithstanding the 140 years of separation, are almost identical. Or, consider the combined views of Karl Marx and Friedrich Engels: ". . . bribery, deceit, the exploitation of disunity (often artificially incited or maintained) are traditional features of that [Russian foreign] policy."[4]

Officially, the Soviet Union rejects both cheating and deception. Both are touted as capitalistic pursuits. Wherever a plan or an office is dedicated to these activities, it is referred to euphemistically as the "political" plan, or active operations, or, in the case of the Operations Main Administration, "special state interests."

THE PLANNING AND DECISION PROCESS

Cheating and deception are not frivolous pursuits. To the contrary, they are serious, high-level activities that are regarded as the most important weapon of the party. Whenever a major decision is made by the Defense Council, Sejna explains, that decision is fully prepared. The plans for implementation are carefully laid out. Additionally, the plans governing how secrecy is to be handled, who is to be informed about what, how implementation is to be monitored, when progress will be reported and to whom, and what means of deception (the political plan) will be employed are also fully prepared as an integral part of the decision.

Similarly, before any treaty is signed, the Defense Council or the Politburo, depending on the nature of the treaty, approves a plan for the secret violation of the treaty. Treaties are recognized as a "means of gaining strength."[5] Insofar as the communists understand that they are at war and always will be at war until capitalism is eradicated, this statement applies equally to treaties during what the West refers to as peacetime. Accordingly, when a treaty is being considered, Sejna explains, an analysis is presented on how the treaty will operate to the benefit of the USSR through a resultant increase in Soviet strength.[6] The plan for cheating usually is incorporated into this analysis.

As an example, in the fall of 1962, officials from the Soviet International Department briefed the top Czechoslovak leadership on the progress of the nuclear test ban treaty negotiations. They explained that the major objectives for the treaty were political. In its final form, the treaty would show the Soviets leading the battle to control the arms race and forcing the United States to capitulate. It would enhance the Soviet "peace-loving" image and whet the appetite for arms control of those in the West with influence over policy—academics, journalists, scientists—by demonstrating that it was possible to pressure the imperialists into signing agreements. At the same time, the treaty would not stop the development of Soviet nuclear forces; any treaty that obstructed the development of Soviet forces would be a crime and not considered.[7] There would be no break in the research and development of nuclear weapons in the USSR. When the resumption of testing became necessary, the Soviets would not hesitate to do so, and the satellites would be notified in advance so that they could join the Soviets in blaming the West for breaking the treaty. General A.I. Antonov, Chief of Staff of the Warsaw Pact forces, explained that the Soviets would wait six months after the treaty was signed and then begin again with small tests. The Soviets believed the tests would not be detected, but, if they were, that would tell the Soviets much about U.S. monitoring technology.

Another example from this period with relevance to current U.S.-Soviet relations concerns Soviet interests in space weapons. Following the signing of the limited test ban treaty, the Soviet Union ceased linking an agreement prohibiting weapons in outer space with the question of foreign bases. On September 19, 1963, Foreign Minister Gromyko told the UN General Assembly that the Soviet Union wished to conclude an agreement banning the orbiting of objects carrying nuclear weapons. On October 17, 1963, the General Assembly unanimously adopted a resolution calling upon all states to refrain from introducing weapons of mass destruction in outer space.[8] This then led to the signing, on January 27, 1967, of the Treaty on Principles Governing the Activities of States in the Exploration and Use of Outer Space, Including the Moon and Other Celestial Bodies, which incorporated the 1963 General Assembly resolution.

In 1964, Jan Sejna became First Secretary at the Czechoslovak Ministry of Defense. In reviewing documents dealing with Warsaw Pact treaties as part of his new duties, he read a Soviet report on a Soviet Defense Council decision in 1963 stating that the Soviets would not adhere to the UN resolution banning weapons in outer space. Attached to the document was a special order from the Soviet Defense Council to the USSR Minister of Defense, Minister of Interior, and President of the Academy of Sciences directing that Soviet activities in violation of the resolution were to be kept secret.

In 1966, according to Sejna, the Czechoslovak Defense Council discussed the 1963 Soviet Defense Council decision not to comply with the UN resolution in the context of a decision on Czechoslovak exploitation of scientific programs for the military use of space and how those programs were to be hidden. The items that the Czechoslovak scientists were directed to work on included: (1) weapons that could be used to destroy satellites in space; (2) space weapons capable of destroying ground targets; (3) biological weapons that could be stored in space and used in future conflicts; (4) laser weapons for offensive and defensive purposes; and (5) communications for command and control of space-based systems. To maintain secrecy, the Czechoslovak Defense Council ordered that: (1) there would be no mention of military applications of space below the top secret level; (2) the portions of the Czechoslovak Academy of Sciences program in this area would be deleted from all Academy plans and reports that went to the Politburo (that is, the Politburo would not be informed about this work)[9]; (3) all Czechoslovak scientists working in this area would have to pass an additional security background investigation in which the Soviet KGB military counterintelligence would participate; and (4) all of this work would be directed by the Ministry of Defense, which meant that Academy of Sciences participants would work under Soviet direction channeled through the Czechoslovak Ministry of Defense. The "political plan" designed to assist in this activity began with an order from the Czechoslovak Defense Council to the Department of Special Propaganda at the Ministry of

Defense, the Ministry of Interior, the Administration Department, and the Foreign Department. This order directed these departments to prepare, based on Soviet guidance and for approval by the Czechoslovak Secretariat (responsible for oversight of such operations), a propaganda campaign to be employed against the West, accusing it of exploiting space for military purposes.

In January 1967, when the treaty banning weapons of mass destruction in outer space was signed, an official report presented at the 13th Czechoslovak Party Congress was printed and distributed. This report referred to the work in progress on using space as a base for military operations: "What will be obviously important for the future development of military affairs is the question of providing an adequate amount of energy and sufficient means for reliable anti-rocket and anti-space defense of the entire hinterland of the state and of the coalition, and for the possibility of conducting warfare in cosmic space."[10] This is the manner in which the military space research and development programs were described in an official secret-level Czechoslovak Ministry of Defense document.

In September 1967, Sejna reports, Czechoslovak leaders went to Moscow to obtain approval of a comprehensive plan for modernizing the Czechoslovak military forces that had been initiated at Soviet direction in 1965. This plan also pointed to the military use of outer space: "The strategic fire (strike) system will reach higher possibilities and from the fire point of view will cover the cosmos [space]."[11] Again, this statement referred to the military space research and development that was undertaken with specific intent to violate the 1963 resolution and 1967 treaty. It also predicted that the results of this effort would emerge in the third phase (1975–1980) of the plan. Unfortunately for the Czechoslovak leaders, the classification attached to this Ministry of Defense document was only top secret. When Marshal Zakharov, Chief of the Soviet General Staff, discovered that the above statement and another one related to military space systems had been inserted into a top secret document, he became extremely angry. The inclusion of this material, he stressed, was impermissible in top secret documents. It was only permissible in documents that carried the highest classification, namely, "State Importance."

While plans for cheating and deception are formulated, additional plans are developed to deal with the possibility that the cheating or deception will be recognized by the enemy. A good example of this kind of advance preparation can be found in the Berlin Wall crisis. The planning for this action was revealed to the East Europeans on March 28, 1961. To prepare for Western reaction, the Soviet plan was to provide a context in which the Soviets could claim that the wall was built only as a necessary response to "well-founded" fears of West German and NATO military adventurism.

The Soviet propaganda and disinformation apparatus initiated an operation to create through the U.S. and West European press an image of West German militarism, coupled to the issues of nuclear war and nuclear deployment. The effectiveness of this campaign and its additional success in discrediting West German Defense Minister Franz Josef Strauss is reflected in the *"Der Spiegel* Affair." A good example, uncovered by Sir James Goldsmith in preparing for his defense against a libel action brought by *Der Spiegel*, is an article written by Rudolf Augstein, writing in *Der Spiegel* under the name "Jens Daniel" five weeks before the erection of the Berlin Wall. He writes: "It was the policy of the Federal Government which left the Soviets only the choice either to put the screws on Berlin or to wait until Federal Chancellor Strauss had nuclear weapons at his disposal. Now he will not have them at his disposal, but only because the Soviets put the screws on Berlin."[12] Here is the essence of how the Soviets wanted the political environment to be perceived in the West in preparation for the building of the Berlin Wall.

Another revealing example of the Soviet techniques of cheating and deception can be drawn from the arena of chemical and biological weapons (CBW). In the mid-1950s, the Soviets reasoned that it might be possible to get the West to disarm unilaterally in CBW. To do so, however, the Soviet Union must be seen to be complying with the 1925 Geneva Protocol. Accordingly, Soviet offensive chemical and biological warfare capabilities were to be treated as extremely sensitive matters, and CBW research and development was to be carried on in secret. In the mid-1960s, the Soviets placed high priority on research and development for advanced chemical and biological agents, which were regarded as eventual alternatives to nuclear weapons, and on the production of CB weapons and their integration into the operational plans of all Warsaw Pact forces. A twenty-year plan was set in motion in 1965, calling for the training of workers, equipping of factories, and general preparations for production of CBW from 1965 to 1971, production and stockpiling of CBW during the 1971–1976 period, and the development of a family of qualitatively new chemical and biological weapons by 1985.

While engaged in this massive buildup, the Soviets undertook a combined propaganda and deception operation designed to shut down U.S. development and manufacture of chemical weapons and ultimately to disarm the United States in chemical and biological weapons through political pressure and adverse media exposure, and to entrap the United States into accepting a Soviet offer to exercise mutual restraint in the CBW field. The Soviet propaganda apparatus, building on anti-war feelings in the United States, capitalized on the U.S. use of Agent Orange, a defoliant, in Vietnam, and on the death of some 6,000 sheep near the Dugway Proving Grounds that was linked to U.S. Army testing of a nerve agent. The sheep became a cause célèbre used against the U.S. military. In an effort to put an end to the unfavorable publicity, the Army was directed to pay off the sheep farmers, but this did even more damage because of the Army's implicit acknowledgment of guilt in the process. In retrospect, it now appears nearly impossible for the deaths to have been caused by nerve agent testing. Years after the testing was stopped, several additional episodes occurred in which large numbers of sheep died, and state veterinarians concluded that the deaths were due to the ingestion of a noxious weed, common to the area. None of the reporters or newspapers who reported on the Dugway sheep "accident" paid any attention to the follow-on "accidents."[13]

The negative publicity was used in the Soviet operation as the stick. The carrot was the offer of mutual restraint. As reported in the *Washington Star* in 1978:

> The Soviet Union attempted to influence President Richard M. Nixon in 1969 to halt chemical and biological weapons development by transmitting information through double agents working for the FBI, according to American intelligence officials.
>
> The aim of the agents' messages was to convince Nixon that if the United States continued its build-up of chemical weapons, especially nerve gas, the Soviet Union would be compelled to start a "crash program" to match American capabilities, the officials remarked.
>
> In effect, it was an invitation to mutual restraint in the field of chemical weapons, an intelligence officer remarked.[14]

A more detailed explanation by Edward J. Epstein in 1980 deserves lengthy citation:

> The FBI received information from two Soviet agents at the United Nations in 1969, code-named Fedora and Top Hat, who it assumed were anti-Soviet and FBI double-agents, which greatly affected the Nixon Administration's perception of the Soviet Union. Specifically, they provided dovetailing pieces of information, putatively from one of their colleagues in the Politburo, which sugested that the Soviet Union was on the verge of a crash program to develop chemical and biological weapons. According to these agents, the Soviets had found out through an intelligence gathering program that the United States was many years ahead of the Soviet Union in both research and production of chemical and biological weapons, and that Soviet leaders, including Leonid Brezhnev, had been "shocked" by this disparity. Presumably, the Soviets did not want to squander precious resources on research on such weapons, but it would have no choice if the United States persisted in developing them.
>
> After J. Edgar Hoover personally brought this message to his attention, President Nixon decided to avert a Soviet-American arms race in these lethal weapons by dramatically announcing that the United States was unilaterally terminating its build-up of such weapons. Nixon apparently believed, as these FBI reports indicated, that the United States had an indisputable lead in these weapons and that his embargo of further development would

preemptively discourage the Soviets from their reported "crash program." In 1973, however, U.S. military intelligence was able to determine from an analysis of weapons captured by Israel from Syria in the Yom Kippur War that the reported American lead in chemical-biological weapons was nonexistent, and even in 1969, when some of these weapons were designed, the Soviet Union could not have been far behind the United States in this area. This finding, as well as other evidence developed in prior cases, suggested that the agents Fedora and Top Hat were Soviet disinformation agents.[15]

As it turned out, the Soviets were ahead of the United States in 1969 in both CBW stockpiles and research and, as later acknowledged by the FBI, Fedora and Top Hat were Soviet double-agents.[16]

The President went on to renounce the manufacture and stockpiling of toxins and to sign the 1972 Biological and Toxin Weapons Convention, which Congress ratified along with the Geneva Protocol in 1975. This decision not to develop biological and toxin weapons—or chemical weapons as it turned out—was ideally timed from the Soviet perspective, because the early 1970s marked the beginning of what became known as the biotechnology revolution, in which knowledge in the life sciences was greatly expanded and, along with it, the technology of biological and chemical warfare took a quantum leap.

The Soviets artfully eased the United States out of the field that the Soviets knew would be of special importance. Moreover, they provided a base of false information that would lead the unwary to discount any news of a Soviet CBW buildup that leaked out as being only a paranoid reaction to U.S. capabilities; in the process, they shifted the blame—should any blame be necessary—onto the shoulders of the United States. Moreover, the intelligence information provided by Top Hat and Fedora, it should be noted, was not the only "tainted" data that the Soviets provided the West in this deception operation.

The Biological and Toxin Weapons Convention of 1972 was icing on the cake. It would guarantee the nonparticipation of the United States in developing biological and toxin weapons, and even cause the United States to lose touch with what was happening in this field, which in fact is exactly what happened. The Soviets had no intention of complying with the convention; they were in the midst of a major buildup in all dimensions of chemical and biological warfare. Their research and development, besides being cloaked in secrecy, was hidden within academic institutes and hospitals. A special division of the Soviet microbiology industry organization was even created for the express purpose of coordinating and managing the development of new biological weapons *at the same time* the convention was being negotiated. This is corroborated by the Soviet diplomatic defector, Arkady N. Shevchenko, who wrote that at the time of the Soviet decision to sign the Biological and Toxin Weapons Convention,

General Aleksei A. Gryzlov told Shevchenko that the Soviet biological weapons program would not be affected by the convention.[17]

The foregoing examples show how cheating is prepared in advance and how the groundwork is laid to counteract anticipated Western reactions. Additionally, the preparations are a good example of how the Soviet propaganda apparatus fuels the action-reaction and arms "race" arguments that are often used by Western arms control advocates to explain or justify Soviet actions.

Moreover, as part of their preparations to anticipate the need for a counterattack, Soviet leaders carefully observe U.S. reactions to Soviet actions that violate or even circumvent the various treaties. Thus, in July 1976, Rurarz was asked to read Western newspapers carefully while he was in Poland or during his trips to the West, and report on anything concerning alleged Soviet cheating while testing missiles. Specifically, he was asked by the ZII (Poland's military intelligence, and Rurarz's affiliation) to look for discussions on telemetry encryption, precision targeting, hot/cold mode of launching, booster thrust power, and numbers of warheads. The fact that such information was sought by the ZII indicated to Rurarz that Moscow had an interest in U.S. monitoring of Soviet cheating, since such information was not of direct interest to Poland.

Sejna suggests that Rurarz's asssignment was probably part of an operation carried out by joint Warsaw Pact teams to assess what the world knew—especially what the United States knew—of secret communist activities. Joint military research teams were formed and managed by the Soviet Main Political Administration, and, in scientific disciplines, by the Soviet International Department and Science Department. The Czechoslovak component of the military research team that met in Moscow numbered twelve senior professionals, and a group—the Administration for Science and Technology—was set up in the Czechoslovak General Staff to manage work in Czechoslovakia. Joint assignments within the Warsaw Pact were established by Soviet leaders. Within the various assigned areas, the teams were responsible for assessing how much the West knew and how accurate the knowledge of various Western experts was. This data was used for planning and as feedback to test the effectiveness of deception operations run against the West. Rurarz quite possibly had been ordered by one of these groups to provide specialized data in a preselected area, a common practice of these teams.

SOVIET STRATEGY FOR RESPONDING TO CHEATING CHARGES

The basic strategy employed when cheating is uncovered by the enemy is to deny everything. The Soviets always deny that they engage in cheating, deception, and disinformation. This poses no moral dilemma, because these actions are all justified by Marxist-Leninist morality: that is, nothing done to advance the revolutionary cause is immoral or improper. The only crime is to fail to cheat to gain an advantage over the imperialist adversary whenever the opportunity arises. Moreover, in Soviet strategy, such denial must be "offensive": It must transfer the guilt or blame to the other side.

A good example of offensive denial is the denial by the Soviets of their role in sponsoring international terrorism. The United States accused the Soviet Union and its satellites of sponsoring international terrorism. The Soviet Union denied the accusation and in response accused the United States of state terrorism. This is illustrated in a booklet by former Chief of the Soviet General Staff, Marshal N.V. Ogarkov, published in 1985. In reference to international terrorism, he explains,

> This began to be manifested especially distinctly with the arrival of the Reagan administration in the White House. Raising international terrorism, lying, provocations and slander to the status of state policy, U.S. ruling circles in their search for the mirage of world domination declared from the mouth of their President a new "crusade" against the USSR and socialism as a social and political system. . . . The U.S. is organizing flagrant provocations and campaigns of threats; encouraging state terrorism and committing diversions and unconcealed acts of banditry and piracy against the sovereign countries of the Middle East, Africa, and Central America.[18]

This same accusation was made by V.M. Chebrikov, Chairman of the KGB, at the 27th Party Congress: "Washington continues to interfere in the affairs of sovereign states and pursues a policy of state terrorism."[19]

Another good example of offensive denial in the Ogarkov booklet is his description of the shooting down of Korean Airlines Flight 007:

> A vivid example of such flagrant provocation was the violation of the USSR state border in the Far East on the night of 1 September 1983, organized by the U.S. intelligence services, which was carried out by a Boeing 747 aircraft belonging to a South Korean airline. As has already been irrefutably proven, the incursion of this aircraft into Soviet air space was an intentional, carefully planned, provocative reconnaissance action, which for its entire duration was precisely controlled from certain centers on the territory of the U.S. and Japan.[20]

It is important to remember that the military publishing house responsible for printing these two documents operates directly under the supervision of the Main Political Administration, which itself is a Department of the Party's Central Committee. This means the article has the approval of the CPSU and the General Secretary himself.

A classic example of Soviet offensive denial in the arms control arena, identified by William F. Scott and Harriet Fast Scott,[21] is contained in Khrushchev's remarks related to the resumption of U.S. nuclear testing after the Soviet Union broke the test moratorium in the fall of 1961.

Following the massive Soviet atmospheric test series, by far the largest and most extensive any nation had ever conducted—including instrumented high-altitude shots, ABM experiments, and two detonations in the 40 to 70 megaton range—the United States conducted several small underground tests. Khrushchev then announced:

> The Central Committee of our Party and the Soviet Government are responsible to the Soviet people for the security of our homeland, and we see to it all the time that the defenses of our socialist land are at the proper level. It should be clear that if the United States holds another series of experimental explosions in the atmosphere, and it is already making underground explosions, the Soviet Union will be compelled to reply to this by holding its own tests. Thus, the United States Government will not achieve any military advantage by holding nuclear weapons tests. But there is one thing it will indeed achieve—it will usher in a new stage in the arms race and thus earn the censure of the peoples who want the Soviet Union and the United States to compete peacefully, and not in the manufacture of increasingly terrible weapons of destruction.
>
> We regret the decision of the United States Government to resume nuclear tests. It has thereby assumed a serious responsibility before the peoples of the world. But I should like to assure you, comrades, that this decision of the United States Government, far from weakening our efforts in the struggle for disarmament, including a nuclear test ban, will, on the contrary, redouble them.[22]

On July 13, 1962, Khrushchev received a group of U.S. journalists. During the interview, Felix McKnight, editor of the *Dallas Times Herald*, brought up the Soviet breaking of the moratorium. Khrushchev responded to one aspect of the question and then turned to the issue of nuclear testing.

> Now about the tests. In this, too, you have been misled and have probably not followed the Soviet, and even the American, press.
>
> No one can claim that the Soviet Union was the first to begin tests, just as you cannot say that the United States was the first in outer space. You can only say that you have visited outer space after we had already been there. Just as Columbus discovered America, so Garagin discovered outer space. The Soviet Union was the first, and this fact will go down in history and live down the ages.
>
> Who was the first to begin atomic tests? It was the United States of America.
>
> Who used atomic weapons to kill people in Hiroshima and Nagasaki? It was the United States of America.
>
> This too will go down in history.
>
> You say that we terminated the moratorium. Actually, it was all different. When carrying out nuclear weapons tests, the Soviet Union was from the outset replying to a corresponding series of tests carried out by the U.S.A. The negotiations on ending nuclear tests began after a series of American tests to which the Soviet Union did not reply in the hope that a treaty ending all nuclear tests would be signed. The Soviet Union honestly took part in the talks, until the U.S. President declared a mobilization of the armed forces

and began to threaten us with war. It was then that we decided to carry out nuclear weapons tests in order to prepare our army better in case the U.S. President actually carries out his threat and unleashes war against the Soviet Union. But even in that case the Soviet tests were a reply to tests previously made by the U.S.A.

No one can say that we broke the moratorium. As far as the number of series of tests is concerned, the United States is continuously in the fore, and the Soviet Union will be able to catch up with the U.S.A.—and then only in the number of test series, but not in the number of actual explosions—if it makes new tests after the current American series. We hope that after this the U.S.A. will finally agree to signing a treaty banning tests for all time.

However, if the Americans end their nuclear weapons tests now, and if we reach an agreement on general and complete disarmament and the destruction of nuclear weapons, we would no longer need to make our tests. On the other hand, if America pursues the policy of testing, stockpiling and improving nuclear weapons, then, of course, we shall be compelled to do the same. That is the true state of affairs on this question.[23]

These statements by Khrushchev are especially interesting when compared with Gorbachev's response to Reagan's announcement at the end of May 1986 that the United States would not comply with SALT II unless the Soviets stopped cheating. Gorbachev's response was, like Khrushchev's, an excellent example of offensive denial coupled with a threat that U.S. actions would require Soviet counteractions that would only lead to another needless escalation of the "arms race."[24]

SOVIET INSTRUCTIONS ON CHEATING AND DECEPTION

In 1963 the Soviet Union sent Czechoslovak leaders special instructions on how to weaken the enemy politically and militarily. The Czechoslovak Administrative Organs Department extracted those portions of the instructions that were relevant to Czechoslovakia and presented them to the Defense Council.

The instructions explained that cheating, deception, disinformation, and misleading the enemy were essential functions of both party and government organizations because they helped protect socialism and blinded the enemy to the nature of the main strategic goals. Of special significance, they covered the methods used to achieve the main strategic goals and, therefore, the final victory of communism. Accordingly, these activities were described as the most important responsibility of the highest party and government officials.

The instructions stated that the activities undertaken should deny the enemy the ability to evaluate accurately the strength of Soviet defenses, the economy, and agriculture, and the development of each. The activities should be designed to minimize the ability of the enemy to exploit the weaknesses of the Soviet Union on the one hand, and, on the other, to diminish and eventually eliminate the military superiority of the United States and NATO.

The instructions set forth principles of cheating and deception, as well as the tasks where cheating and deception would be important tools for accomplishing the tasks. Because of the importance of the year 1963, when Soviet military strategy shifted to the offensive, when efforts to integrate and intensify disinformation and intelligence operations were undertaken, and when arms control became a strategic military and intelligence operation, these instructions are worth repeating in detail. The principles were divided into three groups, military, political, and economic, and set forth as follows:

1. *Military*
    a. Preserve the secrecy of the main goals of military decisions and the real level of Soviet Union and Warsaw Pact defenses; that is, the development and production of weapons, organization and numbers of troops and weapons, especially those of strategic importance, and the mobilization system.
    b. Mislead the enemy about the major targets of the intelligence services of the Soviet Union and Warsaw Pact.
    c. Compromise the enemy's information about the real military power of the Soviet Union and Warsaw Pact.
    d. Discredit the military buildup of the United States and NATO.
    e. Convince the world that Soviet military forces are only for defensive purposes.
    f. Slow down scientific development and production of weapons and military technology in the United States and NATO countries.
    g. Discredit any accusations of a Soviet military buildup and shift the responsibility to the enemy; that is, make the United States and NATO the guilty parties.
    h. Mislead the enemy about military and state strategic reserves.
2. *Political*
    The main objective is to draw the attention of the enemy away from the main political-strategic goals and the steps being taken to achieve these goals. In general, activities should help the Soviet Union achieve strategic superiority on the political, military, and territorial fields.
    a. Strictly deny that there is any unity between Soviet foreign policy and Marxist-Leninist ideology.
    b. Hide the provision of material help to revolutionary movements and groups by the Soviet Union and deny any related accusations.
    c. Conceal the activity of the Soviet Union that creates political and military tensions and draw the attention of the imperialists away from the main strategic zone.

d. Disorient the masses and anti-right-wing factions about the strategy and intentions of capitalist governments.
e. Convince the enemy that the achievement of tactical goals is final; that is, that the Soviet Union will be satisfied and stop with the achievement of the tactical goals.
f. Convince the masses that cheating and deception are not socialist activities, but are capitalist activities.
g. Convince Third World countries that the Soviet Union has no desire to interfere in the internal affairs of other countries.

3. *Economic*
   a. Create a situation that allows the Soviet economy and science to make the maximum contribution to the buildup of the strongest possible military posture, and that enables the Soviet Union to exploit the science and technology of the enemy.
   b. Conceal information and mislead the enemy on the scientific achievements of the Soviet Union and the Warsaw Pact.
   c. Hide information on the real level of production of strategic importance.
   d. Hide information on the buildup of state and strategic reserves.
   e. Create conflict between capitalist governments and their financial and industrial institutions.
   f. Help create antagonisms between capitalist states and generate competition among the capitalists to do business with the Soviet Union.

The only difference between this enumeration of the roles of cheating and deception in Soviet political strategy and other descriptions is one of detail. Many of the same "principles" are clearly identified in Golitsyn's analysis of Soviet deception objectives. The enumeration may also be viewed as a guide for the use of strategic disinformation, a euphemism for strategic deception, set forth in a KGB training manual:

> Strategic disinformation assists in the execution of State tasks and is directed at misleading the enemy concerning the basic questions of State policy, the military-economic status, and the scientific-technical achievement of the Soviet Union; the policy of certain imperialist states with respect to each other and to other countries; and the specific counterintelligence tasks of the organs of State Security.[25]

There is a tendency in the West to discount lists of principles,[26] such as the one above, just as there is a tendency to discount the elaborate Soviet discussions of principles of military art. This is a dangerous mirror-imaging of Western practices in which there is a distinct separation and difference between theory and practice, between strategy and capabilities. However, this does not seem to be a Soviet practice. While there are strong and continuing conflicts between Soviet theorists and organizers, the theoretical principles more often than not are carefully applied to the operational plans. This is especially evident in top secret Soviet documents detailing attack strategy, documents which show clearly that the plans have been thoroughly examined from the perspective of each and every principle to ensure maximum effectiveness. Lists of principles are carefully constructed and then used for many years. This is a basic Marxist-Leninist modus operandi. It is another reflection of the long-term approach of Soviet strategy and operations, which applies with special vigor to cheating and deception operations that are carefully reviewed at the highest level on a regular basis.

THE USE OF "LEARNED PROFESSIONALS"

One of the more sophisticated and dangerous means of Soviet cheating and deception, independently identified as such by Rurarz, Sejna, Voslensky,[27] Golitsyn, and others, is the Soviet use of "learned professionals," such as scientists and academicians.

Golitsyn's warning of this activity is quite specific. When Shelepin took charge of the KGB, Golitsyn writes, it was with the intent to reorganize the KGB and turn it into a more activist instrument of Soviet policy. One of the changes was to adopt an "activist approach" toward Western scientists. Under this scheme, the Soviets would use various recruitment schemes, deception, and disinformation to influence Western scientists (and world opinion) in directions required by Soviet long-range policy, in the expectation that these scientists would then bring pressure to bear on Western governments. A special KGB-controlled section was created within the Academy of Sciences. Special institutes were formed to widen the opportunity for Soviet scientists to develop contacts with American scientists and influence them toward the objectives of Soviet policy. Thousands of KGB agents were recruited from among Soviet scientists and trained for assignments abroad, for international conferences, and for meetings with foreign scientists in the Soviet Union. Most Soviet scientists who participated in the Pugwash meetings from 1958 onward were KGB agents. (Schuman estimates that at least 50 percent were KGB agents.)

This data dovetails with that provided by Sejna, who explains that in the Soviet strategy formulated under Khrushchev the primary target of peaceful coexistence deception was the "intellectual middle class" in the West. Academicians and research scientists throughout the socialist nations were recruited to this cause. Intelligence agencies had priority in the recruiting of the best university students, and were assisted in this effort by the Academy of Sciences and other scientific research institutes that participated in defense research. The Academy of Sciences itself was heavily involved in national security work. Roughly 70 percent of military defense research was managed by the Academy of Sciences under guidance provided by the Operations Administration to meet the needs of the Operations Plan.[28] Moreover, when the arms control process became serious in the mid-1960s, the need to hide military R&D within the Academy of Sciences and nonmilitary sectors of science and industry was stressed by Soviet military and party officials to their Czechoslovak counterparts. This was also the time when the Soviets initiated an intensified effort to improve their ability to influence the Western press, both overtly and covertly (see Chapter 4).

A good example of the dual-hatted role of communist scientists is provided by Czechoslovak academician Ivan Malek. Malek, a world-class microbiologist, was the director of the main military biological warfare institute. His wife, Sejna recalled, was a doctor who worked at the main military hospital in Prague conducting biological warfare experiments. All of this was secret. His public image was quite different. He is described at a 1968 arms control conference on chemical and biological warfare as follows: "Member of the Czechoslovak Academy of Sciences and Director of the Czechoslovak Biological Institute where he conducts research into antibiotics and continuous cultivation of micro-organisms. He has been associated with peace movements for many years including Pugwash and the World Federation of Scientific Workers and was awarded the Lenin Peace Prize in 1967."[29] In the advance publicity for the Thirteenth Pugwash meeting (September 1964, Karlovy Vary, Czechoslovakia), Malek is listed as a member of the working group on aims and methods for peaceful collaboration among nations.[30]

The use of scientists in these types of operations came under the purview of the Administrative Organs and Science Departments of the Central Committee. They selected the scientists and planned the meetings. Scientists were carefully selected so that there would be a mixture of those working with the KGB or GRU and those who were unconnected and were, in effect, used as uwitting agents. Czechoslovakia participated in Pugwash but did not have a major role. The Czechoslovak Pugwash operation was run by the Ministry of Interior, specifically by a special section in the Intelligence Administration No. 2 that had been set up to handle scientists involved in "peace" propaganda, disinformation, and technical espionage. They were assisted by extremely competent scientists from the Academy of Sciences who were highly motivated to work with the intelligence services, in part because the latter were able to obtain Western equipment and supplies for the laboratories of these academicians.

Rurarz, who was in Poland's military intelligence (ZII) for twenty-five years, explained that in Poland the military officially operates several scientific research institutes and laboratories. Many more of them are controlled indirectly and semi-covertly, for example, factory and university research centers related to defense. Similarly, the secret police operates its own scientific research institutes and laboratories, albeit to a lesser extent than the military.

Moreover, both the military and the police have easy access to all scientists and research personnel and may recruit them at will. This is especially true of those who travel in the West or have access to Western literature, or both. Such people are coopted to either of the services, even in cases when the disciplines they represent only remotely suggest such connections. In Poland, thousands of such scientists may have intelligence roles. There are about 1,500 different fields of specialization in the Polish armed forces and about 2,500 in the Soviet armed forces. This means that the tentacles of the military must penetrate deeply throughout the scientific community and not just for Pugwash-like tasks, although they are high on the agenda.

Michael Voslensky provides additional insight into this disinformation and recruitment process. Since the early 1950s, Voslensky was affiliated with the International Department of the CPSU Central Committee. The International Department is the present-day successor to the Comintern. Together with the Administration Department, it has the main role in the development and implementation of global deception operations and direction of the world revolutionary movement.[31] In the mid-1950s, Voslensky worked for the World Peace Council, the major Soviet front organization responsible for propaganda and active measures on questions of disarmament. (As explained by Schuman, the President of the World Peace Council, Romesh Chandra, was strictly the product of Soviet recruitment and placement.) Later, Voslensky participated in the Pugwash conferences and became a member of the Commission on Disarmament of the Soviet Academy of Sciences. One of the objectives of the International Department, he has explained, was "to use the meetings as a vehicle to ignite a genuine disarmament movement among elites in the West, in order to create an atmosphere conducive to arms control talks in general and, therefore, responsive to Soviet proposals as likely to enhance this process." As a member of the Soviet delegation to Pugwash, Voslensky received instructions along these lines from the International Department. This was also true of his work with the Disarmament Commission when it interacted with Western officials and specialists.[32]

Voslensky further explained that the Soviet Pugwash strategy was coordinated with representatives from the East European satellites. Based on detailed profile analyses of Western representatives to Pugwash, the Soviets concluded that the Westerners were somewhat idealistic and naive, and hence likely to be receptive to Soviet disinformation. As an operational tactic, the Soviets deliberately included in the Soviet delegation scientists who were also idealistic to aid in the deception. However, Voslensky was careful to point out that the Soviet representatives who directed the Soviet delegation to Pugwash, and those who were in charge of the Commission on Disarmament, were under no such illusions. They were all members of the International Department or worked for the department. Based on his personal experience, Voslensky stressed that "certainly the USSR has no interest in arms control as a whole, but only in arms control of the West."[33]

Another prominent former Soviet official to provide supporting data is Arkady Shevchenko. He explains that in sponsoring Soviet disarmament proposals at various Pugwash conferences, the United Nations, and so forth, the International Department and the Foreign Ministry divided the tasks between them, with the ministry more involved with details such as scheduling and meetings. Shevchenko believes that Soviet leaders viewed the SALT talks as a mechanism that could be used to help shift the military balance of power; that SALT was a tactical move rather than a first step toward mutual arms reduction and eventual disarmament. He noted that strategic deception was a Soviet objective in SALT; specifically, the Soviet Union sought to communicate the false impression that it was committed to the SALT process and shared U.S. concepts such as mutual assured destruction (MAD), and that its strategic purpose constituted a mirror image of American concepts. He also said that the various research institutes of the USSR Academy of Sciences had a role in promoting this image and in influencing operations directed against Western policy and research institutes. Both the International Department and the KGB, he explained, have important responsibilities in directing this aspect of the work of these "research institutes."[34]

Rurarz adds that many types of contemporary Soviet cheating and deception may assume the form even of scientific theories, which, as is the case in many theories, may not be subject to proof or verification. One good example of such Soviet efforts is the view of Soviet scientists, vigorously advanced, that the Strategic Defense Initiative cannot possibly work.[35] The manner in which Soviet scientists have participated in the nuclear winter phenomenon is another good example of this "political" use of scientists.[36]

"Of the various forms of Soviet cheating," Rurarz concludes, "I have no doubt that 'learned' ones are the most dangerous, insidious, and difficult to combat."[37]

THE PROBLEMS OF LANGUAGE

The ingrained nature of cheating and deception in the Soviet Union and its sophisticated practice is perhaps nowhere more evident than in their language. Careful attention, beginning with the General Secretary, is placed on the use of language to influence perceptions. Indeed, as pointed out by Dr. Igor Lukes, "The very foundation of Soviet long-term deception *is* language."

The deception begins with the name of the country, the Union of Soviet Socialist Republics. Like the Holy Roman Empire, which was neither holy nor an empire, and certainly not Roman, not one of the political concepts implied by the words in the name is present in reality. In the case of the USSR, Schuman, a former Soviet propaganda expert, explains that there is no Union; there is no Soviet, a Russian term that means a group such as a parliament or council where decisionmaking is done by mutual agreement and consent; there is no Socialism, in its classical meaning; and the USSR could hardly be defined as a Republic. He recalls a Russian anecdote in which Winston Churchill asks Stalin why he had chosen such a clumsy name for his country. Stalin is described as answering, "So that every time you pronounce the name of my country, you participate in the lie."

The same holds for descriptions of apparent policy. For example, peaceful coexistence does not relate to peace, as that word is defined in the West, nor to coexistence. Peaceful coexistence is merely a form of the struggle between revolutionary forces and capitalists. It is in reality a low-intensity war whose purpose is to end the class struggle by destroying the opposition in a controlled manner. Peace is the condition that will exist when capitalism has been completely destroyed.

Certainly, this raises a basic question: How to communicate when words are defined differently by one party seeking to deceive the other? In effect, this kind of communication at best becomes miscommunication; at worst, it becomes a charade designed to provide the trappings of respectability to a process that is in reality just a deception and whose ultimate goal is not the reduction of armaments but rather the destruction of free societies.

For the most part, the meanings of words are spelled out in Soviet literature; thus, to the extent that we are deceived, we do it to ourselves through inattentiveness or self-deception that comes from an overpowering desire to see the world as we wish it were. This is especially true of Americans who find it exceedingly difficult to recognize that some kinds of evils exist, especially when disbelief is easier and when belief would bring into question cherished policies. This is especially evident in The Declaration on Basic Principles of Relations that was signed at the time of SALT I, as analyzed by Igor Lukes in his paper, "Linguistic Deception and Arms-Control Treaties" (Appendix C).

NOTES

1. As explained by Tomas Schuman: "The Soviet system is an elaborate maze of compulsive lies. We cheat everywhere, on any occasion, through all the ages, and for a variety of purposes, or without any."
2. "At times pulling the wool over foreigners' eyes approaches a national sport. 'We do it naturally,' a bright young government consultant on foreign policy admitted to me one evening in the privacy of his apartment. 'It is to our advantage. Deceit is a compensation for weakness, for a feeling of inferiority before foreigners. As a nation, we cannot deal with others equally. Either we are more powerful or they are. And if they are, and we feel it, we compensate by deceiving them. It is a very important feature of our national character.'" Hedrick Smith, *The Russians* (New York: Quadrangle/The New York Times Book Co., 1976), p. 17.
3. *Journey For Our Time*, the journals of the Marquis de Custine, edited and translated by Phyllis Penn Kohler (London: Arthur Barker, Ltd., 1951).
4. Blackstock and Hoselitz, editors, op. cit., p. 8.
5. V. I. Lenin, Speech in Reply to the Debate on the Report on War and Peace (1918), in *Selected Works*, Vol. 7 (New York: International Publishers, 1937), p. 309.
6. This is precisely the message conveyed to the East European satellite leadership by Brezhnev in the months immediately following the signing of the ABM Treaty and the Interim Agreement in 1972.
7. This was also part of the message communicated by Brezhnev to the satellites following the signing of the ABM Treaty and Interim Agreement, as discussed at the end of Chapter 1.
8. *Arms Control and Disarmament Agreements*, U.S. Arms Control and Disarmament Agency, August 1980, pp. 48–49.
9. The Politburo does not have access to secret defense and intelligence matters. They are informed only to the extent the Defense Council deems prudent or appropriate. See Sejna and Douglass, op. cit., Chapters 2 and 3.
10. *Problems of the Party's Military Policy in Light of the 13th Congress of the Communist Party of Czechoslovakia*, Czech Secret; Defense Intelligence Agency (DIA) translation LN 048-79, January 5, 1979, pp. 4–5.
11. Ministry of National Defense, *Analyses of Activities of MoD Under the Order of the Ministry of National Defense 13 April 1965*, Czech Top Secret, p. 533.
12. Quoted in Chapman Pincher, *The Secret Offensive* (London: Sidgwick & Jackson, 1985), p. 41.
13. Additional background and supporting documentation on this sheep propaganda operation is contained in Joseph D. Douglass, Jr., "Chemical Weapons: An Imbalance of Terror," *Strategic Review*, Summer 1982, pp. 40–42.
14. "Trickery on Chemical War," *Washington Star*, June 5, 1978, p. A-5.
15. Edward J. Epstein, "Incorporating Analysis of Foreign Governments' Deception into the U.S. Analytical System," in Roy Godson, editor, *Intelligence Requirements for the 1980s: Analysis and Estimates* (Washington, D.C.: National Strategy Information Center, 1980), pp. 124–125.
16. Henry Hurt, "Is This American a Soviet Spy?," *Reader's Digest*, October 1981, pp. 92–93.

17. Arkady N. Shevchenko, *Breaking With Moscow* (New York: Alfred A. Knopf, 1985), p. 179.
18. Marshal N.V. Ogarkov, *History Teaches Vigilance* (Moscow: Voyenizdat, 1985); translation in JPRS-UMA-85-021-L, August 30, 1985, pp. 13–15.
19. FBIS, *Party Congress*, March 3, 1986, p. O-11.
20. Ogarkov, op. cit., p. 16.
21. See Appendix E, "A Soviet View of Arms Control: Lessons from the Past."
22. N.S. Khrushchev, *Prevent War, Safeguard Peace* (Moscow: Progress Publishers, 1962), p. 29.
23. Ibid., pp. 281–282.
24. For an excellent recent example of Soviet duplicity, see the short article by the Soviet Ambassador to the United States, Yuri V. Dubinin, "We're Willing to Negotiate," *Parade* Magazine, March 1, 1986.
25. Deputy Director of Operations, CIA, "Soviet Covert Action and Propaganda," edited and reprinted in U.S. Congress, House, *Soviet Covert Action (The Forgery Offensive)*, Hearings before the Subcommittee on Oversight of the Permanent Select Committee on Intelligence, February 6, 1980 (Washington, D.C.: U.S. Government Printing Office, 1980), p. 63.
26. For example, as discussed in Chapter 1.
27. Michael Voslensky, *Nomenklatura* (Garden City, N.Y.: Doubleday, 1984).
28. See, for example, Sejna and Douglass, op. cit., pp. 33, 53.
29. Steven Rose, editor, *CBW: Chemical and Biological Warfare* (Boston, Mass.: Beacon Press, 1968), p. 190.
30. Duane Thorin, *The Pugwash Movement and U.S. Arms Policy* (Oakton, Va.: Monte Cristo Press, 1965), p. 76.
31. Sejna and Douglass, op. cit., p. 20.
32. Oral History Project, International Security Studies Program, The Fletcher School of Law and Diplomacy, as reported in Uri Ra'anan and Richard H. Shultz, "Methodologies for Assessing and Projecting Soviet Strategic Defense and Arms Control Policy," paper presented at the Conference on Emerging Doctrines and Technologies: Implications for Global and Regional Political-Military Balances, April 16–18, 1986, pp. 45–50.
33. Ibid., p. 47.
34. Ibid., p. 49.
35. For example, *Perspectives on the Development of a U.S. Space-Based Anti-Missile System and its Probable Effect Upon the Politico-Military Situation in the World*, by the Committee of Soviet Scientists in Defense of Peace Against the Threat of Nuclear War (Moscow: 1983).
36. See Leon Gouré, " 'Nuclear Winter' in Soviet Mirrors," *Strategic Review*, Summer 1985.
37. See Appendix A, p. 144.

7

RISK ASSESSMENT

The Soviets divide their assessment of risk into three segments: short-term and long-term risk, local and global risk, and temporary tactical reaction and long-term strategic reaction. Additionally, the analysis of risk is a two-sided process in which the risks and benefits are compared side by side.

For example, the occupations of Hungary and Czechoslovakia were for the Soviet Union short-term risks and the reactions of the whole world were of a temporary nature. From a strategic point of view, the Soviets believed the action would show that they were not afraid to take military action if necessary to protect their investment. In the case of Czechoslovakia, the action would help improve the posture of the Warsaw Pact forces along the Czechoslovak/NATO border. These examples illustrate how positive as well as negative factors enter into the Soviet assessment of risk in deciding on a course of action.

Another good example is the risk assessment that accompanied the decision to build the Berlin Wall. On March 28, 1961, the first secretaries and ministers of defense of the East European satellites were summoned to Moscow to discuss a forthcoming course of action: the building of the Berlin Wall. Sejna was present at this meeting. The Soviets explained that a wall dividing Berlin was to be built, but not until after Khrushchev had met with the new U.S. President to discuss improvements in relations and the need to base relations on peaceful coexistence. The possible risks that had been assessed were: (1) the possibility that the Western powers might encourage demonstrations and provocations that could cause problems in Eastern Europe; (2) the United States might undertake actions against Cuba in response; (3) there could be an adverse impact on the Soviet policy of peaceful coexistence that had made such good progress in the preceding five years; and (4) there might be a negative economic impact, that is, the curtailing of economic and trade assistance from the West. The last risk, which was also coupled to the third risk, was of great concern to Romania and Bulgaria. No risk of possible military action, such as the Western forces in Berlin tearing down the wall, was raised at this meeting. Alternatively, the positive aspects of the course of action that were discussed were: (1) the wall would stop the infiltration of intelligence agents into the East; (2) it would stop the outflow of skilled tradesmen and professionals; (3) it would stop the economic ruin of the East that had been generated by the above outflow[1]; and (4) it would provide a test of the United States and the West. If successful, and the Soviets believed it would be, there would be no adverse reaction and the event would demonstrate to all that the United States could not be counted upon to support its allies. The implication of the last point is that Soviet agents would then use the success of the Berlin Wall to exacerbate relations between the United States and Europe.[2]

The Cuban crisis provides another good example of the Soviet assessment of risk. Following the crisis, Khrushchev met with the Warsaw Pact leaders. Sejna was present at the meeting and recalls Khrushchev's remarks as follows:

> "You can ask us if we counted the risk, especially the military risk?" he asked. "Yes," he answered, "We did."
>
> "The highest risk was the possibility that we might lose Cuba. We discounted this risk because we believed that the combination of our peaceful coexistence policy and our agreements with Kennedy would act to prevent Kennedy from undertaking any military action. We concluded that his reaction would be strictly political gesturing. In this regard we underestimated Kennedy. On the other hand, some comrades overestimated the Americans. They thought the Americans would go much farther than they went, but we did not accept that estimate."
>
> "Comrades," Khrushchev then continued, "the risk was worth it. Cuba is still a socialist state. The crisis demonstrated the inability of the United States to liquidate a socialist state, even one under their own windows. This has opened for us new possibilities throughout the whole world. Additionally, it has helped us wake up many realistic thinking politicians and scared many people because it demonstrated that America is no longer untouchable."[3]

The Soviet assessment of risk is seen to be a risk/benefit trade-off analysis in which the goals and strategy are set by the Marxist-Leninist ideology influenced by Russian tradition, and in which the risks reflect a cold appraisal of reactions that might be generated, the most important of which would be American, European, Third World, and those of progressive movements around the globe. In addition, Moscow's risk assessment is a flexible process, and lessons learned from past events are fully incorporated. Current analyses will differ from those of the late 1960s as a result of detailed Soviet analysis of events during the intervening years. In this regard, today there are at least five major lessons learned by the Soviets that would condition their consideration of the risks and benefits. To a considerable degree, these are not new lessons learned in recent years but old lessons confirmed by recent events.

Perhaps the most important lesson learned by the Soviets is the unwillingness of nations around the globe to react to Soviet violations of treaties—not just arms control agreements, but a wide variety of international agreements. The only example of a reaction to a violation by the Soviet Union of an international agreement was its expulsion from the League of Nations following its violation of the territorial integrity of Finland on November 30, 1939. Except for this single instance, the Soviet Union repeatedly violates treaties, and the rest of the world turns their heads and proceeds to enter into still more treaties, which the Soviets also violate with impunity.

The reluctance of the West to respond to Soviet cheating, deception, and deliberate violations is nowhere more evident than in the arms control arena today. Notwithstanding a succession of U.S. government studies that have found deliberate Soviet noncompliance with the majority of operationally significant treaty provisions, many current and former high-level U.S. officials remain unable to conclude that Soviet behavior is inconsistent with U.S. security or that the arms control process has been compromised. One of the best examples of this attitude is the statement of Jack Matlock, former senior Soviet expert on the National Security Council staff. In a statement that is reminiscent of administration statements in 1976 downplaying the possibility that the Soviets might be cheating on the chemical and biological warfare treaties, Matlock is quoted in the *Los Angeles Times* on April 16, 1986, as assuring us that "They have too much at stake to be the first to break the overall SALT II ceilings (on missiles) or to flagrantly start putting in a whole national ABM system." For future agreements, he said, "It is probably not possible to write an agreement that is absolutely unambiguous in every respect." Current arms talks "take us into areas where verification is more and more difficult," thus making it all the more important to persuade Soviet leaders to adhere to the treaties of the future.[4]

Notwithstanding the official findings of noncompliance and the President's expressed belief that the United States should not be bound by the unratified SALT II treaty, the U.S. policymaking apparatus not only refuses to discuss the possibility of the United States pulling out of even those treaties most flagrantly violated, but works hard at making sure that the United States remains in full compliance even with unratified and violated "agreements."

Given this state of affairs, the obvious conclusion is that the Soviets risk very little, if anything, in violating any and all international agreements between countries whenever it suits their purposes. It seems equally evident that this is not true of contracts with commercial organizations; the Soviets can be and have been very businesslike in situations where they are getting something they need.

The second lesson relates to the effectiveness of Soviet propaganda. The Soviets spend large quantities of rubles on their international propaganda and disinformation apparatus, in excess of $3 billion per year by CIA estimates.[5] They must have considerable confidence in their ability to use propaganda in their favor. Soviet propaganda, it is important to bear in mind, is not defensive. Like their approach to denial of cheating, propaganda is designed to be an offensive weapon. An excellent example of the effectiveness of Soviet propaganda coupled with the reluctance of people to call the Soviets on their violations was the worldwide press response to the Soviet resumption of nuclear testing in 1961. The main reaction of the media did not occur until the U.S. decision to resume atmospheric testing was announced in the spring of 1962, and then the main thrust of its reaction was to protest the American decision.

The third lesson the Soviets have learned—and everyone else should have learned—is how difficult it is to prove violations in a sufficiently dramatic manner so that the Soviets cannot simply deny their cheating and pass the blame to the United States or other capitalist countries. The Soviets' ability to lie with a "straight face," coupled with their massive international propaganda machine, almost guarantees their security from American protests over Soviet violations. The only example one can point to where the United States was able effectively to use a "smoking gun" was in the Cuban missile crisis, and even that ended as a victory for the Soviets. At the same time, there are indications of Soviet concern over cheating where data are subject to collection by its enemies; for example, the use of chemical weapons and toxins in Afghanistan, Laos, and Kampuchea. Following the signing of the 1925 Geneva Protocol and the 1972 Biological and Toxin Weapons Convention by Kampuchea on March 9 and 21, 1983, the Vietnamese stopped using chemical and toxin weapons in Kampuchea. The last reported "Yellow Rain" in that area was March 4–5, 1983.

A fourth lesson the Soviets are certainly aware of is the failure of the United States to come up with credible responses, and the ease with which the Soviets are able to derail U.S. criticism and citations of violations. The Soviets are aware of the absence of strategic thinking in the United States in both political and military affairs. In both areas, U.S. officials are seen in Moscow as responding to private, rather than state, interests, with political thinking driven by various commercial interests and military thinking by the military-industrial complex. In neither case is there perceived to be any serious U.S. consideration of strategy or of the nature of the threat posed by the Soviet Union. Consequently, the types of responses likely to be formulated and made public by the U.S. government are almost guaranteed to be tactical rather than strategic: partial, expedient measures that are of little consequence and susceptible to retraction or counteraction. The inability of the United States to act in a responsible manner is evident in the U.S. approach to coping with the survivability of strategic land-based forces; in President Reagan's short-lived attempt to stimulate the national security community to become concerned about defense; in the many abortive attempts to constrain trade and economic assistance to Eastern bloc countries; and in the numerous half-measures undertaken to counteract Soviet espionage and active measures. Even when the United States feels compelled to respond, the responses the United States is most likely to field can be anticipated by the Soviets to be ineffective and subject to rapid reversal. No violation the Soviets have committed, however substantial or blatant, has been sufficient to provoke any serious, long-term response on the part of the capitalists.

Finally, the Soviets have learned through experience that events, while possibly generating substantial adverse press at the time, quickly pass from memory in the West; moreover, the nature of the violations they are accused of need to be more serious than anything they have previously done before there is any likelihood of generating a reaction that goes beyond mere rhetoric. Indeed, in the arms control arena there has been only one instance of a tentative reaction—the U.S. resumption of atmospheric testing for a brief duration in 1962—and even in that case, as in the case of Cuba, the Soviets came out far ahead in the process.

Given the record of Western nonresponse to Soviet cheating, Soviet leaders have no doubt concluded that there has been and will be no unacceptable adverse reaction from Washington associated with any of their arms control violations.

PROBABLE DOMINANT RISKS

There are a variety of risks that the Soviets take into consideration when deciding to violate arms control treaties. Some decisions may have to be concerned with all risks; others may be involved in only one or two of the risk categories. All risks are ultimately related to possible responses by the West: no perceived response, little risk. Further, the assessment of risk likely would take place in the context of a specific decision on cheating, which would be a complex decision involving treaties and their terms, deception, intelligence capabilities, and plans to deal with accusations of cheating. Without knowledge of all these factors, it is only possible to speak of risks in general terms.

The risks identified fall into five basic categories: increased likelihood of major military actions; compromise or loss of Soviet state secrets;

increased Western military or political awareness; degradation of the Soviet peace image; and economic repercussions.

The Soviets traditionally have been concerned about the possibility of nuclear war. Their efforts generally have been directed toward reducing the risk of nuclear war and pushing the possibility of war with the United States further into the future. Open hostilities would be viewed as counterproductive and to be avoided if possible. The Soviets would be reluctant to undertake any action that would increase the risk of nuclear war. However, this Soviet concern is less now than it was in the 1960s, and should they grow confident in their defenses, this concern would diminish still further.

Today, the risk of nuclear war, while present, is unlikely to be associated with a decision to violate arms control treaties. Quite the contrary. The threat of nuclear war is still employed as a tool to intimidate the West and promote the Soviet versions of peaceful coexistence and the arms control process. This has been a most successful tactic and one that is likely to continue.

Second, the Soviets believe that obtaining intelligence on Soviet capabilities and plans is a U.S. arms control goal. Loss of state secrets would always be at the forefront of Soviet considerations, including those pertaining to risks associated with violations.[6] Further, U.S. concern over possible violations can easily be seen by the Soviets as resulting in an increase in U.S. intelligence efforts.

Alternatively, on the plus side, the arms control and violations process provides a mechanism to distract U.S. intelligence or keep its efforts focused on areas where harm to Soviet interests would be minimal. This important tactic is emphasized in both the political and military literature, and its application to arms control is only a natural extension. Further, arms control can be used to provide a feedback mechanism to help in the design of important facilities or activities: for example, the creation of hidden strategic missile reserves, a task almost certainly undertaken as a hedge against the possibility that those weapons might be outlawed some day. It is likely that the Soviets, at least as early as 1960, began to plan how they could secretly deploy and maintain land-based missile reserves. As stated by Khrushchev on January 14, 1960:

> We are aware that our country is ringed with foreign military bases. This is why we locate our rockets in such a way as to ensure a double and even triple margin of safety. We have a vast territory and we are able to disperse our rockets and camouflage them well. We are developing such a system that if some means of retaliation were knocked out, we could always fall back on others and strike the enemy from reserve installations.[7]

This policy has continued to the present day as an integral part of Soviet military doctrine. Two obvious possibilities for locating secret land-based reserves are underground and imbedded in a complex of above-ground facilities, such as fake urban areas, large enough to hide missiles and related activities but small enough not to be nuclear targets. This type of concealment at the strategic level is mentioned in the classified General Staff journal, *Voyennaya mysl'*.[8] The Soviets might well experiment with various techniques designed to test U.S. intelligence capabilities before determining which location(s) to use.

On the minus side, the Soviets could be concerned over any actions that might cause U.S. intelligence to bore in on extremely important subjects—perhaps unrelated to the terms of any treaty—such as secret facilities, new weapons systems, previously unrecognized research and development (R&D), or missile reserves. The Soviets would not want to lead the fox to the chicken coop.

A third risk is that concern over Soviet violations could lead to an awareness, within political or military circles in the United States, that the Soviet threat is serious. Arousing the United States to stronger policies and actions could have a detrimental effect on Soviet political or military strategy and would be regarded in Moscow as a serious setback. The political actions that would worry Moscow are discussed as part of the fourth and fifth risks below. On the military side, the United States could react by building more weapon systems. The Soviets would certainly be concerned over this development, but they would expect to find help in the perceived ability of the antiwar and antidefense groups in the United States to prevent such a response; moreover, even if the United States does respond, the arms control process will have delayed the U.S. weapons program by many years. This risk would seem to be outweighed by the benefits of cheating and by the fact that even a failure could be evaluated as a limited success.

Certainly today the main potential U.S. weapon system of concern to the Soviets is the Strategic Defense Initiative (SDI). SDI is of concern for four reasons: (1) it might neutralize a major fraction of Soviet strategic forces; (2) it could destroy the Soviet nuclear blackmail strategy that has been so effective; (3) it might enable the United States to recapture the "strategic initiative"; and (4) it would interfere with, if not effectively block, Soviet plans to control space, which seems to have been a major objective of Soviet research and development, at least since 1963 when Soviet leaders decided they would not comply with the UN resolution against placing weapons of mass destruction in space.

How arms control and the whole host of covert activities can be used to sabotage SDI is certainly receiving the highest priority in Soviet strategic planning. While SDI might be viewed by Moscow as a U.S. response to Soviet ABM violations, it seems more likely that it is viewed as a product of selected interests of the military-industrial complex and the President's own agenda. The only Soviet risk associated with SDI would seem to be that of possibly strengthening its support through new violations, and this might well be a strong consideration. However, it seems unlikely that any ongoing Soviet programs would be sacrificed to stop SDI. SDI is still too much in its infancy and the Soviets are likely aware of the considerable opposition to SDI, even within the Department of Defense and military services, not to mention other segments of American society.[9] Although SDI today is far from being a serious threat to Soviet strategic plans, it logically would be a prime target for espionage and sabotage. It is quite possible that, because of the emphasis placed on SDI in the United States, one of the major political reasons the Soviets would like to kill the program is the consequent negative effect that such an outcome would have on U.S. morale and on the technological reputation of the United States.

Fourth, Soviet strategy leans heavily on the ability to mislead the world as to the nature of the Soviet Union, its strategy and its ideology. The image that Soviet strategy seeks to promote—legitimate, morally superior, peace-loving, reasonable, defense-minded, and so forth—is very important to the Soviets in their relations with Third World countries, with "progressive" movements around the world, and with "realistic thinking" intellectuals, powerbrokers, and politicians in the West. This image is crucial in helping to prevent a resurgence of serious concerns about defense and military preparedness in the United States and Western Europe, not just within the defense establishment, but in the even more critical nondefense components of government, industry, and academia, which have been prime targets of Soviet strategy for many years. In brief, the Soviet Union's image of being paranoid about defense for historical reasons, and of being sincerely concerned about the arms race, is an essential linchpin in Soviet political strategy.

The Soviet Union's concern for its image is reflected in the $3 billion or more they spend each year on propaganda and related activities; in the importance it attaches to penetrating and sabotaging institutes and organizations that study the Soviet Union; in the strong counterpropaganda it unleashes when anyone criticizes the Soviet Union, as President Reagan did early in his presidency; and in its "offensive denials" in dealing with accusations of Soviet cheating. Hence, Soviet leaders are concerned about the possibility that their willful violations could have an adverse impact on their image, and thus on their strategy. On the other hand, the perceived impact on their political strategy would be in direct proportion to their assessment of the U.S. ability to use Soviet violations deliberately to undermine their image.

The Soviet image is also important to them in an economic sense. The combination of trade and financial assistance is one of two primary objectives behind the Soviet strategy of peaceful coexistence—the other being a reduction in U.S. military power. The economic aspect of the Soviet peaceful coexistence image is that of a nation interested in restricting competition with the West to what the West would regard as normal healthy economic competition.

The arms control process provides an aura of respectability for trade and economic assistance. As long as the U.S. government is negotiating arms reductions with its Soviet counterpart, the Soviet Union is implicitly recognized as a nation with which one can conduct business. As stated just prior to the 1972 agreements, "A mutual willingness to curb arms competition indicates constructive intentions in political as well as strategic areas. Progress in controlling arms can reinforce progress in a much wider area of international relations."[10] This rationale was reiterated with greater specificity the following year: "In fact, trade and other aspects of economic relations could never flourish if political relations remained largely hostile. . . . Nor would the Congress support an expanding economic relationship while our basic relations with the Soviet Union were antagonistic."[11]

The types of economic relationships mentioned in the *U.S. Foreign Policy for the 1970s* statements of 1972 and 1973 include expanded trade, scientific and technical cooperation and exchanges, participation by American firms in the Kama River manufacturing project, cooperation in medical research, granting of most-favored-nation status to the Soviet Union, establishment of a trade center complex in Moscow, authorization for the Export-Import Bank to engage in credit transactions with the Soviet Union, long-term cooperative ventures including the use of American capital and technology to help develop Soviet natural resources such as natural gas, and so forth. If the Soviet Union's image is tarnished, the rationale for trading with it and financing its projects is undermined. Indeed, it requires little imagination to hypothesize that the main forces behind arms control policy in the United States are the same forces that would benefit from most types of economic relations identified in the 1972 and 1973 Presidential reports. Today, these benefits could be the main reason the Soviets continue to pursue the arms control negotiation process. These benefits could also be the main reason for the distorted image of the Soviet Union that underlies U.S. policy, for the reluctance of the United States to address Soviet arms control violations, and for the State Department's reintroduction of detente in 1983.

The possible impact of Soviet violations on the trade and financial benefits of peaceful coexistence and detente—a subject treated above in a different context (the Soviet image) under the fourth risk—has to be an important consideration. Peaceful coexistence, which has been a major thrust of Soviet strategy since the 1920s, is the Soviet long-term strategic deception designed to lull the West into a false sense of security, and provide an atmosphere within which the Soviet Union and its satellites are able to make maximum use of Western technology, trade, and loans. These economic benefits, in turn, are used to increase Soviet power and thereby hasten the decline of the West.

As demonstrated following the Soviet invasion of Afghanistan and the imposition of martial law in Poland, the United States can react by imposing economic sanctions and restricting trade agreements. This was one of the few times the United States has actually responded to Soviet behavior in a manner that, while not too damaging, might have provided some reason for Soviet concern. Export controls are one of the few ways in which the U.S. government can react, and they probably represent one of the risks the Soviets evaluate carefully.

In drawing up any plans to violate arms control agreements, the Soviets need to consider the possibility of upsetting the arms control negotiations process and the ultimately detrimental effect this might have on U.S. trade and economic assistance. However, given the manner in which trade and financial agreements that had been restricted following the events in Afghanistan and Poland were revived in the mid-1980s, even this risk would appear to be minimal. The reestablishment of trade and financial assistance occurred precisely at the time when all of the Presidential assessments of Soviet noncompliance with arms control treaties were coming to light. In 1985 alone, roughly $5 billion in credits were made available to Moscow—clear evidence of the success the Soviets have had in enlisting the support of "nonmilitary" industries and financial circles. It is also evidence of how effective the false theory that increased trade and financial assistance will lead to better relations has been. Here, as in the previously discussed cases, the Soviet Union seems to have little trouble coping with the limited risks involved in violation of international agreements.

NOTES

1. Brian Crozier has noted that "East Germany's growth as a real centre of economic power dates from the Berlin Wall. Before that, too many skilled people, too many brains, were escaping to West Germany." Crozier, *Strategy of Survival*, op. cit., p. 114.
2. In this regard, one later action whose origins might stem from the Berlin Wall crisis is Charles de Gaulle's decision to pull French troops out of NATO in February 1966. For example, Aleksei Myagkov reported that the head of KGB School No. 311 stated to future KGB officers in 1968 that "events in France were a positive result of the efforts of the Soviet Government and of the successes of the KGB." *Inside the KGB* (London: Foreign Affairs Publishing Company, 1976), p. 24.

3. See Appendix B, p.136.
4. Robert C. Toth, "U.S. Faces Arms Decision Amid Soviet Cheating," *Los Angeles Times*, April 16, 1986.
5. U.S. Congress, House, *Soviet Covert Actions (The Forgery Offensive)*, op. cit., p. 60.
6. At the same time, there is a tendency to overreact to Soviet secrecy. The Soviets do deliberately sacrifice state secrets when it is in their interests, for example, to establish the bona fides of an agent. This practice is also explicitly indicated in KGB studies undertaken in the late 1950s. One Soviet study on disinformation reported by Golitsyn was titled *State Secrets and How They Can Be Disclosed In The Interests Of Policy*.
7. *Disarmament—The Way to Secure Peace and Friendship Between Nations*, report by N.S. Khrushchev to the Supreme Soviet of the USSR and the Appeal to the Governments and Parliaments of the World, January 14–15, 1960, Soviet Booklet No. 64, p. 30.
8. For example, Lt. Col. Kh. Adam and Lt. Col. R. Gebel, "Military Camouflage," *Voyennaya mysl'*, No. 11, November 1971; Foreign Press Digest translation FPD 0004/74, January 1971, reprinted in Joseph D. Douglass, Jr., and Amoretta M. Hoeber, *Selected Readings From Military Thought 1963-1973: Studies in Communist Affairs*, Vol. 5, Part II (Washington, D.C.: U.S. Government Printing Office), p. 159.
9. See, for example, Angelo M. Codevilla, "How SDI is Being Undone from Within," *Commentary*, May 1986.
10. *U.S. Foreign Policy for the 1970s*, 1972, op. cit., p. 171.
11. Ibid., 1973, p. 33.

8

CONCLUSIONS

For the Soviets, arms control is a serious strategic military and intelligence operation. Goals are carefully set, a wide variety of resources are used in a coordinated fashion, and the progress is carefully monitored from many different perspectives.

Soviet arms control goals are quite different from those of the United States, which is why Soviet arms control is referred to in this study as a strategic military and intelligence operation. The main Soviet goals or uses of the arms control process are to debilitate the U.S. defense planning and weapons acquisition process; act as a wedge to split Western alliances and the Western bourgeoisie, and raise antagonisms between military and nonmilitary industries; promote the image of the Soviet Union as a peace-loving country and that of the United States as a warmonger; facilitate trade, credits, and the transfer of technology from the West; confirm intelligence; provide a cover for expanding Soviet military programs; prod the West to disarm; and shift the balance of power irreversibly in favor of the Soviet Union. At the same time, the Soviets expend major resources to convince the United States that the situation is exactly the opposite, that Soviet strategic interests mirror-image those of the United States.

Soviet planning for cheating and deception on arms control accords begins well in advance of any specific agreement. This planning encompasses concealing research and development, testing and deployment, and misleading the United States about the nature of Soviet weapons programs, technology, and military interests. Specific details on cheating and deception are approved when agreements are reached, and, at the same time, the Soviets also formulate their responses to possible U.S. reactions to Soviet cheating. Finally, as cheating and deception measures are implemented, the reaction of the United States is carefully monitored to determine whether the enemy is alert and is able to detect Soviet cheating.

The risks involved in being caught are weighed against the benefits. The benefits are assessed in terms of contributions to the goals. The risks can generally be categorized as possible U.S. and West European reactions that would be detrimental to Soviet political strategy, which since 1955 has been dominated by Lenin's concept of peaceful coexistence. The three principal risks the Soviets run are an adverse impact on their peace-loving and defensive image, the development of a political and military awareness in the West, and the curtailment of trade and financial assistance. These risks are interrelated.

The analysis of risks and benefits will be conditioned by historical experience, especially by the arms control experience of the past twenty-five years. Thus, within limits, the Soviets appear to run few risks when they violate or circumvent arms control agreements because there have been few significant adverse reactions on the part of the United States.

To a considerable degree, the risk of serious adverse reaction is countered by six forces that operate in the Soviet favor. First, there is a decided tendency in the West to mirror-image, to see the Soviets as only a slightly different version of ourselves, to see only what we want to believe, and to deceive ourselves about the nature of Soviet interests. Second, the Soviets have built up an extensive propaganda, disinformation, and influence apparatus that has demonstrated its ability to sway public opinion. Third, antidefense lobbies have grown up within the United States and Western Europe that are highly vocal and constantly challenging Western governments, especially pressuring for arms control agreements and for ignoring Soviet violations. Fourth, the Soviets have gained the support of major elements of what they perceive to be the real power in the United States and other Western nations, namely, the business and finance communities, and these elements favor the expansion of trade—irrespective of Soviet actions in the arms control or military arena. Fifth, the West does not have a long-term political strategy and lacks a coordinating mechanism adequate for the task of challenging the Soviet threat. Sixth, whenever a U.S. reaction begins to develop, the Soviets retain the policy of taking "two steps back" to defuse the reaction, a tactic that has been successful time and again.

To the extent the United States is serious in negotiating arms control agreements that enhance international security and can be enforced—as appears to have been the case in the early 1980s—the Soviet Union's strategy is to negotiate at length but strive to achieve its objectives through political pressure applied indirectly through the media and influential individuals. To the extent the United States stands firm, an agreement is unlikely because Soviet goals would not be served, and this would be publicly evident. To the Soviets, a "public" agreement, such as an arms control treaty, needs to be received as a Soviet victory, not as a mutually derived resolution of a problem. For Moscow, it is better just to negotiate than to accede to a meaningful treaty, especially today when the principal Soviet goals of peaceful coexistence are being attained through negotiation alone. At present, it is difficult to believe that any evidence of cheating or deception would be so alarming as to awaken the United States or shut down the flow of desired trade, finance, and technology.

However, until the Soviets are militarily superior to the extent that they are able to intimidate the United States, they can be expected to exercise some restraint in violating agreements. At present, the Soviets should be expected to exercise caution where the United States has direct access to irrefutable data, where the issue is important to the point of being a threat to vital Western interests, where Soviet guilt would be clear even to the professional skeptics, where the nonprofessional would be aware of the cheating, where the media would give the event widespread and continuing publicity, and where the cheating is not really vital to Soviet military security.

Although they operate with restraint, the Soviets appear to run only minor risks in cheating on arms control agreements and have every reason to use all such agreements to enhance achievement of their goals, which have little to do with arms control as understood in the West.

APPENDIX A

THE SOVIET APPROACH TO ARMS CONTROL

by Zdzislaw M. Rurarz

Soviet actions—various Russian traditions and state interests apart—are ideologically driven. Having embraced Leninism as gospel, the Soviets genuinely believe that this ideology can explain anything happening in the world and can even predict the future.

It is wrong to dismiss their frequent quotations of Lenin as mere rhetoric. Any such quotations—whether used to justify present Soviet policy, or to determine its course for the future—should be taken most seriously. At the same time, the importance of Soviet political considerations should not be underestimated as they may outweigh even Lenin's teachings. Put another way, ideology serves the interests of the state.

The issue of Soviet violations of arms control treaties cannot be isolated from the overall Soviet assessment of "imperialism," especially when seen in light of the many detailed statements on imperialism left by Lenin, which constitute to this day a valid reflection of Soviet thought. Two of his less familiar statements are worth repeating:

> [Imperialism] because of its basic economic characteristics, distinguishes itself by the least peace-loving and freedom-loving trait, which it does by the biggest and multifaceted development of militarism.[1]
>
> There was an epoch of relatively "peaceful" capitalism. . . . This epoch is gone for good; it has given way to an epoch which is relatively much more violent, spasmodic, disastrous and conflicting; an epoch which for the mass of the population is typified not so much by a "horror without end" as by a "horrible end."[2]

These words, and many others conveying the same message, still influence the Soviet view of the contemporary world. For example, in 1985, Major General M. Yasyukov warned that

> Mankind is again confronted with a challenge, this time by U.S. imperialism. . . . The increased irresponsibility of the White House and its war policy is linked directly to a general crisis of capitalism. . . . Because of class hatred toward socialism, the ruling circles of imperialist countries are losing their sense of reality, and often their common sense, too. This leads ever more to the irrational character of the policy of imperialism. . . . The adventuristic nature of its policies becomes ever stronger as a result of close interlocks between the state apparatus, aggressive militarism, and the transnational companies incredibly fattening on the arms race and the exploitation of developing countries.[3]

As simplistic as such views may be, they should not be taken lightly or dismissed as meaningless rhetoric. Even if the Soviets are cynical and may not always believe their own words, they do consistently repeat these views and back them up with deeds whenever possible.

THE RECORD OF SOVIET TREATY VIOLATIONS

The Soviet record of violating nearly all arms control treaties should not be isolated from the general Soviet practice of disregarding *any* treaty signed by them, whether because of sheer contempt for international law or the belief that such transgressions may go unpunished or even unnoticed.

In the case of prewar Poland, the Soviets—by signing the Ribbentrop-Molotov Pact and its secret annex leading to the fourth partition of Poland—violated at least four major treaties and conventions. These included:

- the Treaty of Riga, concluded by Poland, Soviet Russia, and the Ukraine on March 18, 1912;
- the Protocol of Moscow, resulting from the Kellogg-Briand Pact, signed in Moscow by the USSR, Poland, Estonia, Latvia, and Romania on February 9, 1929;
- the Non-Aggression Pact between Poland and the USSR, signed in Moscow on July 25, 1932, for a three-year period, and then, on May 5, 1934, extended until December 31, 1945;
- the Convention for the Definition of Aggression, signed *inter alia* by Poland and the USSR in London on July 3, 1933.

In fact, the Soviet Union violated still more bilateral and multilateral treaties and agreements on occasion, but the above four will serve as specific examples. Similar violations also took place in relation to Estonia, Latvia, and Lithuania.

In all of these cases, no bilateral or multilateral sanctions were applied against the USSR. Neither Poland nor the three Baltic states declared war on the Soviet Union after the integrity of their territories had been violated by the Red Army. The USSR also avoided actually declaring war on these countries, all the while achieving its politico-strategic objectives by breaking the treaties to which it had been a signatory. This situation changed only when the USSR violated the territorial integrity of Finland on November 30, 1939, and was engulfed in an undeclared war with that country. As a result, the Soviet Union was expelled from the League of Nations on December 14, 1939.

That has been, for all practical purposes, the *only* major sanction ever applied against the USSR for its violation of bilateral and multilateral treaties, and even this was limited in scope, due to the fact that such major powers as the United States, Germany, Japan, and Italy were themselves at that time no longer members of the League. Additionally, because war was already raging in Europe and the Far East, the League's activities had little practical effect.

All other treaty violations by the Soviet Union, including those of the Yalta accords, have gone unpunished or even unnoticed. On the contrary, in many ways these violations seem to have been handsomely rewarded. The admission of the Soviet Union to the United Nations—especially the fact that it was offered three seats in the General Assembly (e.g., USSR, the Ukraine, and Byelorussia) and a permanent seat in the Security Council with veto power—is the best example of such rewards.

Soviet aggression in Eastern Europe has gone unpunished and has been largely ignored. The Soviet invasion of Afghanistan, for example, despite limited sanctions imposed temporarily by a few countries, has not even been mentioned by name in the United Nations, where the only "action" taken was an overwhelming vote to withdraw "foreign troops" from that country. Moreover, no important signatory has ever broken any major bilateral or multilateral treaty with the USSR, save Nazi Germany, when it violated the Ribbentrop-Molotov Pact in 1941.

In view of this record, the USSR feels free to violate any treaties and agreements it signs. Arms control treaties, whose strict observance is particularly difficult to monitor, are no exception. On the contrary, the USSR has—quite legitimately from its point of view—good reason to single them out for violation.

ATTITUDES OF SOVIET DECISIONMAKERS TOWARD ARMS CONTROL

Western Sovietologists believe they know who the decisionmakers are in the Soviet Union. Primarily, they seem to be the leaders of the Communist Party (CPSU), either as individuals (as was the case with Stalin), or collectively (in various duos and troikas). Their official views are also known to the West.

My view, contrary to widespread opinion in the West, is that Soviet decisionmakers—especially in military and foreign matters—are predominantly those top-ranking military officers who have been strongly supported by the Committee for State Security (Komitet Gosudarstvennoy Bezopasnosti—KGB) since Yuri Andropov became its head in April 1967.

The voice of the military and the KGB in anything concerning "external security" may, in fact, be more influential than that of the purely political leadership. Concrete evidence in support of this opinion was provided in Moscow in May 1972, during the final stages of the SALT I negotiations between President Nixon and the Brezhnev-Kosygin-Podgorny troika. Brezhnev's consent to certain U.S. proposals was quickly overruled by Vice Premier Leonid V. Smirnov, Chairman of the Military Industrial Commission (Voyenno Promishlennaya Komisya—VPK) during Smirnov's meeting with Henry Kissinger, in the presence of Andrei Gromyko. Brezhnev never attempted to overrule Smirnov.

Today, some serious discrepancies can be seen between Gorbachev's public pronouncements on disarmament and the stand taken by the Soviet negotiators in Geneva. In the final analysis, it is this latter stand—effectively that of the military—which counts.

Based on my knowledge of how military matters are handled in Poland, I can report that these matters are *not* discussed during the sessions of the Politburo or the Council of Ministers. When I was economic advisor to Edward Gierek (September 1971–December 1972), I attended Politburo meetings and was present during discussions on all agenda items. Never were defense matters discussed. I learned then that defense matters are handled exclusively in the country's Defense Committee (KOK) and the Military Council, or the Kolegium, of the Ministry of National Defense. Since political and military institutions in satellite countries are modeled on the Soviet original, it is quite likely that military matters are dealt with in similar fashion in Moscow—that is, by the Defense Council, or the Main Military Council (GVS—Glavnyy Voyennyy Soviet), or the Kolegium, of the Ministry of Defense.

Moreover, because in the Soviet military hierarchy the Chief of the General Staff is second in consequence only to the Minister, and may sometimes be a more knowledgable military expert than the Minister (as was the case with Marshal Nikolai V. Ogarkov and Marshal Dmitri F. Ustinov), it is quite likely that the Chief of the General Staff will be the most important of the Soviet leaders. Recent public pronouncements by Marshal S. Akhromeyev, Chief of the General Staff, on disarmament issues (e.g., on October 17, 1985) may support such a view, particularly because Akhromeyev's opinions were disseminated in the West in an unprecedented way, even more prominently than Gorbachev's own views on the subject.

If the Chief of the General Staff occupies such a critical position, then the real Soviet decisionmakers on all disarmament and arms control issues should be sought in the GVS, to which also belong the heads of the CPSU and the KGB, or perhaps even in the General Staff itself. Moreover, the General Staff runs the Main Intelligence Directorate of the General Staff (Glavnoe Razvedyvatelnoye Upravleniye—GRU), and the GRU is known to be highly instrumental in all disarmament and arms control negotiations. In Poland, the ZII—the Polish Military Intelligence Directorate—is the equivalent of the GRU. As a ZII official, I was briefed regularly on arms control issues and all related developments. I was obliged to report anything I could learn on the subject, whether from my trips to the West or from reading Western publications. When I was chief of the ZII Rezydentura (station) in Geneva (December 1969-August 1971), I was aware of ZII officers attending various disarmament conferences, and was instructed to provide them any assistance they required. During the MBFR talks in Geneva, the same situation existed. Some ZII officers posed as officers on active service, while others were "coopted civilians" posing as ordinary civilians.

The practical implications of this are obvious. Any negotiations on arms control and resulting treaties would be viewed in the USSR as a purely *strategic* matter, with only as much political/diplomatic significance as the former might permit. The negotiations in question amount to a strategic operation, a sort of "reconnaissance by negotiation." To be more precise, Soviet decisionmakers have two primary goals when they engage in negotiations that may ultimately lead to treaties: (1) to seek strategic superiority over the adversary at minimum risk to the Soviet military posture by structuring treaties in such a way that only the adversary would be obliged to follow the stipulations; and (2) to gather as much information as possible on the adversary's strength and determination to use force, while at the same time lowering his vigilance and confusing him through disinformation and deception.[4]

In such an operation, it is doubtful that any civilians in the Soviet leadership—for example, those not associated with the military, KGB, or Ministry of Internal Affairs (Ministerstvo Vnutrenikh Del—MVD)—will have any expertise allowing them to contribute significantly to the "disarmament process." In a sense, this point is confirmed in the previously cited article by General Yasyukov. He writes that party policy is determined by external and internal factors, with the former more important than the latter. The external factors consist of the seriousness of the threat of war, the character of the sources of the external threat, and the strength of the potential enemy.[5] Dealing with these three factors requires the highest degree of professional expertise, which is found in the General Staff and its GRU, as well as in the KGB.

Logically then, any "disarmament process" should be understood as being driven by purely politico-strategic objectives and constituting an integral component of Soviet strategic planning. Any treaties resulting from this process would be designed so that they can be violated in whole or in part, while keeping adverse reaction to a minimum.

SOVIET MOTIVATIONS AND GOALS

The Soviet "military-police complex," which includes party functionaries from the Administration, Personnel, International, and Heavy Industrial departments, does not engage in negotiations for the purpose of reaching agreement on any effective disarmament or arms control treaties—save the ones where the adversary can be convinced to accept measures that will favor the USSR, or where the treaty stipulations are such that they can be easily violated later by the USSR without undue risk.

The Marxist-Leninist ideology emphasizes the inevitability of confrontation between East and West—or between socialism and capitalism. The Soviets want the imperialist powers to disarm and to lower their guard, thereby guaranteeing themselves certain victory in the inevitable confrontation to come. The path to this goal lies in the use of disinformation and the manipulation of treaty language so that the West believes a valid treaty binding to both sides has been concluded; in reality, the treaty is binding only on the West—the Soviets having provided themselves with linguistic loopholes which make it an easy and low-risk task to violate the treaty.

Lacking any motivation to disarm or to join in any effective arms control measures, the Soviets focus their attention on the goals of the "disarmament process": (1) to learn from the adversary as much as possible on anything of interest to the Soviet "military-police complex," and (2) to tell the adversary as little as possible, to lie to him as much as possible, and, when striking deals, to design treaty clauses that will bind the Soviet Union as little as possible. Under these circumstances, treaty violations are not only understandable for the Soviets, but are quite commendable. *Not* to seek to violate a treaty with the imperialist forces is wrong.

SOVIET CONCEPT OF OBLIGATIONS

Obligation, as a category of law, rather than a moral principle, was long ago defined by Lenin: "The source of law is strength."[6] It is clear that Soviet decisionmakers, as true followers of "Lenin's teachings," feel obliged from a purely legal point of view to comply with terms of treaties signed by them *only* when they may fear sanctions, or where the risks of noncompliance exceed the benefits.

When it comes to *commercial* treaties and contracts, the history of Soviet observance is exemplary—though not without exceptions (like Lend-Lease), especially when dealing with other communist countries, most notably Yugoslavia, Albania, and China.[7] The explanation for this is simple: The Soviet Union needs Western goods, knowhow, and credits. The Soviets are also aware of the fact that commercially and financially they will gain nothing by adventurism. In these areas, their sport comes from playing one Western country against another, and private companies and financial institutions against their governments.

With regard to obligations arising from treaties and contracts affecting *external security*, the Soviets—and the pre-Bolshevik Russians before them—would break any of these if they believed that in so doing they could secure some strategic or tactical advantage over an adversary. And they never allow any obligations under international law, or arising from multilateral or bilateral agreements, to stand in their way. Nor do moral considerations concern Soviet decisionmakers, for Lenin decreed that everything and anything done to serve the "Revolution" is morally correct.

Today, because the strategic or tactical advantage (indeed, strategic or tactical *surprise*) has become increasingly important due to technological advances in weaponry, the violation of arms control treaties takes on even more significance. This is especially true if such a violation cannot be detected with certainty or is otherwise played down or ignored by the other contracting parties. Although satellite pictures or electronic intelligence (e.g., the tracking of missile tests by telemetry) are considered hard evidence by military specialists monitoring the observance of arms control treaties, it is hardly conclusive evidence for the Western mass media and is barely perceived by the general public. What is understandable is that the USSR tries to capitalize on this situation, and feels little constraint in violating certain vital provisions of the treaties it signs.

This cold calculation by the Soviet Union regarding treaty violations raises some troubling prospects. For example, with regard to eleven nuclear arms control treaties signed by Moscow—such treaties are the most sensitive ones, whether concluded bilaterally or multilaterally—Soviet risk analysts know that the only country potentially able to cause problems for the USSR is the United States.[8] All others would hardly raise their voices should any Soviet treaty infraction occur. Complaints against the USSR, even if filed with the United Nations or the International Court of Justice at The Hague, are not likely to cause any real harm to the Soviet Union. Only bilateral sanctions might hurt, and as a practical matter, only those employed by the United States.

In fact, the only nuclear arms control treaties which the USSR *may* feel truly obliged to observe, from the point of view of risk analysis, are those concluded with the United States. These would include the Hot Line

Agreement of 1963; the Accidents Measures Agreement of 1971; the SALT I Treaty of 1972; the Prevention of Nuclear War Agreement of 1973; the Threshold Test Ban Treaty of 1974; and the SALT II Treaty of 1979. Of these, the SALT treaties are the most important. If the Soviets feel obliged to observe them at all, it is only because of the fear of adverse consequences that may result from their nonobservance. A similar situation exists in the case of the 1972 ABM Treaty and the 1974 Protocol to the SALT I ABM Treaty concluded bilaterally between the Soviet Union and the United States, and in all conventions on the use of chemical and biological weapons.

The Soviet Union, with its clear-cut, long-range strategic-political goals, which it keeps carefully hidden from public view, attaches great importance to its many bilateral and multilateral treaties and conventions, because it can use them to further its strategic objectives. Moreover, the Soviet leadership enjoys continuity and thus its goals remain constant, unlike the situation in the West.

The Soviet leadership, unshaken in its adherence to Leninist doctrine, believes that the world order is dictated not by any "Divine Force," but rather by the laws of nature—a "survival of the fittest" theory. It is the stronger one who prevails, or, if both contenders are equally strong, then it is the more aggressive one who will wield the scepter. Coupled with some uniquely Russian traditions, such an approach allows the Soviet leadership to make a mockery of the treaty negotiation process—with a clear conscience. This is a fact that should be recognized by all who enter into negotiations with the USSR: The Soviets will stop at nothing, and will honor only those obligations that exclusively serve to further their own strategic objectives.

THE SOVIET PERCEPTION OF U.S. GOALS AND MOTIVATIONS

The standard Soviet view of American goals and motivations derives from Lenin, who stated that as long as imperialism exists there cannot be peace on earth.[9] In the eyes of the Soviet leadership, the United States is the "chief" imperialist, and therefore the major obstacle to attaining Soviet-style "peace."[10]

The Soviets are quite specific in condemning U.S. "ruling circles." For example, four Soviet journalists, who interviewed President Reagan in October 1985, prior to the Geneva Summit, later wrote an article "About the Reagan Interview," in which they made brazenly personal attacks against the U.S. President.[11] The opinions expressed by them were undoubtedly sanctioned by the highest Soviet authorities, and are significant in many ways. The journalists not only ridiculed all U.S. disarmament proposals—calling American intelligence information on the level of Soviet nuclear forces outright lies and fabrications—but they also went so far as to accuse the United States of having the worst intentions toward the USSR. They wrote that as long ago as the autumn of 1945 the United States had already considered the USSR a potential enemy and a target for atomic attack. They specifically referred to U.S. plans to attack the Soviet Union as "Gunpowder" and "Dropshot." They recalled that the United States surrounded the Soviet Union with 1,500 military bases located in 32 countries with 550,000 U.S. servicemen stationed there.

Naturally, neither the journalists nor anyone else in the USSR mentioned the origins of the alleged U.S. concern, nor did anyone discuss why the USSR retained six million troops after World War II, when the United States was demobilizing its own armed forces. In this regard, a question arises: Does the Soviet leadership truly believe what it says?

Drawing on my own experience, based on my participation from 1977 to 1979 in two Soviet-led "think tanks" (Zvedza II and Moment II), the Soviet leadership may in fact believe its own propaganda about U.S. "hostile intentions" toward the USSR. The "true" civilians in the Soviet leadership may not have independent sources of expert knowledge about the highly complex nature of the balance of forces between the United States and the Soviet Union, much less about genuine U.S. intentions toward the Soviet Union. Their knowledge is almost exclusively based on what the authoritative "complex" teaches. For many reasons the Soviet military complex portrays U.S.-Soviet relations, and its own level of forces, in a manner that bears scant relationship to reality.

For example, on November 19, 1985, Colonel General Yu. Yashin, First Deputy Commander-in-Chief of the Soviet Strategic Rocket Forces, when interviewed by the Soviet press on the issue of the U.S. Strategic Defense Initiative (SDI), expressed no doubt that the United States is deploying "space strike arms," and that the American intent is to turn space into a "possible theater of military actions." More specifically, he maintained that the "main aim of this dangerous adventure is to try to find protection behind a space 'shield' and deprive us [the USSR] of the possibility of inflicting an effective **retaliatory** strike."[12] (Boldface in original.)

Hearing such authoritative statements pronounced by the military in the USSR—the unchallenged experts in such matters—any "true" civilians in the leadership are, at best, helpless to distinguish fact from fiction in the rare case where they might have a contradictory opinion to express.

It seems more likely, in fact, that the Soviet military leadership not only openly influences the "official" Soviet view on disarmament and arms race issues, but actually sets this policy itself. In a speech delivered in East Berlin on December 4, 1985, Marshal S. Sokolov, Soviet Minister of Defense, said that the Warsaw Pact "would match any U.S. arms buildup," thus suggesting that the USSR and its satellites must continue or increase their military efforts, allegedly to match the U.S./NATO challenge. Whether such declarations by the Soviet military leadership merely reflect the political "green light" in the USSR, or create the political atmosphere itself is, of course, debatable. I believe the latter is the case. However, one cannot completely rule out the possibility that the Soviet leadership— military-police complex included—can have a clearer, unbiased view of the United States. I have met such Soviets who disbelieve the official line although they continue to support it publicly.

Even the Soviet official party line has greatly evolved over the decades. The best example is the concept of "peaceful coexistence"—popular in the late days of Lenin's reign, later abandoned, and then again reborn under Khrushchev's leadership. Peaceful coexistence (*Mirnoe sosushchestvovanie*) is a political slogan suggesting the renunciation of war as an instrument of foreign policy; but for the Soviets it is also a period during which the Soviet Union can build up its military potential and promote its designs for global domination. While this basic concept implies that the downfall of capitalism can be effected without resort to armed violence, there is some uncertainty among the Soviet leadership as to the practical application of this philosophy. Some, at least privately, may even believe that the coexistence of socialism and capitalism can be seen as the coexistence of plus and minus in physics, or as matter and antimatter—if you have one, you necessarily have the other. Because such a view does not allow a *totally* peaceful coexistence, ideological war, at least, must be relentlessly waged. The Soviets emphatically reject any notion of convergence. They once strongly rebuffed French President Giscard d'Estaing when he raised the issue of convergence during a trip to the Soviet Union.

Many sophisticated Soviets, even within the "complex," do not really fear a first strike by the United States, even if they publicly proclaim the opposite. Telling the Soviet people that the United States is not likely to launch a first strike would be tantamount to admitting that the "predatory nature of imperialism" had changed. In such a case the Soviet military-police complex would be challenging the ideological basis of its authority. Finally, the Soviet leadership, whether out of ignorance or narrowly defined self-interest, may actually believe its own rhetoric. They also know that if there is a nuclear war, the question of who attacked first will be superfluous; the victors are not going to raise that question.

The problem confronting the United States is how to convince the Soviet Union that the West, specifically the United States, does not want to deliberately start World War III. For the time being, the Soviets, at least publicly, continue to believe that American intentions toward the Soviet Union are hostile and inflammatory. The more they talk like that, the more difficult it becomes to convince them that they are wrong. The Soviet system has created a special environment in which lies become truths, believed by many and suspiciously guarded from anyone having differing views. How much this situation has degenerated can best be illustrated by the case of Anatoliy Dobrynin, the former Soviet Ambassador to the United States. Despite having spent twenty-five years in the United States, he seemed not only to believe the Soviet propaganda about the United States, but appeared to be quite instrumental in advancing this nonsense. It is quite likely that in his own mind he did not believe his own words, but he cynically reported what he knew his superiors wanted to hear from him. This state of affairs is highly dangerous, as the Soviets may fall victim to their own deception and disinformation.

It is true that recently Gorbachev's *glasnost* has introduced some new Soviet rhetoric, but it is not yet clear what are the limits of *glasnost* and what in the end it signifies. Although its primary purpose may not be deception, its deceptive aspects are obvious—especially in cases where words are taken for deeds and where the naive want to interpret Gorbachev's words according to their own viewpoint.

Nevertheless, I reiterate my doubt that, in the final analysis, the Soviet leadership has ever truly believed in the likelihood of the United States launching a first strike against the Soviet Union. Take the Cuban missile crisis, for example. Had the Soviets believed that such a strike was in "standing preparedness," they would never have dared provoke the American President to such an extent. Moreover, the very course of the Cuban crisis has surely taught them a lesson; the United States, even in such a dramatic situation, had left open the opportunity for the USSR to back down from its provocation, avoiding war. If the United States pursued a cautious and prudent policy at a time when its superiority in strategic forces was approximately four to one, it seems unlikely that the Soviet leadership could now be so fearful of U.S. goals and intentions when a "rough parity" in strategic forces exists, and when the conventional-chemical forces of the USSR have clear superiority.

Paradoxically, the less the Soviet leadership believes its own official pronouncements on U.S. aims and motivations, the more it portrays the United States in the worst possible light. Since Soviet leaders know that their own public rhetoric is playacting, they tend to believe the American statements of peaceful intent to be dishonest as well. The Soviets have even mastered the technique of displaying publicly their "honest concern" about U.S. policies and goals. They know that the United States credits them with genuine concern about the war and peace issue—based on the Soviet historical experience, especially World War II—so they act even more the aggrieved party. The best example of this is the failure by President Reagan in Geneva to convince Mr. Gorbachev as to his good intentions concerning SDI. The same failure was repeated, even more dramatically, in Reykjavik. In return, the President was told by Gorbachev, in an apparently convincing and emotional manner, that the Soviets are not "simpletons" to be so easily deceived. I think the President believes Gorbachev is sincere in his concern.

In order to confuse the United States still more, the Soviets may make many misleading public statements about American goals and ambitions, or at other times they may say nothing about the United States at all, dumbfounding and frustrating American observers and policymakers. This may even cause a sense of guilt on the part of the Western representatives that somehow they have failed to convince the Soviets of their good intentions. If this is true, and I believe it is, then one must seek an explanation for this Soviet behavior.

My own explanation is that the Soviets are aware of their difficulties, economic ones primarily. Their present defense effort is possible only because Soviet leaders have been willing to live with a stagnating standard of living and cuts in capital spending. Even in the Soviet economy, such a policy cannot last indefinitely. Sooner or later, the point will be reached where the belt can be tightened no more to bolster the defense effort. The deterioration in the standard of living, even in such a country as the USSR, can become an explosive issue. The Polish lesson of the summer of 1980 is a warning: The military-police complex, the most important part of the *nomenklatura*, beset by the deteriorating economic situation and other growing tensions—problems of nationalities, religious faith, incipient democratic aspirations, dissidents—must find an excuse for belt-tightening and harsh social discipline. The military, with its 700,000-strong officer corps, together with over one million in the KGB-MVD subcomplex, have vested interests in controlling external and domestic tensions in order to preserve their own privileges and indispensability within the *nomenklatura* itself.

Thus, the United States serves as scapegoat. Portraying U.S. leaders as warmongers ready to attack the USSR at any moment serves the self-preservation instinct of the complex. Finding "hard evidence" with which to "document" U.S. warlike attitudes and ambitions does not pose a major problem to the complex in such a closed society.

The United States, moreover, by its very existence is truly a threat to the USSR. Presenting such a vigorous and robust example of a democratic system, the United States is an even greater threat to the Soviet system than any Nazi, fascist, or military dictatorship. No authoritarian society could be as attractive to the Soviet peoples as a democratic one could be. The 150 million people forced into the Soviet camp in the postwar period are even more fascinated with democracy and capitalism than are the long-subjugated Russian citizens. The American demonstration of a thriving capitalist democracy penetrates behind the Iron Curtain and creates very real problems for Soviet rulers. They fear anything like a "convergence" or "free flow" of peoples and ideas between East and West. The undermining effect of both is only too obvious to them.

Therefore, the very survivability of the *nomenklatura*, especially its military-police complex, dictates general and specific Soviet external and internal policies. Since external policies have generally assumed precedence, the very existence of the United States and its appeal to the tyrannized peoples of Soviet bloc nations may—even rightly from the *nomenklatura*'s perspective—be considered a "strategic threat." Portraying the United States as ready and willing to launch a first strike against the USSR is a convenient deception available to the Soviet leaders. Allowing the Soviet citizenry a clear and undistorted view of the United States and its allies could spell the end of the *nomenklatura*. Therefore, self-interest and a finely tuned instinct for survival dictate how the Soviets portray the United States. Even if the Soviet leaders clearly recognize that the U.S. system is "working," it matters less what they think in private than what they do in public. They dare not admit that the U.S. example of democracy is flourishing. To do anything but denounce the American example would be suicidal.

The Soviet treatment of the United States is largely determined by Marxism-Leninism, a "modern atheistic religion," despite its claims to be "scientific." The combination of strange religiosity and scientificity has resulted in dogma surprisingly resistant to evolution. They take the form of basic laws and truths. Dogmatists are tolerated in the Soviet bloc, while revisionists are more bitterly fought than even outright opponents of Marxism-Leninism. The Leninist tenets on imperialism are gospel; hence, whatever the United States says or does is not important. What really matters is that Soviet leaders know scientifically how the United States should be acting as an imperialist power, and therefore that is how the United States is acting.

U.S. CONCEPTS OF SOVIET TREATY OBLIGATIONS: THE SOVIET PERSPECTIVE

I believe that Soviet leaders are aware that the American perception of how the Soviets view their treaty obligations is basically correct. Yet their strength lies in not admitting this publicly. The leadership knows only too well that the USSR has succeeded in achieving "rough strategic parity" with the United States—with doubtless first-strike superiority—thereby giving it a serious strategic option: nuclear blackmail.

It is only logical that the USSR wants to capitalize on this state of affairs, and to avoid creating an impression that it in any way accepts the U.S.

version of Soviet obligations. For example, the concept of verifying Soviet obligations infuriates the Soviet leadership. Verifiability is either branded U.S. spying on the USSR, or made conditional on achieving disarmament first, and permitting verification only later—a totally ridiculous proposition. The Soviets are truly apprehensive that any on-site inspection by American teams roaming the country could create unpredictable complications. Once present in the USSR, U.S. verification teams, even unintentionally, would be engaged in something "close to spying" in places until now tightly closed to foreign eyes and ears. Human contacts could create serious dilemmas for Soviet leaders. Hence, they must continue to ridicule American concepts of Soviet treaty obligations.

However, it cannot be excluded that the USSR may create an impression of being flexible in some areas of disarmament and arms control. Gorbachev seems to be especially inventive to this end. But what such Soviet flexibility may mean in the long run is not yet clear. What does seem clear is that effective ways of cheating are in place, and thus partial verification of treaty provisions can be safely advocated by Moscow.

By and large, the Kremlin will muddy the waters even more as "high-tech spying" by the United States is thwarted by Soviet technological advances—the introduction of mobile ICBMs and improved *maskirovka*[13] in general—thus increasing the necessity of human on-site inspection and verification. To decrease the human element and to take advantage of more opportunities to cheat on obligations, the Soviet Union must increasingly distance itself from American ideas of obligations, and must increasingly denounce American verification procedures, or, if it does not, then one must be suspicious of Soviet concessions. I cannot see how this vicious circle can change without changing the nature of the Soviet system itself.

THE SOVIET PERCEPTION OF DIFFERENCES ON THE ISSUE OF ARMS CONTROL

The standard Soviet view of arms control is well known. "Socialism," represented chiefly by the Soviet Union, does not want war, but "imperialism" is propelling the world toward conflict. The Soviet Army, in consequence, is the army of "peace" while all imperialist forces are potential aggressors. For this reason, the USSR asserts that any arms it has are used to "serve peace" and thus there is virtually no need for arms control. The word of the Soviet Union, as that of a "peace-loving country," that weapons will never be used except for defense, is to be unconditionally trusted.

Moreover, the USSR, though regularly parading its forces through Red Square and otherwise glorifying them on all possible occasions, keeps secret the level of spending for arms or any other information relating to the military. As to the defense budget itself, the figures officially reported are ridiculously low: for 1987, Rubles (R) 20.2 billion, or close to $30 billion. No figures on the levels of military personnel or weapons, including types and names, are ever officially mentioned. However, the Soviets reiterate that any aggression against the USSR will be dealt a "mortal blow," and that the USSR is "invincible." Reconciling its invincible armed force and its "peace-loving" nature, the USSR quite willingly enters the disarmament process, at times even initiating it.

During the disarmament process, the USSR very cleverly uses intelligence gathering and disinformation to confuse and disarm the West. Whatever Gorbachev says publicly about the "oncoming crisis" in the Atlantic Alliance, or about the "military-industrial complex" allegedly pushing the United States to escalate the arms race, the Soviets know perfectly well that the Western democracies are ill-suited for war. They also know—though they do not say so publicly—that the "welfare state" has found a solution to the aggregate demand that competes with armaments spending. Additionally, they know that most Western businesses shy away from defense contracts, as defense research is very costly and the length of contracts is an unknown factor.

The Soviets, by engaging in arms control talks, believe that such negotiations may actually influence adversely the level of defense spending in the West. They know that the NATO countries—the United States apart—do not live up to agreed levels of defense spending; and that even in the United States, future levels of spending are in jeopardy. In Geneva in 1983, the tactic of abruptly breaking off talks with the United States gained them nothing, and they will not repeat the same mistake. Today, the situation seems to favor them. With the United States taking the initiative for the Geneva summit, then quickly responding to the Soviet initiative for an ad hoc Reykjavik summit, with more summits probably to follow, and with the current U.S. President having no chance of remaining in office beyond the 1988 elections, the Soviets may well play a "wait-and-see" game, figuring they can outwait any unfavorable developments—most notably the U.S. Strategic Defense Initiative.[14] Assuming this is true, the USSR may be as disinterested in meaningful arms control as the United States is interested.

Moreover, one cannot rule out the possibility that the USSR deliberately breaks arms control treaties with the United States in order to assess the U.S. reaction. The Soviets probably do not believe that they can actually conceal the testing of an SS-24 or -25, or the construction of Krasnoyarsk-like radar stations. It is more likely that they have theorized possible U.S. reactions to such violations and are testing the accuracy of their analyses. As it looks now, nothing serious is really happening to deter the Soviets from further violations, especially since public opinion in the West hardly understands what Soviet violation of the ABM Treaty really means.

The fact that the United States has kept such Soviet violations quiet for so long has greatly helped the USSR counter U.S. accusations once they were made public. When the United States began to raise the question of Soviet treaty violations, the Soviet Union immediately passed to the counterattack by accusing the United States itself of violating the SALT II accords with the MX and Midgetman missile programs.[15]

The Soviet Union is contemptuous of any treaty obligations that no longer serve its purposes. At the same time, it knows democratic countries cannot follow its example of blatantly violating valid treaties. The arms control talks and ensuing accords are exploited by the USSR for its own ends, and the lengthy process encourages deception and disinformation practices. For example, in the case of the SALT I Treaty, Americans were led to believe that the Soviet Union had more weapons delivery systems than the United States, due to the Soviet lag in MIRVing their ICBMs, but this turned out not to be true. The ink had hardly dried on the SALT I Treaty when the Soviets MIRVed their ICBMs and gained an important edge over the United States in the number of ICBM-deliverable warheads.

Disinformation and deception practices are given a special prominence in Soviet strategy, and these "active measures" are undertaken by a group called the Strategic Deception War Board (Voyennoye Upravleniye Strategicheskovo Obmana) linked to the GRU and its Warsaw Pact equivalents.[16]

The Soviet Union has been able to judge the effectiveness of its active measures propaganda by the slowdowns in Western defense efforts. Soviet disinformation tactics have greatly retarded deployment of several major U.S. weapons programs—B-1 bombers, Trident II and MX missiles—and in Western Europe the deployment of Pershing II and cruise missiles was delayed.

Given the miniaturization of weapons and improved means of camouflage, the United States will gradually acquire less intelligence about Soviet weapons systems, and this will make it more difficult for Washington in arms control negotiations with Moscow.

SOVIET VIEWS ON CHEATING

Breaking the rules and trying to beat the system is normal behavior for the average Soviet citizen. He has to cheat to get ahead. The Soviet leaders are no exception; deception and disinformation are, after all, forms of cheating. Cheating, moreover, is deeply steeped in Russian tradition. There is an old Russian proverb that says *"duraka y v tserkvi b'yut,"* which translates as "a fool is roughed up even in church." What this means is that anyone who is naive enough to be cheated *should* be cheated; there is nothing immoral in taking advantage of a fool. This concept has been magnified by the communist regime. One must remember the Marxist concept of truth: Truth "depends on time and place." In the case of Soviet disinformation practices and arms control treaty violations, the United States plays the role of the gullible simpleton. The Soviets view arms control talks as "conflict by negotiation"; for them, cheating on treaties during peacetime is as normal as saving lives and armaments during wartime.

Categories of Cheating

There are many different ways in which the Soviet Union and satellite countries cheat—from simple day-to-day operations designed to transmit disinformation to the West, to complex, long-term plans for circumventing treaty obligations. Perhaps the most dangerous form is what I call "learned cheating," which is used both internally and externally.

The military, at least in Poland, officially runs several scientific and research facilities. Many more such institutes and laboratories, particularly those in high-technology defense research, are covertly directed by the military and/or the secret police. The military and secret police have easy access to scientists or research personnel whom they consider worth recruiting.[17] This is especially true for all those who may travel in the West, or who have access to Western literature, or both. Such people are coopted to serve either the military or police, even in cases when the disciplines they represent only remotely suggest connections to state security.

It is difficult to pin down exact numbers, but my impression is that, in Poland at least, such coopted specialists may number in the thousands. In the Polish armed forces there are about 1,500 specializations, and in the Soviet armed forces there are about 2,500. This allows the tentacles of the military to penetrate deeply throughout the scientific community. Civilians who can be trusted to remain true to their communist masters are sent abroad as undercover operatives. Almost any international gathering can serve to introduce those Soviet operatives to Western scientists and researchers. Two examples are the Pugwash conferences and the World Peace Council: both afford the Soviets the opportunity to gain information from the Western scientific community, as well as to attempt to recruit Western scientists to serve—in most cases, unwittingly—the communist cause.

One of the goals of the Soviet Union is to discredit the West in as many ways as possible, and scientific theories appear to be prime targets.

A theory is an assumption, a belief, a hypothesis; it is not a proven fact. It is relatively simple to cast aspersions on a scientific theory, bringing its accuracy into question. One such recent Soviet propaganda campaign has been directed against the American Strategic Defense Initiative (SDI); specifically, the Soviet Union would like to advance the notion that SDI cannot be made operational. Soviet academician Yevgeny Velikhov is particularly outspoken in his attack on SDI, and has been somewhat successful in his efforts.

When Soviet scientists state emphatically that SDI can never work they speak in vague generalities, and are only reluctantly pinned down on specifics. They assert that a 100 percent effectiveness is impossible to achieve and imply that a defensive system with only 98 percent efficiency is useless. This is, of course, despite the fact that the Soviets continue to work on their own "strategic defense" program.

Unfortunately for the West, various types of Soviet cheating are greatly facilitated by a large number of "concerned scientists" in the West who are being cleverly manipulated through "active measures" by various Soviet "persons of influence." The West is at a visible disadvantage here. The Andrei Sakharovs in the Soviet Union cannot outweigh the Carl Sagans in the West; while the "Tellers," "Jastrows," and the like are probably not representative of a majority among the Western scientific community. The extent to which the Soviet Union has succeeded in deceiving Western communities is best exemplified by the nomination for a Nobel prize of Soviet "peace activist," Dr. Yevgeni I. Chazov, in December 1985, despite worldwide protests by human rights activists. Of the various forms of Soviet cheating, I have no doubt that the "learned" ones are the most dangerous, insidious, and difficult to combat.

SOVIET TREATY VIOLATIONS

The Soviet Union is the world's unsurpassed expert when it comes to negotiating treaties that are "soft" on Soviet obligations and easily circumvented by the Soviet Union. It is incredible that the Soviets might violate any treaty out of ignorance of its contents and stipulations. Soviet treaty violations are deliberate and premeditated. It is their duty to break any accord that does not support official goals and doctrine. Only the conclusion that violating the treaty is riskier than not violating the treaty will prevent them from doing just that; and as history has proven, sanctions against them for cheating are rare and ineffective at best.

For example, both the United States and the Soviet Union are signatories to the 1925 Geneva Convention forbidding the use of chemical and biological weapons, as well as to the 1972 Biological and Toxin Weapons

Convention prohibiting the manufacture and possession of chemical and biological weapons. Nevertheless, the Soviet Union has not complied with these accords; they have used these weapons in Afghanistan, and directed proxies to employ CBW in Laos, Kampuchea, and elsewhere. These Soviet violations have passed unpunished and even unnoticed by many. When the U.S. delegation to the Madrid Conference on European Security charged in February 1982 that the Soviets were operating 20 CBW facilities in direct violation of international law, no action was taken—not even a censure. In fact, the disinformation campaign launched by Soviet authorities has been so successful that even some scientists in the West are doubtful now as to whether traces of T-2, one of the trichothecene mycotoxins, were really found in "yellow rain" samples taken from Kampuchea.

In response, the Soviet Union accused the United States of CBW violations. For example, on July 11, 1985, TASS accused the United States of intending to produce binary weapons—even while this proposal lay defeated in the U.S. House of Representatives—asserting that such action would be a violation of treaty provisions. And Moscow then went so far as to raise the question formally during a session of the Geneva Disarmament Commission. The history of such successful disinformation and offensive denial campaigns encourages the Soviets to continue their treaty violations.

THE ROLE OF DOCTRINE IN THE SOVIET UNION

The Soviet approach to cheating, disinformation, and other forms of "active measures" is determined by their firm belief in Marxist-Leninist doctrine and their vision of world developments. At once orthodox and pragmatic, Soviet leaders will do whatever is necessary to ensure their continued grip on power and pursue state goals. Whenever necessary, they may switch from one extreme to another—from total orthodoxy to excessive flexibility—to advance the cause of communism.

Although cheating, as such, is not officially recommended, it is unofficially strictly demanded. The actions of Soviet *apparatchiki* in deceiving their Western counterparts are not the result of misperceptions and miscommunications, as the Soviet leadership may conveniently claim. In fact, all state and party functionaries having contacts with the West are not only encouraged to find ways in which to deceive the West, but are, in reality, provided with detailed instructions to this end.

The Soviets actually have something like a "cheating doctrine," which is an integral part of the military doctrine—obligatory for the KGB and MVD troops as well. Soviet military doctrine, as formulated by Marshals V.D. Sokolovskiy, A.A. Grechko, and N.V. Ogarkov, can be summarized as follows.

The military doctrine, formulated and adopted by the Soviet state,[18] and applicable within a certain period of time, sets forth the nature and goals of a potential war. As a result, all necessary preparations to emerge victorious from such a conflict are to be undertaken ("active measures" are included, particularly in the area of disarmament and arms control). The military doctrine defines the adversary (the primary adversary being the United States), the proper means with which to fight, and the nature of the war once it has begun. The tasks for the armed services, the art of conducting war in its direction and developments, are determined by the doctrine.

Nothing done by the Soviet Union in its battle against the imperialist West is improvised; rather, it is predetermined by the military doctrine. Since the entire disarmament and arms control treaty negotiations process must be thoroughly examined and approved by the Soviet military, I am inclined to believe that both fall under Soviet military strategy, subordinated to military doctrine. This is because military strategy provides answers to dilemmas presented by future war, and both the arms control and disarmament negotiation processes raise very concrete problems for the Soviet Union. For this simple reason, once the military are directly involved in the process, they must have a "disarmament and arms control sub-doctrine" as well as a "negotiation strategy."

Moreover, I doubt that any "true" civilians are very instrumental in either process because their knowledge of the problems is far more limited than that of the military personnel. This holds true even for such civilians as Gorbachev himself. Gone are the times when a Stalin (who was a civilian) could assume the post of commander-in-chief in wartime. One must remember in those days, despite the German blitzkrieg strategy, there was no chance of conquering the USSR in a matter of days or weeks. Today technology has made the time factor critical. Additionally, Stalin had only one theater of war to concern himself with—about one million square kilometers in all. Today, there could be five to seven such theaters covering the entire globe—or, approximately 500 times more area to worry about. If one adds space as a new theater, the expanse of operations would be far greater. With automated C^3I systems, nuclear weapons, and the great complexity of operations on numerous fronts, any nonmilitary person would be incapable of directing an entire war effort. Ensconced in their remote, hardened shelters and cut off from their civilian power base, Soviet civilian leaders would have to rely on their military commanders to prosecute the war.

One must assume then that the present process of disarmament and arms control lies firmly in the hands of the military cadre, and that the military will try to reap the maximum benefit from the process. The Soviet military leadership has at least two goals: (1) to prevent the United States from making SDI operational and from developing first-strike weapons to the extent that these could nullify the Soviet edge in ICBMs; and (2) to ban all U.S. nuclear weapons from Western Europe and the Far East (and perhaps also foil French and British nuclear weapons plans).

Both of these Soviet aims encounter stiff resistance from most Western governments, but the Soviets will not give up, believing that time is on their side in their efforts to gain superiority in the strategic balance. The Soviets thus already are fighting a nuclear war with the United States at the negotiating table, and that war is waged by the Soviet military—not civilian leaders such as Karpov, Kvitsinski, and Gorbachev. This is the Soviet advantage over the United States: U.S. negotiators, whatever their diplomatic skills may be, are true civilians and are by no means expert on nuclear warfare and U.S. military strategy. It is doubtful that their civilian superiors are better informed than they or that they can assimilate U.S. military doctrine and strategy—to the extent that it exists and is clearly formulated.

A FINAL NOTE

Western knowledge about the Soviet Union is based primarily on past experience and interpretation of current policies and attitudes. Unfortunately, Soviet behavior is not yet clearly understood by Western societies. Add to this the fact that the Soviet Union has become, in military terms, probably the most powerful country in the world, and is the country best prepared for waging conventional or nuclear war. This situation is a dangerous one for the Free World, and is probably with us for the foreseeable future.

Pre-revolutionary Russia, although a major world power for at least two and a half centuries, always confronted adversaries who were stronger or at least equal in military strength. Post-revolutionary Russia, on the other hand, has only one adversary as its equal: the United States. The People's Republic of China does not yet pose a worrisome threat to the Soviet Union. The consequence of this situation, together with the fact that the USSR appears to have conventional and strategic superiority over the United States, is difficult to predict. I fear that the Soviet Union will try to capitalize on this new balance of power, and will have many strategic surprises in store for the United States. The international state of affairs is favorable for Soviet aims—given the conditions in South Africa, the Philippines, and Central America, as well as the possibility of a Soviet rapprochement with the PRC, waning enthusiasm for defense spending in the West, and so on.

The Soviet Union has been actively preparing for war, and I believe that, under the right conditions, Moscow might risk starting a war. If anything makes such a decision risky, it would be the combination of U.S. strength and unpredictability. The USSR may, in the end, have some doubts as to the American determination to go to all-out nuclear war. Put quite simply, the Soviet Union may believe that the United States is, by its very nature, a responsible and peace-loving nation. Soviet leaders know, even if they pretend otherwise, that the United States had no hand in starting the two world wars, or the Korean and Vietnam conflicts.

The Kremlin is aware that it could ultimately lose the arms race. Hence, it must try to make the most of superiority (or parity) achieved with so much effort. It may never again have such an oportunity to win a war as it has now. Whether this attack would come in the form of a limited nuclear assault in one region of the globe, or as a conventional-CBW conflict in, say, northern Europe, or even as a series of confrontations using proxies in many parts of the world is hard to predict. What is clear is that the Kremlin is agitated greatly by alleged U.S. actions to upset "strategic parity." If the United States can be deterred from pursuing an SDI shield and from completing the modernization of its strategic forces, the Soviet Union may enjoy a distinct global strategic superiority over the Western allies, with the option of a surprise first strike, and they may exercise that advantage to its fullest.

Neither can a sheer miscalculation by the Soviets be excluded. The Soviets know that the NATO allies assume them to be prudent. Hence, the West may not really believe that the Soviet Union would risk starting a major war. It is precisely on this premise that the Soviets may capitalize: As firmly as they believe in strategic surprise, anyone relying on their lack of adventurism may actually be helping to make their strategy work. Given the current world situation, I am very concerned that the Soviet Union may be approaching just such a dramatic decision.

The foregoing analysis of Soviet doctrine and strategy means that meaningful and substantive negotiations between the United States and the Soviet Union on the subject of disarmament and/or arms control will lead nowhere. This pessimistic outlook was confirmed by Leonid Zamyatin when he addressed a closed forum in Warsaw, which I attended in 1978 or 1979. He asserted that the USSR must be both conventionally and strategically stronger than the United States because the USSR has more potential enemies, including the Western nuclear powers and China. Therefore, the Soviet nuclear potential should be at least equal to the combined potential of the United States, the United Kingdom, France, and China. Moreover, he pointed out, the Soviet territory is the largest in the world and requires more armed forces, aircraft, naval units, and other defensive means than any other country. What he did not mention was that the USSR also needs larger forces than any other country because it must police the Soviet empire, including Eastern Europe.

With Zamyatin's analysis in mind, it seems unlikely that U.S. arms control negotiators will ever succeed in coaxing the Soviet Union to abandon its goal of strategic superiority. The United States may think it can out-negotiate the USSR. Indeed, it is conceivable that the Kremlin would even deliberately create such an impression to lull the West into letting down its guard. In the nuclear missile age, there will not be time to redress the military balance.

NOTES

1. Vladimir Ilyich Lenin, *Collected Works*, Vol. 37, Russian edition, p. 248.
2. Vladimir Ilyich Lenin, *Collected Works*, Vol. 22, English edition (Moscow: Progress Publishers, 1977), p. 104.
3. Major General M. Yasyukov, "Voyennaya Politika KPSS: Suschnost', Sodernzhaniye" (CPSU's War Policy: Essence, Contents), *Kommunist Vooruzhyonnykh Sil* (Communist of the Armed Forces), October 1985, No. 20, p. 16.
4. During arms control negotiations, the Soviets have regularly used deception as to the accuracy of their missiles, a practice not without influence on the course of negotiations. For example, true impact craters of the warheads of tested SS-19s were immediately filled, while false ones were dug and moved some distance from the actual target. I was first alerted to such practices by the ZII when I was asked to read Western newspapers carefully, whether in Poland or during my trips to the West after I returned from Geneva in July 1976. I was to report on anything concerning alleged Soviet cheating while testing missiles. Specifically, I was advised to look for discussions on telemetry encryption, precision targeting, hot/cold mode of launching, booster thrust power, and numbers of warheads. The fact that such information was sought by the ZII suggests Soviet interest in U.S. monitoring of Soviet cheating, since such information was not of direct interest to Poland.
5. Yasyukov, op.cit., p. 15.
6. This is a paraphrase from Lenin's article in *Pravda*, June 21 (8), 1917, No. 76, entitled, "An Epidemic of Credulity." Lenin wrote: "Power based not on law or elections, but directly on the armed forces . . . ." See Lenin, op. cit. (English edition), Vol. 25, p. 65.
7. However, undertakings agreed to by the USSR within Soviet-led COMECON—the Council for Mutual Economic Assistance—are also violated. For example, the USSR, Poland, Romania, East Germany, Czechoslovakia, and Bulgaria agreed in November 1983 to notify each other on nuclear accidents "as quickly as possible." There is no trace of such a notification following the Chernobyl disaster.
8. Of these eleven treaties, five are multilateral treaties to which both the USSR and the United States are parties: Antarctic Treaty of 1961, Limited Test Ban Treaty of 1963, Outer Space Treaty of 1967, Nuclear Non-Proliferation Treaty of 1970, and Seabed Arms Control Treaty of 1972.

9. More recently, this doctrinal precept was restated by Marshal Sergei Akhromeyev: "WWII has shown that the source of war was, and continues to be, international imperialism." *Kommunist*, No. 3, 1985.
10. Can "international imperialism" change? Apparently not, according to Lenin, who said, "Imperialism cannot be transformed in any way that would accord with the interests of the working class [i.e., communism]." Lenin, op. cit. (English edition), Vol. 39, p. 757.
11. G. Shishkin, V. Ovchinnikov, S. Kondrashov, G. Borovik, "About the Reagan Interview," *New Times* (KGB-sponsored weekly), No. 46, November 1985.
12. *Sotsialisticheskaya Industriya* (Socialist Industry), November 19, 1985, p. 4.
13. *Maskirovka* refers to techniques of camouflage and concealment. It is also used occasionally as a synonym for deception.
14. I am by no means certain that the Soviets are really as concerned about the SDI program as they say they are. After all, SDI is years away from becoming operational. In the meantime, it may drain away many of America's shrinking resources destined for defense, something quite possible should the Congress drastically cut the defense budget. In such a case, many defense programs would never see the light of day, while SDI, probably also underfinanced, may be held up by many years.
15. TASS, November 29, 1985.
16. This is believed to have been once led by Marshal N. Ogarkov. I was always told that he was the "brain" in the Soviet armed forces and that he was once engaged in some kind of intelligence operations before he became Chief of the General Staff. I also heard about the existence of the Board, though I was, at that time, unaware that Ogarkov might have been its head.
17. By the terms of the Soviet-Polish long-term treaty of September 19, 1985, it appears that the USSR has secured for itself *direct* access to Polish scientists and technicians, some of whom are even to be on the Soviet payroll.
18. On the basis of my experience, the party may have a "war policy" but not a "military doctrine."

APPENDIX B

ARMS CONTROL AND SOVIET STRATEGY

by Jan Sejna

THE IMPORTANCE OF IDEOLOGY

Soviet decisionmaking and risk assessment are based on Marxism-Leninism. To understand Soviet reasoning, it is necessary first to understand Marxist-Leninist theory and Russian philosophy. Marxism-Leninism is not just the ideology of the Communist party; it is the official ideology of the state and constitutes the basis for all Soviet strategy and tactics.

Chapter one, Article six of the Soviet Constitution states:

> The leading and guiding force of the Soviet society and the nucleus of its political system, of all state organizations and public organizations, is the Communist Party of the Soviet Union [CPSU]. The CPSU exists for the people and serves the people.
> The Communist Party, armed with Marxism-Leninism, determines the general perspectives of the development of society and the course of the domestic and foreign policy of the USSR, directs the great constructive work of the Soviet people, and imparts a planned, systematic and theoretically substantiated character to their struggle for the victory of communism . . . .

There is a tendency among many Western commentators on Soviet affairs to talk about Marxist-Leninist ideology as if it were dead. They expect to see modifications in Soviet policy, especially when the top level strategic leadership of the Soviet Union changes. Changes there are, although these are most often tactical innovations, not substantive changes. Occasionally there are even variations in strategy. However, since the original formation of the Communist party, and the adoption of Marxism-Leninism as the official Soviet state ideology, there have been no significant changes in the strategic goals to establish a "dictatorship of the proletariat" in every country worldwide, each controlled according to the principle of proletarian internationalism.

For all practical purposes, Marxist-Leninist ideology is as alive and pertinent in the 1980s as it was in the 1920s; moreover, there is no basis for Western hopes that changes are imminent or even possible. Indeed, if anything, the ideology is more sophisticated and mature now than at any time in the past.

Nikita Khrushchev was accomplished in communicating concepts. In November 1955—a time when major post-Stalin "changes" were being planned and implemented in the Soviet Union—Khrushchev visited India and spoke of Soviet ideology and the political line. He said, "We have never abandoned, and never will abandon, our political line, which was mapped by Lenin. . . . And so we say to the gentry who are expecting the Soviet Union to change its political program: Wait until the crab whistles."[1]

DECEPTION AND IDEOLOGY

Although many Soviet goals are clearly stated and many of their tactics are easily discernible, the Soviet Union at the same time seeks to conceal its strategic goals and the means employed to achieve those ends from its adversaries in the West. This is particularly true of a main tenet of Marxism-Leninism, which clearly calls for the liquidation of capitalism. While consistently reaffirming the importance of ideology in official publications and statements, the Soviet Union is informally seeking to deflect attention from the ideology, and to project images that cause the West to conclude incorrectly that the ideology is dead, that the party is composed of technocrats not ideologues, that ideology and foreign policy are not connected, and that the Soviet Union is slowly drifting toward ideological accommodation with the West.

This latter deceptive ploy is intended to foster hope in the West that if the Western democracies would only help the Soviet Union, with technology and bread, the Soviet Union would cease its aggressiveness and turn its attention to the home front. This is intended to promote trade and financial assistance in consonance with the concept of "peaceful coexistence." In reality, this deceptive stratagem is patently false: capitalism and socialism are irreconcilable in official Soviet ideology, and the few seeds of private enterprise that are tolerated are carefully controlled and utilized as merely a temporary expedient for political (deceptive) or economic reasons.

Another deceptive tactic employed by the Soviet Union is that of creating a feeling of guilt in the West for its military buildup of conventional and nuclear forces. The Soviet Union creates the appearance that it is only responding to Western aggressiveness out of fear and concern for its own defense. In fact, anyone who has worked on Soviet defense plans cannot help but recognize that since the mid-1960s they have been offense-oriented, and that their strategy is to attain dominant superiority at all levels. Soviet acknowledgment of "parity" is strictly a deceptive gambit designed to undermine those in the West who voice concern over the shifting military balance of power.

In many areas, the Soviet Union now has achieved military superiority over the Western allies. Accordingly, since the mid-1970s and with increased vigor in recent years, the Soviets have been proclaiming the presence of parity; they claim that they do not have a policy to gain superiority—that superiority is an American policy to which the Soviets are opposed. The fact is that the Soviet goal is superiority, and any statements to the contrary are deceptions. One valid hypothetical projection of future Soviet strategy is that this particular deception will continue for perhaps another decade, at the end of which time the Soviets will be able to announce boldly that they have achieved complete superiority over the West, and that the West should recognize this and act accordingly.

THE ROLE OF ARMS CONTROL IN POLITICAL STRATEGY

Important Soviet deceptions used to conceal aggressive policies are so-called peace proposals and defense treaties. It is useful to keep in mind two of Lenin's well-known statements: first, from September 27, 1905, "Promises are like pie crusts, made to be broken"; and second, from *Reply to Debate on War and Peace* (1919), "It is ridiculous not to know the history of war, not to know that a treaty is a means of gaining strength." Insofar as the communists recognize that they are at war and will always be at war until capitalism is eradicated, this latter statement applies equally to treaties concluded during what the West thinks of as peacetime.

The efforts of Soviet satellite countries in the arena of arms control and disarmament have been integrated into Soviet strategy almost since the satellite countries came into being. These efforts, however, were noticeably expanded and intensified beginning in 1963, due in all likelihood to the major change in Soviet political strategy that emerged in that year. That change sought increasingly to emphasize military might as an active element in Soviet political strategy. This is reflected in Khrushchev's well-known speech, printed in *Pravda* on January 10, 1960, in which he asserted that the Soviet Union would henceforth assume the policy of "maximum retaliation" as its deterrent; and in Marshal Malinovskiy's speech in September 1960 that "the best means of defense is warning the opponent of our strength and readiness to destroy him at the first attempt to commit an act of aggression."[2]

During the period 1960 to 1963, the Soviet military came to realize that arms control was an effective instrument that could be used to achieve military objectives. The military began a campaign to gain control of the arms control process and attained their objective by 1963. In addition to recognizing that the strategic value of arms control extended far beyond its mere propaganda value (previously the main purpose of Soviet arms control and disarmament strategy), the military argued that the civilian diplomats conducting negotiations were not expert on the subject matter, and that the most effective manner in which to use arms control as a political tool—that is, to get the capitalists to devote more serious attention to arms control—was to have the military in charge.

1963 represents a watershed year for Soviet and Warsaw Pact strategy. Several events emerged as part of what was clearly an integrated strategic politico-military operation. The dominant event was the shift from defense to offense in operations strategy. In effect, this was an extension of the 1960 change of Soviet political strategy in the satellite nations. The Soviet decision in this regard was communicated "unofficially" by Marshal Malinovskiy in May 1963 when he met in Prague with the Kolegium of the Czechoslovak Ministry of Defense.[3] Malinovskiy explained that the balance of power was shifting enough to allow the Soviet and Warsaw Pact nations to pursue an offensive strategy.

Furthermore, by 1963 the Soviets began to believe that at some time in the distant future, nuclear weapons might be prohibited. Nuclear weapons were regarded as too destructive and, as more countries obtained nuclear arms capabilities, too dangerous. This message was first conveyed to the Czechoslovak strategic leadership in April 1963 by Soviet Marshal Grechko, Chief of the Main Political Administration of the Army and Navy, when he met with the Czechoslovak Defense Council to approve the new Operations Plan. This intent was repeated, in September 1963, when the Czechoslovak leadership met with the Soviets in Moscow to receive their instructions prior to developing plans for the next year's program. At this meeting, the Soviets expressed their concern that should nuclear weapons be eliminated, this would deprive them of one of their most powerful tools. They further stated that they would need something else, therefore, to prevent U.S. and NATO forces from taking strong responsive actions as the communist revolutionary war movement went forward. That is, the Soviets recognized that nuclear blackmail as a major political tool had a limited lifetime. Eventually, they realized, their threats and tactics that relied heavily on the use of nuclear blackmail would begin to lose their efficacy.

The Soviet leadership did not believe that the abolition of nuclear weapons was a near-term possibility, but saw this gradually evolving over the long term, twenty years and beyond. Accordingly, they believed it necessary to develop substitutes to keep and even to augment their military edge over the West. In 1963 the substitute envisioned was chemical and biological weapons (CBW). Superiority in CBW, combined with strong conventional forces and control of space, would enable the Soviets actually to increase their strength in a future era where nuclear weapons would be banned.[4] However, this did not mean that the Soviet Union would discard its nuclear weapons; on the contrary, the Soviets would retain a substantial hidden reserve, because they could not trust the Western "imperialists" to destroy their nuclear stockpiles.

By 1963, the arms control process had become the bailiwick of the military. Overall responsibility for arms control continued to be that of the Deputy General Secretary. In 1959 this charge had been given to Leonid Brezhnev, and when he was promoted after Khrushchev's downfall, the responsibility passed to A.P. Kirilenko. (In Czechoslovakia, Novotny himself was in charge.) When arms control negotiation became a strategic operation, its day-to-day coordination and direction was headquartered in the Administration Department (often referred to as the Administrative Organs Department), which has authority over Defense, KGB, and Justice. The head of the Administration Department, both in Czechoslovakia and in the Soviet Union, was named as the deputy to the Deputy General Secretary in order to elevate his status and secure more effective coordination between him and other departments in the CPSU, such the International and Propaganda departments.

As the arms control process came within the military realm, it rapidly assumed the form of a strategic operation. In this operation, the satellite countries were heavily involved. In multilateral negotiations, representatives from the satellites took part in the negotiation process itself. In Czechoslovakia, the lead delegate to Geneva was General Egit Pepich who was deputy to, as I recall, Deputy Foreign Minister Jiri Hajek, who provided a "diplomatic cover." The delegates were required to spend several days in Moscow at the Administration Department obtaining specific instructions prior to attending negotiating sessions. Among other subjects covered were detailed analyses of all the Western delegates who would be attending the conference.

The entire arms control process was integrated into Soviet world strategy. The satellite nations were involved in the strategic nuclear arms control arenas, as well as in multilateral negotiations. The tasks they performed in the strategic and multilateral areas included the recruitment of foreign delegates to serve as agents of the Soviet Union; collection of intelligence on materiel, and details on Western negotiation instructions and limits; recruitment of public support for Soviet negotiating positions; development and implementation of pro-Soviet/anti-West propaganda throughout the world (in the late 1960s most of this activity was keyed to the Vietnam War); and, of special importance, assessments of Western negotiating positions, which the Soviets used as a check on the accuracy of their own pre-negotiations analyses.

The role of the satellites in Soviet propaganda campaigns was substantial, especially in Czechoslovakia due primarily to the use of Prague as a coordination center for the world communist movement. This was established in 1958 in what was a covert continuation of the Comintern (the third Communist International) operation. Direction and management remained in the hands of the International Department in Moscow, with Prague providing cover and serving as a mailing address. The satellite countries were regarded merely as extensions of the Soviet Union, and their primary duty was to safeguard the interests of the socialist fatherland—the Soviet Union. Their secondary duty was to help the Soviet Union promote the world communist revolution. Prague is the home of *Problems of Peace and Socialism (World Marxist Review)*, which is the primary coordinating journal of the world revolutionary movement.

SOVIET ARMS CONTROL ORGANIZATION

As mentioned earlier, the Deputy General Secretary was in charge of this effort; the head of the Administration Department, acting as his deputy, performed the functions of coordination and direction. From approximately 1965 or 1966, the primary interface for Czechoslovak operations was Major-General Savinkin.

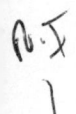

The main responsibility for preparation of the arms control process was assigned to the Chief of the General Staff. The person who actually performed this work, however, was the head of the Main Operations Administration. Within that organization, primary staffing was from within the Operations Administration, where the Operations Plan is prepared. The Operations Plan is the most important plan in the Soviet Union; all other plans (i.e., economic, R&D, mobilization, intelligence, industrial expansion and production, etc.) are keyed to it. Thus, the greater significance attached to the arms control process in 1963 was determined by strategic operations, particularly by the new shift to offensive operations first seen in that year. This further explains the military control over this process, especially the lead role taken by the Operations Administration of the Main Operations Administration. The Operations Administration is, in fact, one of the most sensitive organizations in the Soviet Union. Access is strictly limited to the head of the Main Operations Administration and members of the Defense Council. Neither the KGB nor the ID (International Department) have direct access to this organization, or are even permitted inside its chambers.

The first task in the process required the Operations Administration to determine how far the Soviet Union could go in negotiating arms reductions, what could be done to achieve Soviet objectives, how the process could be developed in support of Soviet force augmentation plans, and so forth. At this stage the GRU also participated, especially the deputy in charge of strategic intelligence. Other important contributors were the Main Administration for Material and Technical Supply, responsible for producing weapons, and the Science and Technology Main Administration, responsible for development. While not part of the General Staff, the KGB was also involved, both in its traditional role of military counterintelligence and in its other roles (for example, conduct of deception, information collection, and influence operations) coordinated through the head of the Administration Department, which has authority over the KGB. After the preliminary work was completed, the package was sent to the Administration of Special State Interests—the administration that is responsible for strategic deception—within the Main Operations Administration.

To compose the basic package, estimates were made in the mid-1960s on what weapons the Soviet Union would possess in the 1980s, and what would be in the process of development. The arms control plan also indicated that if Moscow wanted to achieve certain results, it would be necessary to hide specific weapons. The Administration of Special State Interests had the task of determining how to do that. This process of weapons concealment involved the satellite countries as well as the Soviet Union. The Soviets discussed with the satellites how to conceal this or that weapon, what could be shown in maneuvers, and how to prepare the maneuvers. Arms sales to Third World countries were also examined, as they might bear on this activity and would be required to fit into the deceptive cover. Other administrations had to adhere to the decisions rendered by the Administration of Special State Interests, beginning with those who had important deception responsibilities, such as the Administration for Foreign Relations and the Administration for Special Propaganda.

When the package was completed and the time to make decisions had been reached, the head of the Administration Department, together with the heads of other agencies and departments involved, went before the Deputy General Secretary (Brezhnev, and later Kirilenko) and presented the overall plan.

The main people involved in the negotiations process were from the General Staff and the KGB. Other agencies, such as the Foreign Ministry, would receive directives after the decisions had been prepared. People going to Geneva, such as Czechoslovak General Pepich, spent several days in Moscow at the Administration Department obtaining instructions.

ARMS CONTROL OBJECTIVES

The Soviet Union has just two tightly coupled strategic obligations: global socialism and proletarian internationalism. All other obligations are secondary and transient. The manner in which arms control was to contribute to these overriding objectives is well illustrated by the instructions Marshal Grechko gave to the Ministers of Defense and Chiefs of the General Staffs of the Warsaw Pact countries in September 1966, at the conclusion of the Vltava exercise. Marshal Grechko explained the following to us:

1. Our (Warsaw Pact) agreements must not enable the United States and Western Europe to learn the "whole picture" about our military technology and weapons. We must never "lay our cards on the table" for them to see.
2. Our pressure for arms control and possible treaties must be used as weapons against the military-industrial complex in the United States and Western Europe.
3. This process should be used to recruit to our cause nonmilitary industries in the West, by helping to shift U.S. public interests and demands toward nonmilitary industry and expenditures, and in so doing, to drive a wedge between the military and nonmilitary industry.
4. The arms control process must be designed so as to win over Third World countries to the Soviet view.
5. The arms control process must help us to secure more information about NATO developments in military technology and weapons research, and thus provide us with possibilities to improve our own scientific development of military technologies and production of weapons systems.
6. It must be used to improve the preparedness of Soviet bloc forces and the mobilization system—for example, by using the facade of pressure for arms control agreements as a cover for the Soviet bloc military buildup.
7. Most importantly, it must help the Soviet bloc to halt or delay scientific development of military technologies and production of weapons in the Atlantic Alliance.

These were the primary Soviet goals for arms control and other treaties in the 1960s. Potential agreements and accords would be assessed first by the various officials in Moscow, and ultimately by the Defense Council, to determine how they would help the Soviet Union achieve its arms control goals. Of these goals, by far the dominant one in the 1960s was to achieve military parity with NATO. Today, this is likely to have been furthered by the goals of tilting the military balance of power to greatly favor the Soviets, and of eliminating the U.S edge in many areas of military power where it is still seen as being superior to the Soviet Union.

LONG-RANGE PLAN

The East European satellites were first brought into the Soviet long-range (ten to fifteen years and beyond) planning process in 1967. Guidelines for developing a coordinated plan were provided to all satellite countries for their use in what would be a major two-year planning process. The plan explained what the Soviets believed the arms control process would accomplish, and how the process could be exploited by the Kremlin in its various stages. To the extent possible, these stages were matched to the phases of predicted major global strategic changes around which the long-range plan was structured. These stages were: 1956–1959, preparation for peaceful coexistence; 1960–1972, peaceful coexistence struggle; 1973–1985, period of dynamic social change; thereafter, global democratic peace. The final phase, the period of social democratic peace, was expected to be the longest and the most difficult. It is important to recognize that this process was not viewed by the Soviets as a "straight line"; rather, they conceived of it as a "zigzag" consisting of a series of advances, setbacks, and pauses.

The major issue revolved around how to design arms control agreements so that the United States and other NATO nations would ultimately be compelled to eliminate their own strategic weapons, while the Soviet Union and Warsaw Pact countries would be able to retain enough of their strategic forces to tilt the global balance of power in their favor. The Soviets expressed their belief that in the long run, nuclear weapons would be the first to be eliminated. If this happened, what would be the substitute for nuclear forces? The answer was chemical and biological weapons, and control of space. Additionally, the long-range plan addressed the question of how to prevent future scientific and technological advances from being translated into new weapons systems, while at the same time enabling the Soviet Union to conceal its development of new weapons and technologies within the civilian sector, the Academy of Sciences, and so forth.

The Soviet leaders believed that the negotiations process could be turned into a very important propaganda tool: It could be used to show the imperialists to be guilty of preparing for war, and to recruit and mobilize Western public opinion to pressure their governments urgently to reach arms reduction agreements with the Soviets. This continuing conviction can be seen today in Gorbachev's statement to the 27th Party Congress:

That is why it is not easy at all, in the current circumstances, to predict the future of the relations between the socialist and the capitalist countries, the USSR and the United States. The decisive factors here will be the correlation of forces on the world scene, the growth and activity of the peace potential, and its capability of effectively repulsing the threat of nuclear war.[5]

This explains why Gorbachev says the Soviet Union must use "tactical flexibility" in the negotiations, and must use influence on every level, even religion.

The long-range plan also delineated the use of the arms control process to drive a wedge between the United States and Western Europe. As Gorbachev stated:

> For the first time, governments of some West European countries, the Social Democratic and Liberal parties, and the public at large have begun to openly discuss whether present U.S. policy coincides with Western Europe's notions about its own security and whether the United States is going too far in its claims to leadership. The partners of the United States have had more than one occasion to see that someone else's spectacles cannot substitute for one's own eyes.[6]

Important objectives of the arms control process are, through subversion and deception, to mobilize the masses, influence the European governments to isolate the United States, and create a more revolutionary situation within the United States. This latter aim would be helped by the unemployment that the Kremlin believes would accompany a cutback in defense efforts. As Gorbachev affirmed: "For them [the groups tied most to the military-industrial complex] disarmament means a loss in profits, a political risk. For us it means good in all respects: economic, political, moral."

HOW THE SOVIET UNION VIEWS THE POSITION OF THE UNITED STATES

First, the Soviet Union knows it is extremely easy to exploit the U.S. democratic system because of the very freedoms the United States holds so dear—freedom of the opposition, freedom of the press, free speech, and so forth. They can also exploit the weaknesses of the U.S. security systems and intelligence programs. They know that U.S. policy is not generally determined by political strategy, but rather by economic and budgetary pressures. Soviet strategy is to force the United States into accepting Soviet arms proposals by the careful orchestration of pressure from opposition groups in the West, the international peace movement, financial and industrial lobby groups, and budgetary crises. The Soviet leadership firmly believes in its ability to alter U.S. policies in this way to the benefit of Soviet strategic goals. As stated by the famous Soviet commentator, Bovin, "President Reagan will go only as far as we let him go."[7]

THE SOVIET VIEW OF CHEATING

Cheating that supports the main strategic goals of the Soviet Union is viewed in Moscow as entirely moral. To cheat and deceive the enemy is the duty of all party and government organizations and individuals. This is why all internal Soviet proposals and counterproposals must clearly state how and when deception operations will be carried out against the enemy.

A prime example of this process was the announced Soviet reduction of military forces by 1,300,000 in 1956, and by 300,000 in 1958. The satellite nations, which were ordered to support this Soviet deception plan, received explicit directions from the Soviet Defense Council: Announce force reductions, but do not actually reduce your forces. Czechoslovakia, for example, declared it would reduce its military forces by 15,000. The actual process, however, involved (1) demobilizing soldiers who were concluding their tour of duty anyway; and (2) retiring immediately those officers who were due to retire in the following six months and giving them six months' advance salary. Most of those officers who were retired immediately were so-called bourgeois officers, so this ploy enabled the Defense Council to rid the military forces of those individuals they did not trust. At the same time, the Defense Council ordered the Ministry of Defense to recruit for military service more officers from the reserves.

Cheating often requires the collaboration of different sectors of the Soviet system: political, military, and intelligence. An example of the way in which these different categories merge is the Soviet occupation of Czechoslovakia in 1968, which was not just an intelligence operation; top Soviet political and military leaders were deeply involved. The operation also relied on military deception which was accomplished through the misleading nature of communist tactics and language. The Soviet logic for "assisting" Czechoslovakia was that the achievements of socialist internationalism must be defended, and Czechoslovakia needed Soviet aid to adequately defend these achievements. The possibility of direct Soviet military intervention in Czechoslovakia was never admitted.

In June 1968, a Czechoslovak parliamentary delegation visited the Soviet Union and met with Brezhnev. When they returned, one member of the Catholic (people's) party, Zednik, gave an interview to the party newspaper. He said Comrade Brezhnev had tears in his eyes when he spoke of the efforts of bourgeois propaganda to convince the Czechoslovak people that the Soviet Union would use troops against Czechoslovakia. "How can people believe that?" he asked. "We are your best friends and brothers."[8] Two months later, Soviet troops occupied Czechoslovakia.

The second lie concerns the purpose of the Soviet troops which were stationed on Czechoslovak territory and conducted military exercises in May and June 1968. Soviet propaganda said that these maneuvers had nothing to do with the situation in Czechoslovakia, as the exercise had been planned a year before. However, in a book published in 1971, entitled *The Truth Remained the Truth*, the author, Vasil Bielok, who had been the Second Secretary of the Communist Party of Czechoslovakia in 1968, asserted that the Soviet troops which participated in the maneuvers had been assigned to play a much more important role. Under an agreement between Soviet party leaders and some party leaders in Czechoslovakia, these troops were supposed to help rid the party, the government, and the media of antisocialist forces and to establish a true socialist order in Czechoslovakia. The reason this did not occur was that, in the final analysis, Czechoslovak Premier Alexander Dubcek did not approve such action.

A third case of deception in the Czechoslovak operation concerns Soviet tactics and language that are deliberately designed to mislead untutored observers. When the Soviet leadership met with the Czechoslovak Communist party leadership on the Czechoslovak/Soviet border, the world perceived this confrontation as a victory for the Dubcek-led Czechoslovaks because of the fact that the Soviet leaders traveled all the way to the Czechoslovak border to meet with them. Immediately after this meeting, there was a conclave in Bratislava, Czechoslovakia, of all Warsaw Pact leaders, except the Romanian leader. At that meeting, on August 5, 1968, a resolution was unanimously passed that stated:

> Support, consolidation, and protection of these gains achieved at the price of heroic efforts and selfless labor of every people is a common internationalist duty of all socialist countries. Such is the unanimous opinion of all participants in the conference, who expressed their unbending determination to develop and defend socialist gains in their countries and to work for the new achievements in socialist construction.[9]

This declaration was signed by all Warsaw Pact countries present, including Czechoslovakia. There is no question that anyone who understands Marxist-Leninist doublespeak fully comprehends this paragraph: it meant the capitulation of the Czechoslovak leaders. It signified agreement on the rights of, and the justification for, other socialist states to occupy Czechoslovakia. The world, nevertheless, received this declaration as a victory for the Czechoslovak leadership. This operation proved to be an extremely slick and effective deception.

To deal successfully with the Soviet Union, it is essential to understand the Marxist-Leninist language and Russian psychology. For example, the language in a treaty such as the Helsinki Accords is designed to be beneficial to the Soviet Union. The word "people," for example, does not refer to the citizens or inhabitants of a nation; it refers to those who support the "Red Revolution." In contrast, the word "nation" includes all the population.

Another term used by the Soviets with increasing frequency is "social progress." On the surface, this seems to be an innocent enough term because all countries seek social progress, improvement of the standard of living, and so on. However, in Soviet usage it means only Marxist-Leninist progress, that is, progress toward the world socialist revolution. Social progress in the West connotes evolution; to the Soviets, revolution.

CHEATING IN SOVIET STRATEGY

The Soviet Union and the Warsaw Pact countries know when they are violating treaties. The issue is not their recognition of the fact, but rather that such action is preplanned, even prior to negotiating the treaty. Before any treaty is signed, the Defense Council or Politburo approves a program for the secret violation of the treaty.

In 1963 an event occurred that should be seen as part of an integrated package whose overall thrust was a shift to a decidedly offensive strategy. A set of special instructions was sent from the Soviet Union to Czechoslovakia delineating the use of cheating and deception to weaken the enemy politically and militarily. The Czechoslovak Administration Department extracted those portions of the instructions that were relevant to Czechoslovakia and presented them to the Defense Council, which in turn issued directions to all agencies, for example, to the Ministries of Interior, Defense, Foreign Affairs, and so forth. The Administration Department then acted as coordinator and overseer to ensure that the Defense Council directives were properly implemented.

The instructions explained that cheating, deceiving, disinforming, and misleading the enemy were very important functions of both party and government organizations because they helped to protect socialism, blinded the enemy to the nature of the main strategic goals, and specifically covered the methods used to achieve the main strategic goals and, therefore, the final victory of communism. These activities were considered the preeminent responsibility of highest party and government officials.

These activities should deny the enemy the ability to evaluate realistically the level of Soviet defense, and the health of the economy and the agricultural sector, and their future prospects. They should, furthermore, minimize the ability of the enemy to exploit the weaknesses of the Soviet

Union, while providing means for diminishing and eliminating the military superiority of the West. The instructions set forth three sets of principles—military, political, and economic—that were to guide Czechoslovak leaders in mounting a deliberate deception campaign.

1. *Military*
   a. Preserve the secrecy of the main goals of military decisions and the real level of Soviet and Warsaw Pact defenses including such items as the development and production of weapons, the organization and numbers of troops and weapons—especially those of strategic importance—and mobilization systems.
   b. Mislead the enemy about the major targets of the intelligence services of the Soviet Union and the Warsaw Pact.
   c. Compromise the enemy's information about the real military power of the Soviet Union and Warsaw Pact.
   d. Discredit the military buildup of the United States and NATO.
   e. Convince the whole world that Soviet forces are to be used only for defensive purposes.
   f. Slow down the scientific development and production of weapons and the progress of military technology in the United States and NATO.
   g. Discredit any accusations of a Soviet military buildup and shift the responsibility to the enemy; that is, make the United States and NATO the guilty parties.
   h. Mislead the enemy about military and state strategic reserves.
2. *Political*
   The main political objective is to draw the attention of the enemy away from the main political strategic goals and the steps being taken to achieve those goals. In general, activities should assist the Soviet Union to achieve strategic superiority.
   a. Deny that there is any unity between Soviet foreign policy and Marxist-Leninist ideology.
   b. Conceal the provision of material help to revolutionary movements and groups by the Soviet Union and deny any related accusations.
   c. Hide the activities of the Soviet Union that create political and military tensions for the purpose of drawing the attention of the imperialists away from the main strategic zones.
   d. Disorient the masses and anti-right-wing factions regarding the strategies and intentions of capitalist governments.
   e. Convince the enemy that the achievement of tactical goals is final; that is, that the Soviet Union will be satisfied and will stop with the achievement of its tactical goals.

f. Convince the masses that cheating and deception are not socialist activities, but are exclusively capitalist activities.
g. Convince Third World countries that the Soviet Union has no desire to interfere in the internal affairs of other countries.
3. *Economic*
   a. Pursue any and all measures to strengthen the Soviet economy and its scientific and technological resources—including a maximum level of technological transfer from the West through espionage and trade—in order to create the strongest possible military force.
   b. Hide sensitive weapons information and mislead the enemy on the scientific achievements of the Soviet Union and the Warsaw Pact.
   c. Conceal information on the true level of production of strategic weapons and other war materiel.
   d. Suppress information on the buildup of state and strategic reserves.
   e. Create conflict between capitalist governments and their financial and industrial institutions.
   f. Help to create antagonism between capitalist states, and generate competition among the capitalists to do business with the Soviet Union.

THE DENIAL OF CHEATING

The Soviets deny all accusations that they engage in cheating, deception, and disinformation; all Soviet actions are justified by Marxism-Leninism. According to Soviet doctrine, denial should take the form of an offensive retort; it must transfer guilt and blame to the other side.

Good examples of Soviet offensive denial appear in newspapers almost daily. A recent one was related to terrorism. When the United States and other Western governments accused the Soviet Union and the Warsaw Pact of supporting terrorist organizations, the Kremlin vehemently denied the accusation, and instead accused the United States of state terrorism, specifically citing the American actions in Grenada.

SOVIET CALCULATIONS OF RISK

Any recommendation proposing a particular course of action in the Soviet system must present with it an analysis of its positive and negative aspects. In general, the highest risk for the Soviet Union is global thermonuclear war. The second highest risk is an action that would precipitate negative worldwide opinion which might adversely affect the revolutionary war movement.

The Soviet Union divides its risk assessment into three segments: (1) short- and long-term risk; (2) local and global risk; and (3) temporary tactical risk and long-term strategic risk. For example, the occupations of Hungary and Czechoslovakia were for the Soviet Union short-term risks, and the global reaction was temporary. However, from a strategic point of view, Moscow believed the actions would show that the Soviets were not afraid to take military action, if necessary, to protect their allies. Moreover, in the case of Czechoslovakia, the action would help improve the posture of the Warsaw Pact forces along the Czechoslovak/NATO border. These latter two assessments serve as examples of positive aspects of a recommended course of action.

At present, a U.S. strategic reaction that the Soviet Union is exerting great efforts to avert is a Presidential decision to proceed with the deployment of an SDI system.

The Cuban missile crisis provides another example of the Soviet calculation of risk. Following this crisis, Khrushchev met with other Warsaw Pact leaders. I was present and remember his remarks on that occasion. "You asked us if we counted the risk, especially the military risk?" he asked. "Yes," he answered, "we did." He went on to explain:

> The highest risk was the possibility that we might lose Cuba. We discounted this risk because we believed that the combination of our peaceful coexistence policy and our agreements with Kennedy would act to prevent Kennedy from undertaking any military action. We concluded that his reaction would be strictly political gesturing. In this regard we underestimated Kennedy. On the other hand, some comrades overestimated the Americans. They thought the Americans would go much farther than they went, but we did not accept that estimate.
>
> Comrades, the risk was worth it. Cuba is still a socialist state. The crisis demonstrated the inability of the United States to liquidate a socialist state, even one under their own windows. This has opened for us new possibilities throughout the whole world. Additionally, it has helped us wake up many realistic thinking politicians and scared many people because it demonstrated that America is no longer untouchable.

NOTES

1. "Speech by N.S. Khrushchev at Reception in Indo-Soviet Cultural Society in Bombay," November 24, 1955, *International Affairs* (Moscow), No. 1, January 1956, p. 195.
2. *Pravda*, January 15, 1960, and Malinovsky, *Bditelno Stoyat na Strazhe Mira* (Moscow, 1962), p. 25, quoted in C.G. Jacobsen, *Soviet Strategy—Soviet Foreign Policy* (Glasgow, U.K.: The University Press, 1972), p. 58.
3. See Jan Sejna and Joseph D. Douglass, Jr., *Decisionmaking in Communist Countries: An Inside View* (McLean, Va.: Pergamon-Brassey's, for the Institute for Foreign Policy Analysis, 1986), pp. 69-72.

4. This is explicitly stated in an important secret speech, "Problems of the Party's Military Policy in the Light of the 13th Congress of the Communist Party of Czechoslovakia," prepared by the Czech Ministry of Defense under guidance received from Moscow, DIA Translation LN 048-79.
5. FBIS, February 26, 1985, p. 5.
6. Ibid.
7. *Izvestia*, July 28, 1985.
8. *Lidova Demokracie*, June 12, 1968.
9. *Rude Pravo*, August 6, 1968.

APPENDIX C

LINGUISTIC DECEPTION AND U.S.–SOVIET ARMS CONTROL TREATIES

by Igor Lukes

> What wealth is to a capitalist, what organization is to the old-style political boss, what manpower is to the trade unionist, words are to the new class.
> Jeane Kirkpatrick
> *Encounter*, November 1983, p. 16

On June 25, 1950, the Korean War broke out and the whole world stood on the threshold of yet another conflagration.

Nevertheless, only six days later, Joseph Stalin, undisturbed by the thundering cannons in East Asia, found enough time to enter into a discussion with a hitherto unknown woman comrade, Krasheninnikova.[1] The topic of their exchange? Language.

Stalin's essay, promptly published in the late summer of 1950 under the title *Marxism and the Problems of Linguistics*, was circulated in editions of millions of copies throughout the world. Most of the topics analyzed in this work appeared highly technical, certainly not the kind of stuff the Soviet Generalissimo ought to have busied himself with in wartime: "Should linguistics occupy itself with the semantic aspect of language?" or "Is language a superstructure on the base?"

Given the obscurity of these topics, it is little wonder that most Western observers dismissed Stalin's venture into the realm of linguistics as irrelevant. Some analysts even thought that the great dictator had merely pulled a practical joke on them. Knowing as he did that anything he wrote would be closely examined, the argument ran, Stalin chose to pollute Western analysts with gibberish.

Nevertheless, the patient reader of this work appreciates that this is a statement of seminal importance.[2] The conclusion from Stalin's essay on linguistics is that there exist national peculiarities that are inherently and permanently present in the language of the nation concerned. Of great importance is the passage opened by Stalin's rhetorical questions of "whether classes influence language, whether they contribute their specific words and expressions to language, whether there are cases when people attach a different meaning, in accordance with the class to which they belong, to one and the same words and expressions?" Stalin's answer? "Yes, *classes* do influence language, contribute their own specific words and expressions to language, and *at times understand one and the same words and expressions differently*. This is unquestionably so."[3] (Emphasis added.)

In a clear form and before a worldwide audience, Stalin announced that the language he uses, as a representative of socialism, consists of words the meaning of which is at times understood differently by his opponents, the capitalists.

DECEPTION AS A WAY OF LIFE: *KITMAN*

It is a matter of historical record that, centuries before the Soviets assumed power in Russia, certain political and religious establishments had expressed their dogma in a highly rigorous style and terminology. Moreover, deception, based inter alia on a linguistic ritual, had become a way of life in several, and often quite distinct, political and religious systems. Byzantium, and also Tudor and Stuart England, had seen their share of deception.

Nothing was expressed directly: "What is important is not what someone said but what he wanted to say, disguising his thought by removing a comma, inserting an 'and,' establishing this rather than another sequence in the problems discussed."[4]

The best embodiment of deception as a way of life is the principle of *kitman*. This is an Arabic word, which is also used in Persia. Its dictionary entry reads: "secrecy, concealment, secretion, silence, restraint, control, suppression (esp. of an emotion)."[5] In its broader meaning, *kitman* can be described as a survival-through-deception technique practiced by certain minorities in the Middle East.

This technique is said to be practiced by those who find themselves surrounded by members of another sect that is in control of political and economic power. Under such circumstances, it is permissible to disguise one's true faith, intentions, and even join the adversary's elite.

Kitman was not rejected even by the most extreme wing of the strictest believers: "God gave the believers freedom of movement . . . ; therefore conceal thyself!" *Kitman* is a cloak for the believer; he who does not practice it has no religion. "If anyone is compelled and professes unbelief with his tongue, while his heart contradicts him, to escape his enemies, no blame falls on him."[6]

Most notably, as recorded by a nineteenth-century French diplomat in Persia, the *kitman*-style linguistic deception was practiced by the people of the Mussulman East. "He who is in possession of truth," writes the French minister, "must not expose his person, his relatives or his reputation to the blindness, the folly, the perversity of those whom it has pleased God to place and maintain in error. . . . Not only must one deny one's true opinion, but one is commanded to resort to all ruses in order to deceive one's adversary. One makes all the protestations of faith that can please him, one performs all the rites one recognizes to be the most vain, one falsifies one's own books, one exhausts all possible means of deceit."[7]

The man living by such principles can say that something is white while he is certain that it is black; he can smile outwardly when he is solemn inside; when he hates he manifests his love; when he knows he feigns ignorance. Throughout, *kitman* feels no shame whatsoever. On the contrary: ". . . one acquires the multiple satisfactions and merits of having placed oneself and one's relatives under cover, of not having exposed a venerable faith to the horrible contact of the infidel, and finally of having, in cheating the latter and confirming him in his error, imposed on him the shame and spiritual misery that he deserves." All in all, "*Kitman* fills the man who practices it with pride. Thanks to it, a believer raises himself to a permanent state of superiority over the man he deceives. . . ."[8]

It is truly hard to ignore the existence of clear parallels between the defensive deceptions of the Islamic *kitman* and the more global linguistic maneuvers of the Kremlin decisionmakers. In theory, concealment is at variance with the essence of the communist modus operandi.[9] In the immortal words of Marx and Engels, the "Communists disdain to conceal their views and aims. They openly declare that their ends can be attained only by forcible overthrow of all existing social conditions."[10] In reality, deception and conspiracy were to become a way of life of all communist movements. Indeed, the long careers of Philby et al., demonstrate that *kitman* is as Soviet as it is Middle Eastern.

Recently, a one-time Nazi officer, Heinz Felfe, who had worked for a full decade as "the Soviet Union's most highly placed agent in West German intelligence," conducted a press conference in an East Berlin luxury hotel. The purpose of the event was to present his memoirs. The book was written on the eastern side of the Berlin Wall, but its publisher and audience are in the West. The title of Felfe's memoirs: *In Service of the Adversary*. No *kitman* could choose a better title.[11]

LINGUISTIC DECEPTIONS: THE SOVIET STYLE

Throughout history, there has not been any other politico-military elite more keenly aware of the importance of language, general slogans, or specific terminology than Soviet strategists. Indeed, at the very foundation of Soviet long-term deception is language.

It all began with the names of the Bolshevik leadership: Lenin, Stalin, Trotsky, Litvinov, Molotov, Bukharin, Zinoviev . . . the list goes on; not one of these is the real name of the individual.

What about the lofty-sounding "Union of Soviet Socialist Republics"? It has been observed about the Holy Roman Empire that it was neither holy, nor an empire, and certainly not Roman. This fully applies to the USSR: not one of the political concepts implied by the words in the title is present in reality.

Equally deceptive proved to be the very slogan the Bolsheviks used to attract the masses during the final stages of Russia's involvement in World War I. Their first promise consisted of three words: "Peace, bread, and land." Instead of peace, the Soviet people were to receive years of civil war, collectivization, man-made famine in the Ukraine,[12] the purge of the 1930s, as well as some 20 million deaths incurred in World War II, partly because of the incompetence and total disregard for human life demonstrated by Soviet commanders. Bread is still a sought-after article, even in major cities of the Soviet Union. And land? It was collectivized by the state.[13]

The strategy of semantic manipulation continues to the present. For instance, Augusto Sandino, whom the current leaders of Nicaragua portray as their "founding father," was in reality a nationalist who had openly rejected the communist ideology. Nevertheless, Nicaraguan leftists call themselves "Sandinistas." The purpose, of course, is to play upon the nationalist sentiment of the Nicaraguan people. Sandino's name also serves well in the international arena: the Sandinistas are still thought of by many as nationalists rather than communists.[14]

The Soviet mastery of language surpasses in scope and perhaps in depth the linguistic sophistication of the Islamic civilization. The Mussulman used language and deception on the private, personal level, as a means of protecting himself and his family from the wrath of the "doctors of the faith." For the Soviets, language plays a considerably more important part. "While it is a medium of communication," writes Stalin, "it is at the same time an instrument of struggle and development of society."[15]

For Moscow, language is a tool for achieving politico-military objectives, for ideological softening up of the adversary, and for covering the Soviet reality. It is an instrument of active deceit.

An insider testifies that in the Soviet system, "before it leaves the lips, every word must be evaluated as to its consequences. A smile that appears at the wrong moment, a glance that is not all it should be can occasion dangerous suspicions and accusations. Even one's gestures, tone of voice, or preference for certain kinds of neckties are interpreted as signs of one's political tendencies."[16] Language and linguistic deceptions serve as Moscow's defensive camouflage as well as offensive charge that deceive and explode the capitalist enemy's defensive mechanisms.

Many will consider it a paradox, but it is precisely Moscow's addiction to, and need for, esoteric communications that open up new perspectives on the Soviet reality. The Western analyst can take it for granted that anything generated by Soviet media is carefully thought out by the official censorship organ, *Glavlit*, which implements only official instructions. The Soviets have never accepted the Western theory that one of the best methods of concealment is not secrecy but saturation of the adversary with irrelevant information.

This has proved helpful in the past. For instance, on January 4, 1953, an article appeared in East Germany (dealing with the Slansky case in Prague) in which Malenkov was quoted at great length while Stalin was referred to with a mere half-sentence, dating from 1910. Franz Borkenau, who pioneered the art of Sovietology, analyzed this article and in mid-January openly predicted the tyrant's death. Stalin's death was announced seven weeks later.[17]

LINGUISTIC DECEPTION ON THE HOME FRONT

The Soviets have been practicing linguistic deception for well over seven decades. It is not surprising that they have become true masters of this art. Before it is applied on the international level, linguistic deception is exercised on the home front.

William E. Griffith demonstrated in his exquisite paper on communist communications[18] that the use of Aesopian language has been characteristic of all totalitarian and also authoritarian regimes. Any ideologically or theologically oriented society, which depends on a doctrine for its legitimacy, requires a myth of unanimity.[19]

In order to preserve this myth, the existence of any kind of conflict among the Soviet elites must be most definitely hidden. If the wisdom of Marxism is so obvious, how could anyone (especially among the top elite) be involved in factional struggles?

Perhaps the most common mistake made regarding Marxism-Leninism is to look upon it as an abstraction, an intellectual exercise. It is true that both Marx and Lenin utilize the terminology of German classical philosophy. Nevertheless, Marxism-Leninism is not merely a philosophical system. It is also a useful how-to manual on practical politics in the broadest sense of the word. "It is an operational code for a new-style Mafia," as John Roche put it.[20]

The Western tendency to relegate Marxism-Leninism to the ranks of other purely philosophical systems is further strengthened by reports from Soviet-bloc emigrés. Most were forced to sit through seemingly endless university-level indoctrination sessions during which the dogma was presented, memorized, repeated during the examination, and then forgotten. "Even the instructors do not believe it," report former students of the communist ideology from the East, "and the audience can be seen secretly reading books or knitting sweaters." In short, Marxism-Leninism is dead.

Such reports from Eastern bloc arrivals who had never been in positions of power are in sharp contrast with the way Marxism-Leninism is looked upon by those who had been near the apex of the communist pyramid. For them, Marxism-Leninism was not a philosophical construct but, rather, an indispensable methodological tool for analyzing and influencing global events. This was best expressed by Andropov, who stated in 1979 that Marxism-Leninism is "the textbook for achieving world revolution and the building of a new society in every country of the world."[21] In short, Marxism-Leninism is a set of instructions for achieving concrete worldwide objectives.

Voslensky points out that

> whether Marxist theory is correct or not is a matter of complete indifference to the nomenklaturist, since belief in it has been replaced by its terminology and quotations from it. Stalinist careerists loudly declared that communism represented the radiant future of mankind, but in reality nothing interested them less than a society in which everyone would give according to his capacity and receive according to his needs.[22]

Given the Soviet mania for secrecy, and given the fact that struggles between various departments and rivalries and intrigues among the leaders are permanent in the Soviet system, there appears to be a dichotomy between the need to keep all disagreements hidden while, at the same time, preserving lines of communication from the boss to his official and personal clientele (the two are not necessarily the same thing). Under such circumstances, Moscow simply has to resort to the use of Aesopian language, among other forms of linguistic deception.

This is taken quite seriously. We know from former "nomklats," for example, Michael Voslensky, that all functionaries of the Central Committee apparat study *Pravda* with the utmost attention to detail. Voslensky's fictitious hero, Denis Ivanovich, while reading the CPSU daily, comes across the "theoretical article 'The Party as the Guiding Force in Soviet Society.'" This requires more careful attention, says Denis Ivanovich, because "it might contain interesting nuances and turns of phrase, for *Pravda* never publishes anything without a deeper meaning."[23]

It is only natural that people, accustomed to searching for such subtleties, are often able linguistically to outmaneuver the average Westerner. Consequently, the democracies have lost control over several important aspects of verbal communication.

LINGUISTIC DECEPTION: THE INTERNATIONAL DIMENSION

The Soviets have been playing linguistic games from the very beginning. Their vocabulary is replete with concepts that are misunderstood in the West. For instance, when the Soviets took over Eastern Europe, Moscow coined the term "the democratic camp," which was to stand in contrast with capitalist Europe. In reality, "democratic" meant "totalitarian" (this misuse of the word continues to the present: Moscow systematically talks about the "Democratic" Yemen). Similarly, the Western term "popular" means "relating to or carried out by the people in general"; it implies voluntarism and spontaneity. Moscow, however, uses the term to describe political and military movements under strict communist control; these are said to seek the "liberation" of Third World countries—in reality, the imposition of leftist regimes.

Further, the Soviet terms "federal" and "autonomous" stand for "centralized" and "powerless." "Truth" is identical with Soviet white, gray, and black propaganda. "Self-criticism" represents nothing else but a humiliating form of self-indictment. "Discussion" means prearranged reaffirmation of the official line. "Fraternal" is, within the Soviet sphere of influence, synonymous with whatever is Moscow-controlled. In short, the Kremlin embraces words of definitely positive meaning and exploits them for its purposes.

There is, naturally, an intimate connection between Moscow's abuse of words and its manipulation of concepts and values. "Fraternal international assistance" means simply a full-scale occupation by the Warsaw Pact. "Liberation" often indicates that surrogate forces are directed to achieve Moscow's objectives. When Moscow stresses "international solidarity," it is referring to its worldwide logistical network. When the Soviets talk of establishing a "people's democracy," one can rest assured that they aim at unchallenged rule by the top party elite. Similarly, "cooperation," as in COMECON, means enforcement of one, namely the Soviet, line. "Internationalism" stands for Russian chauvinism. When the Kremlin calls for an "international dialogue," it really means a Soviet monologue with subservient echoes from communist parties around the globe.

Moscow also carefully selects different audiences for different concepts. For instance, peasants are never told about collectivization. Pacifists are to remain ignorant of the Soviet belief that, in the long run, a decisive conflict with the West is inevitable. Artists are not told about censorship.

Intellectuals are not warned that absolute uniformity of thinking is strictly required in the Soviet world. Emerging Third World countries are not bothered with the Soviet concepts of internationalism. The middle classes are not to know about the use of terror and purges, and thus the concept of dictatorship is bypassed. At the same time, the concept is fully stressed to the workers who are to profit from its imposition. Religious individuals are presented with liberation theology rather than with the harsh materialism of Marxism-Leninism.

As a consequence of such confusion, those who will suffer when Moscow-controlled governments are established are often coopted in the initial stages of the struggle against the old regime. (They allow themselves to be coopted because they have been seduced by lofty ethical concepts: freedom, equality, end of exploitation.) When the new system is firmly in control, it purges itself of those who had been temporarily accepted as comrades. In the Marxist vocabulary this is called a "temporary alliance."

Who remembers that the Red Army of the early 1920s had consisted almost exclusively of former Tsarist officers who were promptly purged when the civil war was over? Who will remember that the Church in many Third World countries, as in Nicaragua, has collaborated to varying degrees with the communists? When the new regime feels secure, it will sever its temporary alliance with the Church. Any booklet on dialectical materialism will explain why.

Temporarily, however, the government of Nicaragua incorporates symbols of Christianity, such as the cross, into the state (communist) ideology. "Most of the major rallies in Nicaragua today include the symbol of a soldier with his arms outstretched. It is a novel attempt to identify the Sandinista revolution with the cross. Christ is depicted on the cross and in the background there is a sort of shadow with its arms outstretched in the form of a cross. He is a guerilla with a rifle."[24]

"Communism does not grow by disseminating and winning support for its own values," observed Dr. Kirkpatrick. "Neither members nor followers are regularly recruited through the appeal of communist values. Communism grows by identifying itself with the prestige symbols of competing movements and so blurring issues, stakes, and alignments."[25] Communist propaganda no longer pretends that life in the Soviet Union is a replay of the biblical paradise. It does stress, however, that life *elsewhere* is sheer hell.

LINGUISTIC POLLUTION: U.S.-SOVIET ARMS CONTROL TREATIES

"I think language is the larger problem. . . . If there were one single thing that one should do to improve verification, it would not be the addition of a new satellite or even the dispatch of inspectors to Soviet territory. It would be greater precision in the agreements themselves."[26]

Some might argue that, by definition, totalitarian countries are bound to be successful in linguistically deceptive games because of their absolute control over the media. The West, the argument goes, with its lack of central control and its diversity of interests, is necessarily susceptible to all forms of manipulation. This is true, to some extent, particularly in the area of the popular media.

However, it is alarming to discover that Soviet linguistic deception has found its way into texts of U.S.-Soviet arms control treaties. It would seem natural to expect that such documents are written in language which takes into consideration the semantic meaning of both versions, namely English and Russian. The following analysis demonstrates that such is not the case.

I will focus on the Declaration of Basic Principles of Relations Between the United States and the USSR, signed by Nixon and Brezhnev on May 29, 1972. This document is particularly useful for our purposes because its objectives are not technical. Consequently, the language of this treaty is more symptomatic of the problems I seek to surface than other treaties in the area of arms control. It is the best example of the linguistic and, therefore, political problems that characterize virtually every political document signed by representatives of the United States and the Soviet Union. However, this is not the only document polluted with linguistic deception. On the whole, the more technical the treaty, the less ambiguity or outright deception can be found in the language.

Every Westerner assumes that treaties result from negotiations; one hears constantly about "negotiations in Geneva," or "our negotiators." Also, the Declaration of Basic Principles states that both parties "will be prepared to negotiate and settle differences by peaceful means." Let us, therefore, look at the word "negotiation."

An American dictionary of international relations states that negotiation is "a diplomatic technique for the peaceful settlement of differences and the advancement of national interests. The objectives of negotiations are accomplished by compromises and accommodation reached through direct personal contact." The editors go on to explain that the nature of negotiation is often misunderstood. At times of crises, the public finds it difficult to offer any concessions to the adversary. Nevertheless, "reaching agreement through negotiation implies a willingness on both sides to make mutually acceptable concessions (*quid pro quo*). Ultimatums, threatening speeches, boycotts and walkouts, and resort to force . . . are not negotiation."[27]

For comparison, let us check the term negotiation in a contemporary Soviet dictionary. Here the definition is short and to the point. Negotiation is "an exchange of opinions with a concrete goal."[28] Interesting—not a word about the need for compromises, accommodations, or concessions. Equally significant is the absence of claims that ultimatums, walkouts, and resort to force have no business in the negotiating process.

The reason, of course, is quite simple. The Soviets do not share American political scientists' view that negotiations are based on a give-and-take foundation. They do not believe it is wise to divorce walkouts and threats of use of force from the talks. This is elementary Leninism.

Further, the Declaration of Basic Principles, and practically all of the other basic arms control documents, operate with the concept of peace. It seems perfectly understandable: Treaties that are designed to improve international security in general and U.S.-Soviet relations in particular are probably bound to use the word peace. However, before the U.S. negotiating team allowed such a word to enter the text, its members ought to have checked standard Soviet reference manuals.

The accepted meaning of the word peace in the West is "the absence of war or other hostilities. An agreement or treaty to end hostilities; harmonious relations. Public security and order."[29] This seems fair enough.

But the Soviet reading of this word is different. A military commission of authors, led by Marshal Ogarkov, defined peace from a different point of view:

> . . . relations between nations and states characterized by absence of war and conduct of foreign policy without the use of military strength and following of obligations [stipulated in] agreements. The character of peace and of war is defined by politics of the ruling class. In antagonistic societies,[30] peace is often interrupted by wars and it fixes their results. Objectively, striving for peace belongs to [the camp of] socialism. After the victory of the Great October Revolution, it was expressed in Lenin's Decree on Peace and is consistent with peaceful politics of the Soviet Union and other socialist countries. Strengthening of peace is a principle and goal of foreign policies of socialist countries. The most important guarantee of peace is the strengthening of defensibility of fraternal socialist countries and of their fighting union.[31]

Ogarkov's assertion that peaceful policies are identical with the foreign policies of the Soviet camp while capitalist countries inevitably go through periods of wars, demonstrates the relative nature of the concept of Soviet peace. His claim that peace is guaranteed by an increase of Soviet military power tells the rest of the story: Moscow's concept of peace is quite different from the way it is understood in the West.

Another term that appears often in arms control treaties between NATO and the Warsaw Pact is "peaceful coexistence." In fact, the Declaration of Basic Principles goes so far as to claim that the United States and the Soviet Union "will proceed from the common determination that in the nuclear age there is no alternative to conducting their mutual relations on the basis of peaceful coexistence." Voslensky pointed out in 1973 that the Soviets view this concept differently.[32] Let us now look at it from a historical perspective.

The American *International Relations Dictionary* defines peaceful coexistence as "a reinterpretation of Leninism that rejects the inevitability of a major war between the leading Western and communist states."[33] Here, of course, the authors are alluding to Lenin's statement that "we understand that war cannot be abolished unless classes are abolished and Socialism is created."[34] This meaning, they argue, has been rejected. Unfortunately, this does not seem to be the case.

It is good to remember that the policy of peaceful coexistence was born out of sheer necessity. Lenin explained it graphically in 1918. Pressed by the advancing German Imperial troops, Lenin entered into an alliance with the French:

> This did not in the least prevent me from "compromising" with de Lubersac concerning the services which French officers, expert sappers, desired to render us in blowing up railway tracks to hinder the German advance.... The French monarchist and I shook hands, knowing that each of us would willingly have hanged his "partner." For a time, however, our interests coincided.[35]

Elsewhere, Lenin urged that "we must make use of this breathing spell, which circumstance has given us, to heal the wounds that war has inflicted on the social organism of Russia and to raise the economic level of the country."[36]

Throughout, however, Lenin stressed the temporary character of such arrangements: "... the existence of the Soviet republic side by side the imperialist states for a prolonged period of time is unthinkable. In the end either one or the other will conquer."[37] For the time being, however, "so long as we have not conquered the whole world, so long as we remain economically and militarily weaker than the capitalist world ... we must know how to use the contradictions and oppositions among the capitalists."[38]

Such interpretation of peaceful coexistence was fully embraced by Khrushchev. He stated on several occasions that the concept of peaceful coexistence was a tool of ideological warfare:

> I speak of peaceful coexistence not because I want capitalism to exist, but because I cannot help recognizing that this system does exist.... We have never abandoned, and never will abandon, our political line, which was mapped by Lenin.... And so we say to the gentry who are expecting the Soviet Union to change its political program: "Wait until the crab whistles."[39]

Some might argue that both Lenin and Khrushchev are long dead and that their views have been superseded by more realistic evaluations of the current balance of power. That such is not the case is demonstrated by Marshal Ogarkov and his colleagues who claim in the *Military Encyclopedic Dictionary* that peaceful coexistence is a specific form of class struggle on the international arena between capitalism and socialism expressing itself in economic competition and in the struggle of socialist and bourgeois ideologies. Lenin's statement on peaceful coexistence represents the foundation of foreign policies of socialist countries, peace, and friendship among nations. The USSR and other socialist countries are conducting an intensive struggle for peaceful coexistence. . . .

If peaceful coexistence is a specific form of class struggle, what is "class struggle"? According to Ozhegov's dictionary, the Russian word for class means "a group of people of the same social or economic level"; "struggle" is derived from the Russian verb for "to fight" which means "to try to destroy something or somebody." Conclusion: the purpose of class struggle is to try to destroy a group of people on a different social or economic level.

Therefore, the true meaning of Ogarkov's definition of peaceful coexistence, translated into plain English, reads: it is a specific form of the effort to destroy the class enemy.

It is true enough that the Kremlin elite has lately abstained from making definite and public predictions regarding the end of peaceful coexistence and beginning of a more-or-less unopposed Soviet global peace. Nevertheless, Ogarkov's definition makes it clear that Lenin's understanding of peaceful coexistence remains valid to the present. Further, the Soviet marshal's assurance that Moscow is engaged in "an intensive struggle for peaceful coexistence," confirms that there are actually *two forms of peaceful coexistence*.

The ideal form would be unchallenged Soviet global control. This is the actual objective. Meanwhile, Moscow is forced to coexist with hostile states. A direct attack upon them might not produce the required result. Therefore, a temporary form of peaceful coexistence becomes the guiding strategy for the Kremlin. However, it must be understood that from the Soviet perspective the present form of peaceful coexistence is temporary, not only because Moscow has global plans, but also because the very nature of capitalism renders any other approach impossible. In the immortal words of Radio Prague, the Soviets plan to "batter the warmongers to death with peace."[40]

Given such conflicting interpretations of peaceful coexistence, given the fact that this concept is understood differently in Moscow and in Washington, it is truly surprising that the U.S. negotiating team allowed it to be smuggled into the text of the Declaration of Basic Principles.

The Declaration of Basic Principles further asserts that the United States and the Soviet Union "recognize the sovereign equality of all states." What about the concept of "sovereignty"? An English dictionary entry states that sovereignty is "undisputed political power, the state or quality of being sovereign, the status or authority of being sovereign, a sovereign state."

The Soviets do not share this view. Article 28 of the so-called Brezhnev Constitution of the USSR states that "the foreign policy of the USSR shall be aimed at . . . supporting the struggle of peoples for national liberation. . . ." This is a surprisingly frank admission; the previous "Stalin" Constitution did not deal with foreign policy at all.

Interestingly, even satellite "constitutions" contain such frank declarations. Article 12 of the Cuban Constitution of 1976, for example, states that "the Republic of Cuba espouses . . . the combative solidarity of the people and . . . aspires to establish along with the other countries of Latin America and of the Caribbean—freed from foreign domination and internal oppression—one large community of nations joined by . . . the common struggle against colonialism, neocolonialism and imperialism."

Even the authoritative *Problems of Peace and Socialism*, published in Prague under Soviet supervision, stated in April 1985 that "experienced Party workers who are in North America, Latin America and in Europe have begun conducting far-reaching international activities. . . . We have come to realize that the essence of revolution as a historical process is offensive. . . ." It appears that Soviet assistance for "low-intensity operations" is already regarded as constituting an essential element of Moscow's international behavior.

This is, of course, hardly surprising. In August 1968, Moscow presented the world with the so-called Brezhnev Doctrine. It stipulates that spreading Soviet power can be only progressive, never stagnant or regressive. Moreover, it rejects the notion of noninterference in the domestic affairs of other sovereign countries. Soviet leaders maintain that they have the moral duty and legal right to impose and defend communist regimes all over the globe. Should their client governments encounter serious domestic difficulties (an event quite unlikely given the repressive nature of such regimes), the Kremlin and its allies will intervene with all their might. Anyone who doubts Moscow's devotion to this doctrine ought to consult *Pravda*'s articles dealing with the Soviet invasion of Czechoslovakia and Afghanistan.[41]

If the Kremlin is capable of presenting its occupation of Czechoslovakia as an act of defending the country's sovereignty, how can this concept be taken seriously? The notion of sovereignty ought not to have been allowed in the text.

The above applies equally to such poorly understood terms as equality, noninterference in internal affairs, reduction of tension, universal security, international cooperation, mutual understanding, and other terms freely occurring in the Declaration of Basic Principles.

In addition to such semantic traps, the language of the Declaration further shows disregard for reality when it states that "the two Governments welcome and will facilitate an increase in productive contacts between representatives of the legislative bodies of the two countries."

Students of the Soviet system know that the decisionmaking process in Moscow has nothing to do with the Supreme Soviet. Its deputies are not elected; they are chosen to act as a rubber-stamp institution for decisions taken at the highest levels of the Soviet police-military complex under party control. In short, the U.S. Congress has no counterpart in the Soviet decisionmaking hierarchy. To identify the Supreme Soviet as a legislative body is incorrect. But that is not the only problem. The other one is that it implies the existence of moral equivalence between the United States and the Soviet Union.

The theory of moral equivalence between the two superpowers is one of the most powerful weapons of Moscow-directed disinformation. It allows Soviet propagandists to focus not on the "advantages" of living under a communist system—a contention less and less believable—but on the real, as well as imagined, imperfections of the West. Thus, the Kremlin no longer needs to prove the validity of its own values; it attacks the West for its own shortcomings. The result? Westerners feel that they have failed to live up to their values and that they have no right to sit in judgment over the Soviet system. This, in the long run, serves to obfuscate the severity, or even the existence, of the Soviet threat.

The Western public is bombarded daily with disinformation designed to implant the existence of moral equivalence in peoples' minds. One example will suffice:

> The two great world systems—the communist and the capitalist—each have to face their own problems of political stability. Both want to maintain the status quo in the international arena and insist on "peaceful co-existence." Moreover, they depend on each other for a lasting solution of their respective economic problems. Therefore, a new system of international relations would also serve to stabilize internal institutions and procedures.[42]

Virtually every single assertion in this statement is disinformation.

It would be naive to ignore the fact that the moral equivalence theory is not being spread only by Soviet or East European disinformation specialists. In fact, it has been so successful precisely because it plays upon innate Western proclivities toward relativism, self-doubt, and even self-hate. Consequently, it has now become an integral part of Soviet linguistic deception campaigns.

CONCLUSION

Can we "deal" successfully with the Soviets? We must at least try. We ought to remember first of all that the Soviets conduct "total" politics. Whenever Kremlin representatives sit down to negotiate, we can assume that they were instructed to insist on superiority for the Soviet side. In order to achieve that objective, a whole scale of techniques (from regular diplomatic talks to walk-outs and threats of the use of force) will be applied.

In the negotiating process, the West must demonstrate as much patience as it can muster. Open societies tend to expect instant results. But the issues involved in East-West relations are far too complex to be solved during a few meetings. In any case, summits are not solutions in and of themselves. Poorly prepared summits can seriously destabilize international relations.

Finally, no agreement with Moscow should contain references to moral or political concepts. Treaties with the Soviets ought to be restricted to hard data. This essay has attempted to demonstrate why.

NOTES

1. The Soviet elite often pretends that new trends come from the subelites, or from the "constituency." After the Brezhnev years, this deception has now been fully reactivated under General Secretary Gorbachev, who takes time to answer letters from the general public (both Soviet and Western), on the front page of *Pravda*, of course.
2. For a uniquely penetrating analysis of Stalin's "contribution" to linguistics, see Ernst Halperin, *The Triumphant Heretic: Tito's Struggle Against Stalin* (London: Heinemann, 1958), pp. 199–201.
3. Joseph Stalin, *Marxism and Linguistics* (New York: International Publishers, 1951), pp. 36–37.
4. Czeslaw Milosz, *The Captive Mind* (New York: Knopf, 1953), pp. 78–79.
5. J. Milton Cowan, *A Dictionary of Modern Written Arabic* (Ithaca, N.Y.: Cornell University Press, 1961), p. 814.
6. H.A.R. Gibb and J.H. Kramers, editors, *Shorter Encyclopaedia of Islam* (London: Luzac & Co., 1961), pp. 561–562.
7. Milosz, op. cit., pp. 57–58.
8. Ibid., pp. 56–58.
9. The poet of the Bolshevik Revolution, Mayakovskii, put it best: "Molten tin and lead were poured into our mouths: 'Disavow!' But only three words came from our burning throats: 'Long live Communism.'"
10. Karl Marx and Friedrich Engels, *Manifesto of the Communist Party* (Peking: Foreign Languages Press, 1975), p. 77.
11. As reported by James M. Markman, "German Spy Comes in from the Cold," *New York Times*, March 13, 1986. Given the fact that the Soviet agent Felfe has been living on the eastern side of the Wall, the article's title appears strangely misleading. What about "Soviet Spy Remains in the Cold"?
12. For recent literature on this topic, see Robert Conquest, Dana Dalrymple, James Mace, and Michael Novak, *The Man-Made Famine in the Ukraine* (Washington, D.C.: American Enterprise Institute for Public Policy Research, 1984); also Miron Dolot, *Execution by Hunger: The Hidden Holocaust* (New York: W.W. Norton, 1985); and Ewald Ammende, *Human Life in Russia* (Cleveland, Ohio: John T. Zubal, 1986).

13. There is no question that the success of the peace, bread, and land slogan was partly explainable by its similarity with other, considerably more democratic, slogans. As far as many were concerned, they could have been talking about "Liberté, egalité, fraternité" of old glory.
14. This was brought to my attention by Jeane J. Kirkpatrick, "The Myth of Moral Equivalence," *Imprimis*, January 1986, Vol. 15, No. 1, p. 5.
15. Stalin, op. cit., p. 23.
16. Milosz, op. cit., p. 54.
17. This example is quoted from Franz Borkenau's article, "Getting at the Facts Behind the Soviet Facade," *Commentary*, April 1954, No. 17, pp. 393–400. Even today, Sovietologists have a great deal to learn from Borkenau.
18. William E. Griffith, *Communist Esoteric Communications: Explication de Texte* (Cambridge, Mass.: M.I.T. Press, 1967).
19. However, as Franz Neumann showed in *Behemoth*, his brilliant study of closed societies, totalitarian regimes tend to be less monolithic than democracies because no external force, such as public opinion, is ever allowed to intervene in the struggle between various departments, factions, and individuals. Consequently, internal rivalry is permanent and continues even in times of national emergency. Under similar circumstances, democracies can harden and unite virtually overnight.
20. John P. Roche, *The History and Impact of Marxist-Leninist Organizational Theory* (Cambridge, Mass.: Institute for Foreign Policy Analysis, 1984), p. ix.
21. As quoted by Sir William Stephenson on board the *Intrepid* at Intrepid Square, New York, September 22, 1983. Sir William received the William J. Donovan award on that occasion.
22. Michael Voslensky, *Nomenklatura: The Soviet Ruling Class* (Garden City, N.Y.: Doubleday, 1984), p. 415.
23. Voslensky, op. cit., p. 415.
24. Kirkpatrick, op. cit., p. 5.
25. Jeane Kirkpatrick, "American Foreign Policy in a Cold Climate," *Encounter*, November 1983, p. 32.
26. Richard Perle, "Language Problems," *The Defense Monitor* (Washington, D.C.: Center for Defense Information, 1985), p. 5.
27. Jack C. Plano and Roy Olton, editors, *The International Relations Dictionary* (Santa Barbara, Calif.: ABC–CLIO, 1982).
28. Sergei Ivanovich Ozhegov, *Slovar Russkogo Jazyka* (Moscow: Izdatelstvo Russkij Jazyk, 1978).
29. *The American Heritage Dictionary* (Boston: Houghton Mifflin Company, 1982).
30. That is, in societies in which there exists antagonism between classes—in other words, everywhere outside the Soviet Union and Eastern Europe, which are said to be classless.
31. Marshal Ogarkov, et al., editors, *Voennyj Encyklopedicheskij Slovar* (Moscow: Voennoye izdatelstvo, 1983).
32. Michail Woslenskij, "Friedliche Koexistenz aus sowjetischer Sicht," *Osteuropa*, 1973, Vol. 11, pp. 848–855.
33. Plano and Olton, op. cit.

34. V.I. Lenin, *Lenin on War and Peace* (Peking: Foreign Languages Press, 1970).
35. Lenin, "Pismo k amerikanskim rabochim," August 20, 1918, *Sochinenia*, Vol. 23, p. 182.
36. Lenin, "Ocherednye zadachi sovetskoi vlasti," March-April 1918, *Sochinenia*, Vol. 22, p. 440.
37. Lenin, "Otcheyot Tsentralnogo Komiteta," March 18, 1919, *Sochinenia*, Vol. 24, p. 122.
38. Lenin, "Rech na sobranii sekretarei," *Sochinenia*, Vol. 25, p. 498.
39. "Speech by N.S. Khrushchev at Reception in Indo-Soviet Cultural Society in Bombay," November 24, 1955, *International Affairs* (Moscow), No. 1, January 1956, p. 195.
40. Radio Prague, January 17, 1951.
41. "The Soviet Union and other socialist states, in fulfilling their international duty to the fraternal people of Czechoslovakia and defending their own socialist gains, had to act and did act in resolute opposition to the antisocialist forces in Czechoslovakia. . . . The assistance given to the working people of the CSSR by the other socialist countries . . . is in fact a struggle for the Czechoslovak Socialist Republic's sovereignty against those who would like to deprive it of this sovereignty by delivering the country to the imperialists." *Pravda*, September 26, 1968. "People have the right to external assistance when there is interference in their internal affairs. It was aggression from outside, committed by counterrevolutionary bands, organized, armed, and encouraged by American special services against Afghanistan, that caused the lawful government of that republic to turn to the Soviet Union for help in defending the achievements of the Afghan people." *Pravda*, November 5, 1984.
42. Peter Hardi, "Why Do Communist Parties Advocate Pluralism?" *World Politics*, July 1980, Vol. 32, No. 4, pp. 538–539. The author is a professor at the Karl Marx University, Budapest.

APPENDIX D

SUMMARY OF U.S. REPORTS ON SOVIET VIOLATIONS

by William R. Harris[1]

Table 1

Presidential Reports to the Congress on Soviet Noncompliance with Arms Control Obligations Strategic Nuclear Arms Agreements

Obligation	Issue/Report	GAC Report 12/02/83[1]	President 1/23/84[2]	President 2/01/85[3]	President 6/10/85[4]	President 12/23/85[5]
1972 ABM TREATY	Deployment of large Krasnoyarsk radar, neither on periphery nor oriented outward, 1981 to present	violation	almost certainly a violation	violation	violation	violation; no corrective action has been taken
	Testing and deployment of mobile FLAT TWIN ABM radar in 1975, and continuing development 1975 to present	violation	—	potential violation	—	apparent testing and development of ABM components and highly probable
	Concurrent testing of ABM and SAM components	—	—	highly probable violations	—	concurrent testing; SA-X-12 may have some ABM capabilities
	Deliberate concealment measures	violations	—	—	—	—
	ABM and ABM-related actions in preparation for defense of the national territory	—	—	potential violation	serious cause for concern	may be preparing ABM defense
	Rapid reload of ABM launchers	—	—	classified rpt	—	serious cause for concern

155

Table 1
Presidential Reports to the Congress on Soviet Noncompliance with Arms Control Obligations
Strategic Nuclear Arms Agreements (continued)

1972 SALT I INTERIM AGREEMENT	Deployment of large throwweight SS-19 and SS-17 ICBMs despite limit on heavy ICBM launchers, 1972 to present	circumvention defeating object and purpose	—	—	—	—
	Deliberate concealment measures	violations	—	—	—	—
PROTOCOL limiting launchers of modern ballistic missiles	Deployment of "DELTA" modern SLBM launchers exceeding SALT I Protocol limit, 1976–1977; dismantling of older launchers	violations (probably deliberate)	—	currently in compliance (political)	compliance with the letter of the agreement	—
DISMANTLING PROCEDURES effective July 3, 1974	YANKEE SLBM submarine conversion into elongated cruise missile carrier	—	—	not a violation but threat to U.S. and Allies' security	not a violation but threat to U.S. and Allies' security	—
	Mobile missile base (SS-25) at dismantled SS-7 ICBM sites	—	—	future violation		violation; use of SS-7 facilities for SS-25 ICBMs

Table 1
Presidential Reports to the Congress on Soviet Noncompliance with Arms Control Obligations
Strategic Nuclear Arms Agreements (continued)

		[1]	[2]	[3]	[4]	[5]
1979 SALT II TREATY (unratified) (duty not to defeat object and purpose)	Flight testing or deployment of second new type ICBM (SS-X-25)	probable violation	probable violation (political)	violation (political)	irreversible violation	clear and irreversible violation
	Anti-MIRV limit on RV-to-throwweight ratio (SS-X-25)	violation	violation (political)	violation (political)	serious concerns unresolved	violation (political)
	Encryption impeding verification	violation	violation (legal, 79–81) (political, 82–)	violation (legal, 79–81) (political, 82–)	violation	violation (legal, 79–81) (political, 82–)
	Deliberate concealment: — Plesetsk test center	violation	—	—	—	violation (political)
	— association of missiles and launchers during testing	—	—	—	—	—
	Deployment of the SS-16 mobile ICBM at Plesetsk	probable violation	probable violation (legal, 79–81) (political, 82–)	probable violation (legal, 79–81) (political, 82–)	probable violation	probable deployment probable removal in 1985
	Falsification of SALT II database, 1979–	probable violation	—	—	—	—
	Backfire bomber production above 30 per year	—	—	—	—	>30/yr before 1984 <30/yr since 1984
	Exceeding strategic nuclear delivery vehicle ceiling	—	—	—	—	violation (polit) deploying more than 2504 SNDV's

[1] Unclassified summary report of the President's General Advisory Committee on Arms Control and Disarmament, 10/10/84.
[2] Report of the President on Soviet Noncompliance, per FY84 Arms Control Act, 1/23/84.
[3] Report of the President on Soviet Noncompliance, per FY85 Defense Authorization Act, 2/01/85.
[4] Report of the President, Building an Interim Framework for Mutual Restraint, 6/10/85.
[5] Report of the President on Soviet Noncompliance, per PL99-145, 12/23/85.

Table 2
Presidential Reports to the Congress on Soviet Noncompliance with Arms Control Obligations Restraints on Nuclear Weapons Testing

Obligation	Issue/Report	GAC Report 12/02/83[1]	President 1/23/84[2]	President 2/01/85[3]	President 6/10/85[4]	President 12/23/85[5]
NUCLEAR TEST MORATORIUM, 1958-61 (Unilateral Soviet commitments)	Resumption of atmospheric testing, 1961-62, during negotiation of treaty banning atmospheric tests	breach of unilateral commitment	—	—	—	—
1963 LIMITED TEST BAN TREATY	Venting radioactive debris outside the Soviet Union, when available and reasonable precautions could have contained debris, 1965 to present	numerous violations	—	numerous violations	violations	—
1974 THRESHOLD TEST BAN TREATY & 1976 PROTOCOL (unratified, effective March 31, 1976)	Underground nuclear testing with yields in excess of 150 kt. limit	suspicion of repeated violations	likely violation	likely violation	likely violation	likely violations

[1] Unclassified summary report of the President's General Advisory Committee on Arms Control and Disarmament, 10/10/84.
[2] Report of the President on Soviet Noncompliance, per FY84 Arms Control Act, 1/23/84.
[3] Report of the President on Soviet Noncompliance, per FY85 Defense Authorization Act, 2/01/85.
[4] Report of the President, Building an Interim Framework for Mutual Restraint, 6/10/85.
[5] Report of the President on Soviet Noncompliance, per PL99-145, 12/23/85.

Summary of U.S. Reports on Soviet Violations

Table 3
Presidential Reports to the Congress on Soviet Noncompliance with Arms Control Obligations
Other Soviet Arms Control Commitments

Obligation	Issue/Report	GAC Report 12/02/83[1]	President 1/23/84[2]	President 2/01/85[3]	President 6/10/85[4]	President 12/23/85[5]
OFFENSIVE WEAPONS IN CUBA, 1962 (Unilateral)	Deployment of offensive weapons (MRBM and IRBM missiles; medium bombers) in Cuba, Sept.–Oct. '62	Breach of unilateral commitment	—	—	—	—
OFFENSIVE WEAPONS IN CUBA (Reciprocal unilateral commitment) 1970	Deploying and tending Soviet nuclear missile-carrying submarines in Cuban territorial waters, 1970–1974	Breach of unilateral commitments	—	—	—	—
BIOLOGICAL WEAPONS CONVENTION, 1972	Retention of facilities, continued biological munitions production, storage transfer and use; maintaining an offensive biological warfare program and capability; 1972 to present	violations	violations	violations	significant violations	violations; expanded BW and toxin facilities since 1972
GENEVA PROTOCOL OF 1925— CHEMICAL AND TOXIN WEAPONS	Transfer of chemical and toxin weapons to Vietnam, with subsequent use, 1975–83, and Soviet use in Afghanistan, 1980–82, against nationals of Protocol nonparties	circumventions defeating object and purpose	violations (codification of customary international law)	violations (codification of customary international law) – not continued '84	significant violations	violations; no evidence of lethal attacks in 1985
MONTREUX CONVENTION OF 1936 AND LAW OF THE SEA CONVENTION OF 1982	Transit of aircraft carriers through the Turkish Straits; Black Sea construction necessitates future violations	violations	—	—	—	—

Table 3
Presidential Reports to the Congress on Soviet Noncompliance with Arms Control Obligations
Other Soviet Arms Control Commitments (continued)

		violations 1981 and 1983	violation (political) 1981	violation (political) Improved notice – 1983	violation of terms	violation '81; minimal notice provided in 1984-1985
HELSINKI FINAL ACT OF 1975	Failure to provide 21-day notice and specified data before exercises involving more than 25,000 troops, 1981 and 1983					—
CONVENTIONAL WEAPONS CONVENTION, 1981	Use of booby-trap mines and incendiary weapons against civilians in Afghanistan, 1981–1982, before entry-into-force of Protocols in December 1983	violations (codification of customary international law)	—	—	—	
SS-20 MOBILE IRBM DEPLOYMENT MORATORIUM, MARCH 1982–NOV 1983 (Unilateral)	Completion of construction of mobile IRBM launcher bases, despite pledges of March and May 1982	Breach of unilateral commitment	—	—	—	

[1] Unclassified summary report of the President's General Advisory Committee on Arms Control and Disarmament, 10/10/84.
[2] Report of the President on Soviet Noncompliance, per FY84 Arms Control Act, 1/23/84.
[3] Report of the President on Soviet Noncompliance, per FY85 Defense Authorization Act, 2/01/85.
[4] Report of the President, Building an Interim Framework for Mutual Restraint, 6/10/85.
[5] Report of the President on Soviet Noncompliance, per PL99-145, 12/23/85.

Table 4
Arms Control Commitments Regarding which the Soviet Union
is in Apparent Compliance

ACCIDENT AVOIDANCE MEASURES

US-USSR Direct Communications Link Agreement of 1963, amended in 1971 and 1984
US-USSR Accidents Agreement of 1971
 [one violation, judged to be inadvertent]
France-USSR Accidents Agreement of 1976
United Kingdom-USSR Accidents Agreement of 1976

NONPROLIFERATION OF NUCLEAR WEAPONS

Nonproliferation Treaty of 1968
IAEA Guidelines for Nuclear Transfers, INFCIRC/209 of 1974
IAEA Guidelines for Nuclear Transfers, INFCIRC/254 of 1978
Treaty of Tlatelolco (Latin American Nuclear Free Zone), Protocol II, USSR
 ratification 1979
Convention on the Physical Protection of Nuclear Material, USSR ratification 1983

OTHER AGREEMENTS

Antarctic Treaty of 1959
Outer Space Treaty of 1967
Seabed Treaty of 1971
Convention on Environmental Modification of 1977

Sources: Report of the General Advisory Committee on Arms Control and Disarmament, Oct. 10, 1984; Reports of the President to the Congress on Soviet Noncompliance, Jan. 23, 1984; Feb. 1, 1985; and Dec. 23, 1985.

NOTE

1. William R. Harris, "Soviet Maskirovka and Arms Control Verification," in Brian Dailey and Patrick J. Parker, eds., *Soviet Strategic Deception* (Lexington, Mass.: Lexington Books, 1987).

APPENDIX E

A SOVIET VIEW OF ARMS CONTROL: LESSONS FROM THE PAST

by William F. Scott and Harriet Fast Scott

There is a continuity in Soviet policies that is lacking in our own system of government. We are accustomed to a change in political leadership every four to eight years. One administration may have one view of dealing with the Soviet Union; the following, another. When trying to fathom what policies a new Soviet leader might follow with respect to arms control, we tend to mirror-image. We expect a new leader to chart a much different course from that of his predecessors.

However, in the one-party Soviet system there has never been a sudden and complete house cleaning at the top. The nearest approach came with Stalin's purges in the 1930s. Nikita Khrushchev's ouster in October 1964 may have been due primarily to his de-Stalinization program which was beginning to touch too many of the *nomenklatura*, who earlier had been associated with Stalin—as had Khrushchev. The same group, in general, who were ruling the Soviet Union in 1953 at the time of Stalin's death still were ruling in 1964 and some still remained on the Central Committee and Politburo in 1972.

Many of the men at the top of the Soviet power structure in 1986 were powerful leaders in 1972, either in Moscow or in one of the party's "buros" in a "republic." Their perceptions of arms control and of matters such as verification and deliberate violation of agreements are not likely to differ significantly from the views of the party leadership in the 1950s, 1960s, or 1970s.

This does not mean there are no modifications to Soviet policies. As the "correlation of forces in the world arena" changes, Soviet policies are modified accordingly. But at the same time, there are certain fundamentals that appear basic to the Soviet mindset. Among these is the reliance placed on gaining and maintaining overwhelming military power. Another is disregard for treaties.

Soviet actions and policies related to treaties and the buildup of military forces after the death of Stalin and up to the signing of SALT I in 1972 disclose a general pattern that still is followed today. This can be seen in the following analysis with accompanying excerpts from the writings and speeches of the Kremlin leadership in the pre-SALT I period.

WAR IS NO LONGER INEVITABLE

On February 14, 1956, in his address to the 20th Party Congress of the Communist Party of the Soviet Union, Nikita Khrushchev announced a major change in one of the basic tenets of communism. He stated that there exists "the possibility of preventing war in the present era." This was in direct contradiction to the Marxist-Leninist thesis that "wars are inevitable as long as imperialism remains." According to Khrushchev, "there is a world camp of socialism, which has become a mighty force." He went on to assert:

> In these circumstances certainly the Leninist precept that so long as imperialism exists, the economic basis giving rise to wars will also be preserved, remains in force. That is why we must display the greatest vigilance. As long as capitalism survives in the world, the reactionary forces representing the interest of the capitalist monopolies will continue their drive towards military gambles and aggression, and may try to unleash war. *But war is not fatalistically inevitable*. Today there are mighty social and political forces possessing *formidable means* to prevent the imperialists from unleashing war, and if they do try to start it, *to give a smashing rebuff to the aggressors and frustrate their adventurist plans*. To be able to do this all anti-war forces must be vigilant and prepared, they must act as a united front and never relax their efforts in the battle for peace. The more actively the peoples defend peace, the greater the guarantees that there will be no new war.[1] (Emphasis added.)

The "formidable means" and the ability "to give a smashing rebuff . . . and frustrate their adventurist plans" was based on Khrushchev's claim of the importance of the Soviet Union's small but growing stockpile of nuclear weapons.

At that time the Soviets did not discuss "arms control" in the sense of reducing the number of nuclear weapons. Their slogan then was "full and complete disarmament."

In 1959 Khrushchev made his famous trip to the United States. Following this visit, at the request of the editors of *Foreign Affairs*, he wrote an article "On Peaceful Coexistence." In it, he asserted that "the main thing is to keep to the sphere of ideological struggle, without resorting to arms in order to prove that one is right."[2] He stressed the "peace-loving policies" of the Soviet Union as demonstrated, for example, on March 12, 1951, when "the Supreme Soviet of the USSR adopted a Law on the Defense of the Peace," stating:

1. Propaganda of war, in whatever form it may be conducted, undermines the cause of peace, creates the menace of a new war and therefore constitutes a grave crime against humanity.
2. Persons guilty of the propaganda of war shall be brought to court and tried as heinous criminals.[3]

Khrushchev failed to note that at the time this "law" was adopted, Stalin was at the head of the Soviet state, and preparing, if Khrushchev's later secret speech was correct, for another internal purge. As a step toward disarmament, Khrushchev urged:

It is perfectly clear that today the discontinuation of atomic and hydrogen weapons tests is foremost among these questions. Some progress has been achieved in this matter, and this justifies the hope that an agreement on the discontinuation of nuclear weapons tests will shortly be reached. Implementation of this measure will, of course, be an important step towards solving the disarmament problem and the banning of nuclear weapons in general.[4]

A MORATORIUM ON NUCLEAR TESTING

On January 14, 1960, speaking before the Fourth Session of the Supreme Soviet of the USSR, Khrushchev delivered a speech entitled "Disarmament for Durable Peace and Friendship." Later, even after Khrushchev became a nonperson, this speech was referred to as the announcement of a new military doctrine, based on nuclear weapons and their primary carrier, the missile. Among other points made in this speech, Khrushchev emphasized the need to cease nuclear tests:

It is easy enough to imagine what the consequences would be if any country were to resume nuclear weapons tests in the present situation. The other nuclear powers would be compelled to adopt the same course. An impetus would be given to the resumption of an absolutely unlimited race in the testing of nuclear weapons by any power and in any conditions. The government that resumed nuclear weapons tests first would assume a grave responsibility before the peoples. . . .[5]

He then gave the Soviet position:

I should like to re-emphasize in this connection that the Soviet Government, prompted by the desire to provide the most favorable conditions for the earliest possible drafting of a treaty on the discontinuance of tests, will abide by its commitment not to resume experimental nuclear blasts in the Soviet Union unless the Western Powers begin testing atomic and hydrogen weapons.[6]

Later he acknowledged the agreed moratorium on testing, as follows:

> As I have said, no nuclear explosions have been carried out for more than a year—*in accordance with voluntary commitments made by each side*, without an international agreement. Such an agreement, if it is signed, will presumably make it still more obligatory for all the countries concerned to abide strictly by the understanding reached.[7] (Emphasis added.)

On September 10, 1961, *Pravda* reported an interview that Khrushchev had granted to Cyrus Lee Sulzberger, correspondent of the *New York Times*. During the course of the interview, Sulzberger asked the following question:

> In your public statements you have said it is possible to develop a nuclear bomb equal in explosive force to 100 megatons of conventional explosives. I should like to ask what sense you see in developing such a super bomb? It seems to me that the bomb would be too big to use for military purposes. Could you comment on this?

Khrushchev's reply was as follows:

> Yes, that bomb is of enormous capacity and tremendous destructive power. But when war is being imposed upon us and threats are being made to destroy our country and our people, we must take it into account in all earnest. And we shall stop at nothing if the aggressors attack us. . . .
>
> Let those who dream of new aggression know that we shall have a bomb equal in power to 100 million tons of TNT, that we already have such a bomb, and that we shall test the exploding device for it. Let them know that if they attack us it will mean certain death for themselves. We have no choice.[8]

In October 1961, the month following this interview, the Soviet Union broke the moratorium on nuclear testing by conducting a series of tests in the atmosphere. One of these, intended to reach 50 megatons, actually may have exceeded 60 megatons. This apparently was an initial test of Khrushchev's superbomb. The test provided the Soviets invaluable information on the impact of the electromagnetic pulse (EMP) upon communications. There was no admission in the Soviet press that such tests were being, or had been, conducted.

PEACE, LABOR, FREEDOM, EQUALITY, FRATERNITY, AND HAPPINESS

In March 1962, in a speech entitled "Peace, Labor, Freedom, Equality, Fraternity, and Happiness," given in Moscow, Khrushchev claimed:

Among the assets of Soviet foreign policy we have every reason to include the fact that in the last few years the Soviet Union never abandoned the initiative in the search for a solution of the disarmament problem. Of course, the road to disarmament is not an easy one. But if the idea of disarmament has taken firm root in the minds of hundreds upon hundreds of millions of people, this is to be credited mostly to our country, which presented a programme *for general and complete disarmament* two and a half years ago and has since been vigorously promoting it. (Prolonged applause.) (Emphasis added.)

The monstrous destructive force of the modern nuclear devices, the possibility of delivering them to any point in the world are today such convincing arguments that human reason cannot but demand the earliest solution of the disarmament problem.

Can an understanding be reached on disarmament? Yes, it can. The Soviet position is well known to world opinion: we are in favour of *general and complete disarmament* under the strictest international control.[9]

In partial response to the Soviet tests in 1961, the United States conducted a series of tests of its own. Concerning these tests, without admitting that it was the Soviet Union that broke the moratorium, Khrushchev asserted:

The Central Committee of our Party and the Soviet Government are responsible to the Soviet people for the security of our homeland, and we see to it all the time that the defenses of our socialist land are at the proper level. It should be clear that *if the United States holds another series of experimental explosions in the atmosphere*, and it is already making underground explosions, *the Soviet Union will be compelled to reply to this by holding its own tests*. Thus, the United States Government will not achieve any military advantage by holding nuclear weapons tests. But there is one thing it will indeed achieve—it will usher in a new stage in the arms race and thus earn the censure of the peoples who want the Soviet Union and the United States to compete peacefully, and not in the manufacture of increasingly terrible weapons of destruction.

We regret the decision of the United States Government to resume nuclear tests. It has thereby assumed a serious responsibility before the peoples of the world. But I should like to assure you, comrades, that this decision of the United States Government, far from weakening our efforts in the struggle for disarmament, including a nuclear test ban, will, on the contrary, redouble them.[10]

A MATTER OF VERIFICATION

As already noted, approximately three months before this talk was given, the Soviet Union had conducted a series of tests, one of which was of extremely high yield. The data provided on EMP and other phenomena at that time still gives the Soviet Union a significant advantage in certain areas over the United States. Khrushchev wanted to ensure that the tests of the previous October were not matched elsewhere. He now pressed for a nuclear test ban agreement, but without on-site inspection.

The Soviet Government has proposed a sound foundation for a nuclear test ban agreement. We have proposed that national means of detecting nuclear explosions, which the states already possess, should be used for control. The Western representatives allege that national facilities are inadequate to control a nuclear weapons test ban. But this contradicts universally known facts. The nuclear explosions held in the United States were registered in the Soviet Union and the explosions made in the Soviet Union, as one may judge from the statements of the U.S. Atomic Energy Commission, were recorded by American national control facilities.[11]

Later he stated:

The President of the United States and the Prime Minister of Great Britain acknowledged in one of their joint statements that national facilities were quite adequate to control the cessation of nuclear tests in the atmosphere. Yet it is claimed that secret tests of nuclear weapons can be carried out underground.

Let me tell you a secret, comrades. We know that it is scientifically possible to detect underground nuclear explosions by national means of control. The underground nuclear explosions made in the United States, for example, were registered by Soviet scientists and scientists in other countries. We decided to prove that the Western representatives lie when they claim that it is impossible to detect underground explosions.[12]

He then talked about a disarmament agreement.

The Soviet Union sincerely wishes a disarmament agreement, and is working for it perseveringly. We are strongly opposed to the man-hating ideology of imperialism, because communism brings Peace, Labour, Freedom, Equality, Fraternity and Happiness to all peoples of the earth. (Prolonged applause.)[13]

In April 1962, at the time Khrushchev was preparing to place nuclear missiles in Cuba, he met with Gardner Cowles, an American publisher, and his assistant, Edward Korry. Their discussion of verification was as follows:

Cowles: Mr. Chairman, I have read your reply to Prime Minister Macmillan's message very carefully, and must say I can appreciate your viewpoint, your apprehension that inspection in connection with disarmament may be a kind of "fishing expedition" to see what weapons remain and where they are.

But I should like to ask you the following question: Do you see any difference between inspection and verification in the sense that verification is undertaken solely if an event has taken place which a competent international authority presumes to be a nuclear blast? In no other case but this would a commission be entitled to come and make sure what has really taken place—a nuclear blast or an earthquake.

Do you see any difference between inspection and this sort of verification?[14]

In reply Khrushchev digressed on a Civil War experience. He then addressed the question:

> Khrushchev: I do not, in fact, see any great difference between verification, inspection, and intelligence or, as you put it, a "fishing expedition." As the Ukrainians say, "Danila did not die—the plague got him."
>
> Cowles: Mr. Chairman, you often say that you have no confidence in the intentions of the United States. I think that the Soviet Union would itself like to have some kind of inspection and verification with regard to our country. Or do you trust us so implicitly that you will not want to verify or inspect the U.S. if a disarmament agreement is reached?
>
> Khrushchev: No, you have misunderstood me. So far we have been talking about inspection and verification connected with nuclear weapons tests, and not disarmament.
>
> Inspection connected with general and complete disarmament is an entirely different matter, and in that respect we ourselves demand not only verification, but also the strictest and most thorough inspection. We consider that if a disarmament agreement is reached, all countries will have to undergo most rigorous inspection and control. And that is not merely a question of trust or mistrust. We must have a system where every country would be sure that other countries are complying scrupulously with their undertakings and that they have really destroyed, or are destroying the armaments subject to destruction.
>
> This is why we must have our inspection in the United States and other countries, while the United States and other countries should have their inspection in our territory and the territory of other countries party to the agreement on general and complete disarmament. I repeat, it is not a matter of trust or mistrust. There must be an established system: the strictest verification, exhaustive and comprehensive control over disarmament.[15]

As can be seen in the above, Khrushchev professed to be for verification if connected with "general and complete disarmament." One might speculate what would happen to the Soviet power struggle and the Soviet Empire if "general and complete disarmament" were actually achieved.

BEFORE THE CUBAN NUCLEAR CONFRONTATION OF 1962

Again, on July 10, 1962, with the Cuban missile confrontation only three months away, Khrushchev spoke before the World Congress for General Disarmament and Peace. As sites for his missiles to go into Cuba were being surveyed, he stated:

> Dear delegates, the Soviet Government is firmly and consistently carrying on a policy of promoting peace and peaceful coexistence. In putting forward its programme *for general and complete disarmament*, the Soviet Government was prompted by the necessity for radically solving the problem of security for all nations by precluding the very possibility of war.
>
> What is the main point of our programme? The pivot and core of disarmament is the banning and complete destruction of nuclear weapons.
>
> The Soviet Government suggests at least immobilizing all nuclear weapons, paralyzing them by destroying all means of their delivery from the outset, at the very first stage of disarmament. We propose abolishing at one

stroke rockets, aircraft, warships and submarines that can carry nuclear weapons, atomic artillery installations and all military bases on foreign soil and withdrawing all foreign troops from the countries concerned.

Without rockets, aircraft, warships and submarines, nuclear arms would no longer be dangerous even if an unscrupulous government tried to stow away some of them. The destruction of all means of delivery would make it impossible for any country possessing atomic weapons to strike a nuclear blow at other countries. A proposal to this effect was made at one time by the French President, General de Gaulle, and we fully agree with it. Unfortunately, the French Government took no effective steps to ensure the implementation of its proposal. What is more, it refused to take part in the disarmament negotiations at Geneva. . . .

It is said that nuclear weapons can also be carried in TU-114s, Boeing 707s and other civil aircraft. But if there is a real desire for disarmament, the various countries may for a while keep their means of defense—anti-aircraft artillery, and air defense rockets and fighters. Modern means of warfare make it possible to shoot down any aircraft flying at any altitude. As you see, the argument is untenable throughout.

By proposing that disarmament be begun with the abolition of all vehicles of delivery of nuclear weapons, the Soviet Union, which has *the world's most powerful global and intercontinental missiles, relinquishes of its own free will a most important military advantage.* (Applause.) We will not hesitate to take this step because we believe that it would expedite the solution of the disarmament problem.[16] (Emphasis added.)

Khrushchev's claim above of global and intercontinental missiles was much different from assertions of the Soviet leadership in 1986. He explained additional details of his proposal:

For our part, we insist that the Western Powers should agree to dismantle all of their military bases on foreign soil and withdraw their troops from foreign countries. Those bases have been set up for aggression and not for defence. It must be obvious to anyone that, say, the U.S. rocket and nuclear bases on the Japanese island of Okinawa or in Libya, on African soil, or the U.S. bases in Britain, Italy, Turkey, Greece and Thailand are not needed for the defence of the United States. Whoever denies this is trying to pass off black for white. (Applause.)

To greatly ease the threat of armed conflict between countries, the Soviet Union also proposes that at the very beginning of disarmament the numerical strength of national armed forces be substantially cut and conventional armaments reduced accordingly. We think it possible to carry disarmament through to the end in four years. This is a short but perfectly sufficient time limit.

We are willing to seek and find mutually acceptable formulas for all the provisions of our draft treaty, and to compromise wherever necessary—that is, of course, if that will not harm the cause of general and complete disarmament.[17]

It should be noted in the above that Khrushchev is not discussing arms control in the current context, but "general and complete disarmament." Later he stated:

> Peace can be radically safeguarded through the complete abolition of the physical machinery of war. The Soviet Government does not rule out but, on the contrary, considers it indispensable to agree, in advancing to this goal, on the adoption of a series of steps towards lessening international tension, strengthening confidence among countries, and considerably facilitating general and complete disarmament. Among such measures we include the establishment of denuclearized zones in various areas, renunciation of the further spread of nuclear weapons, the withdrawal of troops from foreign territory, the prohibition of war propaganda, and the conclusion of a non-aggression pact between NATO and Warsaw Treaty countries.[18]

He then gave his version of how a Soviet proposal was rejected:

> In 1957 the Soviet Government proposed an agreement on at least partial disarmament measures. Among these measures we included, this time as well, the Western Powers' own proposal for establishing aerial photography zones with a view to discovering secret preparations for aggression. You may remember that aerial photography at that time was a pet idea of President Eisenhower's. We proposed establishing one aerial photography zone in Europe, 800 kilometres deep on either side of the demarcation line between the armed forces of NATO and the Warsaw Treaty. The zone was to have comprised the territories of the German Democratic Republic, Poland, Czechoslovakia and a sizable strip of Soviet territory. The other zone was to have covered our Far East all the way to Lake Baikal, and an equal part of U.S. territory. In the same period we proposed setting up control posts at railway junctions, in harbours, and on highways to prevent surprise attack. In this case too, we took Western suggestions into consideration.
>
> And what was the outcome? What was the lot that befell our proposals for aerial photography zones and control posts? They were rejected by the United States and the other NATO powers, which is regrettable, for anyone realizes that had we at that time succeeded in reaching agreement on the lines suggested by us, the war danger would now be far less. But now that rockets have become our principal means of defence and *NATO generals would readily sell their souls to the devil* if only they could find out their location, these measures can no longer be carried out in the absence of general and complete disarmament. . . . (Emphasis added.)
>
> It is true that nuclear tests are not the same as nuclear war. But their after-effects are very serious for mankind even now. The new major series of nuclear tests which the U.S. Government is carrying out jointly with the British Government is a challenge to mankind. Matters have reached a point where the United States is testing nuclear weapons in space, even though the effect of the tests on people's living conditions may prove very dangerous. . . .[19]

In the above, Khrushchev never acknowledged the Soviet testing that had occurred in 1961. He then made a plea for "general and complete disarmament":

> General and complete disarmament is truly a great goal and calls for great actions and great efforts by all the peoples. Keenly aware that the hour is critical and grave, we should like to declare from this rostrum to all men and

women regardless of their social background and convictions, to the generation that has lived through the terrors of war and to the young people who know about war only from what their elders tell them: *This is the time to act! In the name of life on earth and the happiness of all men, in the name of the future of mankind, show firmness and determination in demanding the atomic weapons ban and general disarmament!*[20] (Emphasis in original.)

ADMISSION OF A VIOLATION

On July 13, 1962, Nikita Khrushchev, referred to as "Chairman of the Council of Ministers, USSR," received a group of U.S. journalists headed by Lee Hills, President of the American Society of Newspaper Editors and Executive Editor of Knight Newspapers.

During the interview, one of the U.S. journalists brought up the matter of the Soviet violation of the moratorium on nuclear testing:

> Felix McKnight (Editor of the *Dallas Times Herald*): Mr. Chairman, during our trip we heard a number of critical remarks regarding the current series of American nuclear tests. This makes us wonder whether the Soviet people know, firstly, that the Soviet Union broke the moratorium on nuclear tests, which had lasted for three years, and made 40 nuclear weapons tests, and that after the Soviet Union had made its tests President Kennedy declared the U.S.A. would not resume testing if a mutually acceptable nuclear test ban were achieved. Secondly, do they know that the recent American explosion in the upper atmosphere was made to test the defensive capabilities of the United States in connection with your statement, Mr. Khrushchev, that the Soviet Union was in possession of a global missile capable of breaking the American defenses.[21]

Before answering McKnight's question, Khrushchev attempted to prove that the United States was seeking to "militarize space." At the same time he bragged about his "global missiles," which "cannot be destroyed by any anti-missile means."

> Khrushchev: I must disillusion you. The high-altitude test carried out by the U.S.A. can in no way interfere with the action of our global missiles. I conclude from what you said that you are not very well informed about rocketry and about the way rockets work. You are a victim of people who have abused your confidence. Better not repeat what you have just said in the presence of an engineer, for you will make a laughing stock of yourself. What you have just said makes no sense at all.
>
> I am not boasting when I say that we really have a global missile which cannot be destroyed by any anti-missile means, and I know what anti-missile means are, because we have them. We thought of showing the delegates of the World Congress for General Disarmament and Peace a documentary film showing our anti-missile missiles in action. But when I spoke with some members of the Congress they advised me against it, because it might have been wrongly interpreted. But if people saw that film, they would realize what kind of machine it is. Our rocket could practically *hit a fly in outer space*. (Emphasis added.)

After this claim, he replied to the question of the October 1961 Soviet test as follows:

> Now about the tests. In this, too, you have been misled and have probably not followed the Soviet, and even the American, press.
>
> No one can claim that the Soviet Union was the first to begin tests, just as you cannot say that the United States was the first in outer space. You can only say that you visited outer space after we had already been there. Just as Columbus discovered America, so Gagarin discovered outer space. The Soviet Union was the first, and this fact will go down in history and live down the ages.
>
> Who was the first to begin atomic tests? It was the United States of America.
>
> Who used atomic weapons to kill people in Hiroshima and Nagasaki? It was the United States of America.
>
> This too will go down in history.
>
> You say that we terminated the moratorium. Actually, it was all different. When carrying out nuclear weapons tests, the Soviet Union was from the outset replying to a corresponding series of tests carried out by the U.S.A. The negotiations on ending nuclear tests began after a series of American tests to which the Soviet Union did not reply in the hope that a treaty ending all nuclear tests would be signed. The Soviet Union honestly took part in the talks, until the U.S. President declared a mobilization of the armed forces and began to threaten us with war. It was then that we decided to carry out nuclear weapons tests in order to prepare our army better in case the U.S. President actually carries out his threat and unleashes war against the Soviet Union. But even in that case the Soviet tests were a reply to tests previously made by the U.S.A.
>
> *So no one can say that we broke the moratorium.* As far as the number of series of tests is concerned, the United States is continuously in the fore, and the Soviet Union will be able to catch up with the U.S.A.—and then only in the number of test series, but not in the number of actual explosions—if it makes new tests after the current American series. We hope that after this the U.S.A. will finally agree to signing a treaty banning tests for all time. However, if the Americans end their nuclear weapons tests now, and if we reach an agreement on general and complete disarmament and the destruction of nuclear weapons, we would no longer need to make our tests. On the other hand, if America pursues the policy of testing, stockpiling and improving nuclear weapons, then, of course, we shall be compelled to do the same. That is the true state of affairs on this question.[22] (Emphasis added.)

As seen above, Khrushchev never admitted that the Soviet series of high altitude tests had broken the moratorium. Instead, he launched a verbal attack against the United States.

WESTERN ASSUMPTIONS

In the spring of 1963 the United States Arms Control and Disarmament Agency (ACDA) awarded a contract to Columbia University to evaluate the Soviet position on arms control and disarmament. A group of distinguished scholars and officials from the United States and Great Britain met for a two-week seminar at Airlie House in Warrenton, Virginia, and again at Arden House, Harriman, New York, to study the issue. Among the conclusions were the following:

- Since about 1960 increased military expenditures, inadequacies in planning and administration, and low agricultural productivity have contributed to a darker mood of anxious preoccupation with economic shortcomings.
- The Cuban fiasco, the test-ban treaty, and the armament reduction in the military sector of the budget in late 1963 form part of a new sequence of policy moves which are evidently based on Moscow's recognition that the USSR has to live in a position of strategic inferiority to the United States insofar as numbers of missiles and delivery vehicles are concerned.
- Thus, the available evidence regarding Soviet doctrine, force structure, and capabilities leads to the conclusion that the USSR has at present no winning strategy—and knows it.[23]

The assumptions about the Soviet Union stated above have a familiar ring. Details may differ, but the popular conclusions in the West concerning Moscow's reasons for wanting an arms control agreement remain much the same today. In the early 1970s Western proponents of arms control argued that Soviet economic concerns would keep the Kremlin from continuing to build up its armed forces. In the mid-1980s many Western analysts write that M.S. Gorbachev, the party's General Secretary, will concentrate on solving Soviet economic problems, and is attempting to reduce military expenditures.

THE 23RD PARTY CONGRESS AND ARMS CONTROL

Nikita Khrushchev was ousted in October 1964, two years after the nuclear confrontation. In March 1966, the meeting of the 23rd Party Congress supposedly set a new course for leadership. A 1967 booklet purported to give the "Results and Prospects of the 23rd Party Congress." Among the statements made were the following:

> Disarmament in its broad aspect is another paramount problem relating to international security.
> It is quite natural that whenever the question of disarmament arises, it concerns first and foremost the economically developed countries which have concentrated the bulk of all armaments in their hands.
> Disarmament does not simply imply a lessening of the temptation to undertake adventures. Disarmament also means a reduction of unproductive expenditures, increased opportunities for creative endeavour and higher

welfare for the peoples. It is a fact that enormous sums of money are being spent on armaments. In the last two decades the military outlays of the United States have totalled over 48 times the military expenditure of that country during the two decades preceding World War II. The growing production of the weapons of war in major imperialist states compels other countries to spend considerable funds on strengthening their defenses as well.

But that is not all. Disarmament would do a great service to the developing countries and the peoples fighting for their national independence and for the consolidation of their sovereignty. Disarmament would result in the dismantling of imperialist military bases on alien territories. And the withdrawal of imperialist forces would promote greater security and the preservation by the emergent nations of their independence.

Reductions in armaments outlays—if they proved possible—would offer opportunities considerably to expand economic, scientific and technical assistance to the developing countries.

In furtherance of the vital interests not only of the Soviet people but also of the broadest masses in all countries, the Soviet Union is waging a consistent struggle to slow down and stop the arms race started by the imperialists, to reach agreement on practical steps towards general and complete disarmament. Soviet policy on these issues enjoys the understanding and support of many countries.[24]

Looking back, we now know that at the time of the meeting of the 23rd Party Congress, the Soviet leadership had begun a massive buildup of ICBMs. In 1965 the U.S. Secretary of Defense had asserted that the Soviet Union had no intention of challenging the U.S. lead in strategic nuclear weaponry[25]; by 1969 the Soviet number of ICBMs exceeded those of the United States.

As shown previously, in the early 1960s Khrushchev claimed that the Soviet Union had an effective ABM system and their ABMs could "hit a fly in outerspace." Claims of this type continued in the early Brezhnev years. For example, in 1967 a prominent Soviet spokesman stated: "The USSR has far outstripped the United States not only in the creation of intercontinental and other rockets, but also in the area of antimissile defense. . . . In our country we have successfully solved the problem of destruction of rockets in flight."[26]

In the latter part of the 1960s the United States undertook two measures to counter the Soviet program: One was to plan for the deployment of an ABM system, Safeguard; the other, to develop MIRVed warheads, against which the Soviet state of the art in ABM defenses could not cope.

SOVIET INTEREST IN "ARMS CONTROL"

In the late 1960s, the Soviets became interested in talks on "arms control," whereas previously they had insisted on only "general and complete disarmament." This may have been a tactic to delay or de-rail the U.S.

ABM system. An indication of the change of thought was reflected in the third edition of Marshal Sokolovskiy's *Military Strategy*, which appeared in 1968.

In the first two editions of the book (1962, 1963), the chapter on the "armed forces of imperialist powers" had ended with the following statement:

> However, the American aggressors are forced to reckon with the might of the Armed Forces of the Soviet Union and the persistent demands of the peoples of the world who protest against nuclear war and actively support the proposals for the prohibition of nuclear weapons, for general and complete disarmament, and for achieving peace on earth.[27]

In the 1968 edition, the last expression, "for achieving peace on earth," had been eliminated, and the expression "for creating a sure system of international security" was substituted. While this work was at the printers, the Soviet leadership was making tentative agreements to begin talks with the United States on the subject of strategic arms limitations.

This change in Sokolovskiy's work reflected a major tactical shift. Foreign Minister Andrei Gromyko, during an address to the Supreme Soviet in June 1968, confirmed a change in Soviet tactics. During his discussion of international affairs, he indicated Soviet willingness to accept U.S. offers to negotiate on arms control. The signal was given as follows:

> Two policies, two lines in international affairs, stand out clearly in the struggle for disarmament.
>
> How often the Soviet Government has placed on the conference table proposals that were thoroughly weighed from the point of view of the broad interests of states and peoples!
>
> The Soviet Union has advanced a detailed program of general and complete disarmament under strict international control. What do we hear in reply? We are told that they are ready to discuss them, but to discuss for years upon years. They do not desire, however, to get down to business. . . .
>
> The Soviet Union's consistency in promoting a line aimed at disarmament, its major initiatives, that rally the forces of peace, make it possible to achieve certain results even if this does not lead at once to concrete agreements.[28]

Gromyko gave a broad review of Soviet efforts to stop the spread of nuclear weapons, and urged that these weapons be liquidated. He called for a nuclear test ban, stating that "no one can explode nuclear weapons underground in secret without being detected." Then, in typical Soviet fashion, he indicated the Kremlin's willingness to accept the U.S. urgings to discuss arms control:

> The Soviet Government is ready to examine the entire complex of other nuclear disarmament proposals together or separately, at one conference or at a series of meetings, having in mind that idle talk must be excluded from the vocabulary of those who are discussing proposals on such serious questions. . . .

> One of the unexplored regions of disarmament is the search for an understanding on mutual restriction and subsequent reduction of strategic vehicles for the delivery of nuclear weapons—offensive and defensive—including antimissiles. The Soviet Government is ready for an exchange of opinion on this question.[29]

Before any significant negotiations took place, Soviet troops invaded Czechoslovakia. To show displeasure at this act of aggression, the United States called off the talks. However, as usual, Washington's anger was short-lived. By early 1969 the new administration in the United States was seeking to resume negotiations. On July 10, 1969, in another address before the Supreme Soviet, Gromyko gave the Soviet position. In his talk, "Questions of the International Situation and the Soviet Union's Foreign Policy," he asserted that "Soviet foreign policy consistently defends the principle of peaceful coexistence of states, independent of this social system, and strives to rid mankind of another world war." In the latter part of this speech he brought up the Soviet willingness to talk on arms limitations.

> One of the most acute problems facing mankind remains the problem of halting the arms race and disarmament. The different aims pursued by states in their policies reflect their different approaches to this problem. . . .
> The Soviet Union has proceeded and is proceeding from the fact that the most radical step aimed at reducing the threat of another world war would be general and complete disarmament by the states. Governments that try to prove that such a decisive step is not yet matured are deceiving the peoples. The thoughts of state leaders and scientists should now be directed not to the determination of the conditions for the use of armament, which is now the favorite occupation at NATO military headquarters, but to disarmament, because the arms race long ago became a folly. . . .
> The Soviet Government has already reported to the Supreme Soviet its readiness to embark upon an exchange of views with the United States of America on so-called strategic arms. The U.S. Government has declared that it is preparing for an exchange of views; the Soviet Government is also preparing for this. One would like to express the hope that the two sides will approach this question taking into consideration its great importance.[30]

THE 24TH PARTY CONGRESS—THE YEAR BEFORE SALT I

Three years later, in March 1971, the 24th Party Congress met in Moscow. There was only occasional mention of "general and complete disarmament." The party had turned to a new course, as indicated by General Secretary Leonid Brezhnev in his "Report to the Central Committee of the Communist Party of the Soviet Union." Those concerned with Soviet policies today should note carefully what Brezhnev referred to as "the three main revolutionary forces of our day—socialism, the international working-class movement, and the peoples' national liberation struggle."

The Soviet Union and the fraternal socialist countries have made a big and active contribution to the struggle for peace and the security of nations. Our country's international positions have become even more secure, and the role of the world socialist system has increased. The great alliance of the three main revolutionary forces of our day—*socialism, the international working-class movement*, and *the peoples' national liberation struggle*—has continued to grow and gain in depth.[31] (Emphasis added.)

With respect to the Soviet Union's foreign policy:

> The Soviet Union is a peace-loving state, and this is determined by the very nature of our socialist system. The goals of Soviet foreign policy, as formulated by the 23rd Congress of the CPSU, consist in ensuring, together with other socialist countries, favourable international conditions for the construction of socialism and communism; in consolidating the unity and cohesion of the socialist countries, their friendship and brotherhood; supporting the national liberation movement and engaging in all-round cooperation with the young developing states; consistently standing up for the principle of peaceful coexistence between states with different social systems, and giving a resolute rebuff to the aggressive forces of imperialism, and safeguarding mankind from another world war.[32]

Although a "peace-loving state," as the Soviet Union modestly claims to be, certain actions still are required. The party's General Secretary explained the invasion of Czechoslovakia in his address to the Congress. The style is much the same as Khrushchev's explanation of why the Soviet Union in 1961 broke the moratorium on nuclear testing.

> In view of the appeals by Party and state leaders, Communists and working people of Czechoslovakia, and considering the danger posed to the socialist gains in that country, we and the fraternal socialist countries then jointly took a decision to render internationalist assistance to Czechoslovakia in defense of socialism. In the extraordinary conditions created by the forces of imperialism and counter-revolution, we were bound to do so by our class duty, loyalty to socialist internationalism, and the concern for the interests of our states and the future of socialism and peace in Europe.
>
> You will recall that in its document, "Lessons of the Crisis Development," a plenary meeting of the CC of the Communist Party of Czechoslovakia gave this assessment of the importance of the fraternal states' collective assistance:
>
> "The entry of the allied troops of the five socialist countries into Czechoslovakia was an act of international solidarity, meeting both the common interests of the Czechoslovakian working people and the interests of the international working class, the socialist community and the class interests of the international communist movement. This internationalist act saved the lives of thousands of men, ensured internal and external conditions for peaceful and tranquil labour, strengthened the Western borders of the socialist camp, and blasted the hopes of the imperialist circles for a revision of the results of the Second World War."[33]

With respect to the "international working-class movement," described earlier as one of the three great movements of the age, General Secretary Brezhnev had this to say:

The international working-class movement continues to play, as it has played in the past, the role of time-tested and militant vanguard of the revolutionary forces. The events of the past five-year period in the capitalist world have fully borne out the importance of the working class as the chief and strongest opponent of the rule of the monopolies, and as a centre rallying all the anti-monopoly forces.[34]

Brezhnev then brought up the question of "disarmament."

Comrades, disarmament is one of the most important international problems of our day. We seek to secure concrete results reducing the danger of war, and to prevent the peoples from accepting the arms race as an inevitable evil. . . .
Treaties banning the stationing of nuclear weapons in outer space and on the sea- and ocean-floor have been concluded. But what has been achieved constitutes only the first few steps. It is our aim to bring about a situation in which nuclear energy shall serve peaceful purposes only.[35]

LIMITATION OF STRATEGIC ARMAMENTS

Brezhnev then switched to a discussion of the "limitation of strategic armaments," rather than disarmament in general.

We are engaged in negotiations with the USA on a limitation of strategic armaments. Their favourable outcome would make it possible to avoid another round in the missile arms race, and to release considerable resources for constructive purposes. We are seeking to have the negotiations produce positive results.
However, one should like to emphasize that disarmament talks in general, to say nothing of those involving discussion of highly delicate military-technical aspects, can be productive only if equal consideration is given to the security interests of the parties, and if no one seeks to obtain unilateral advantages.

He then stressed that the professed Soviet goal still is for "general and complete disarmament."

The struggle for an end to the arms race, both in nuclear and conventional weapons, and for disarmament—all the way to general and complete disarmament—will continue to be one of the most important lines in the foreign-policy activity of the CPSU and the Soviet state.

Brezhnev next turned to a discussion of Moscow's relations with the "capitalist" world. With respect to the United States:

We proceed from the assumption that it is possible to improve relations between the USSR and the USA. Our principal line with respect to the capitalist countries, including the USA, is consistently and fully to practice the principles of peaceful coexistence, to develop mutually advantageous ties, and to cooperate, with states prepared to do so, in strengthening peace, making our relations with them as stable as possible. But we have to consider whether we are dealing with a real desire to settle outstanding issues at the negotiation table or an attempt to conduct a "positions of strength" policy.[36]

Later, Brezhnev assured that:

> *The Soviet Union has countered the aggressive policy of imperialism with its policy of active defence of peace and strengthening of international security.* [Emphasis in original.] The main lines of this policy are well known. Our Party, our Soviet state, in cooperation with the fraternal countries and other peace-loving states, and with the wholehearted support of many millions of people throughout the world, have now for many years been waging a struggle on these lines, taking a stand for the cause of peace and friendship among nations. The CPSU regards the following as the *basic* concrete tasks of this struggle in the present situation.
>
> *First*: To eliminate the hotbeds of war in Southeast Asia and in the Middle East, and to promote a political settlement in these areas on the basis of respect for the legitimate rights of states and peoples subjected to aggression. . . .
>
> *Second*: To proceed from the final recognition of the territorial changes that took place in Europe as a result of the Second World War. To bring about a radical turn towards a detente and peace on this continent. To ensure the convocation and success of an all-European conference. . . .
>
> *Third*: To conclude treaties putting a ban on nuclear, chemical, and bacteriological weapons. . . .
>
> *Fourth*: To invigorate the struggle to halt the race in all types of weapons. We favour the convocation of a world conference to consider disarmament questions to their full extent.
>
> We stand for the dismantling of foreign military bases. We stand for a reduction of armed forces and armaments in areas where the military confrontation is especially dangerous, above all in Central Europe.
>
> We consider it advisable to work out measures reducing the probability of accidental outbreak or deliberate fabrication of armed incidents and their development into international crises, into war.
>
> The Soviet Union is prepared to negotiate agreements on reducing military expenditures, above all by the major powers.[37]

This speech was delivered in March 1971, the year before SALT I. Negotiations were under way at the time, and certain points made by Brezhnev have since been resolved. For example: (1) Communist, Soviet-backed forces forced the United States out of Southeast Asia, and the Soviet Union took over certain bases constructed by the United States. (2) The Helsinki Accords, signed by the United States, legalized the boundaries of Eastern Europe, as drawn up by the Soviet Union.

PROBLEMS OF WAR AND PEACE: A SOVIET PERSPECTIVE

In 1972, the year President Richard Nixon went to Moscow to sign SALT I, Moscow's Progress Publishers issued *Problems of War and Peace: A Critical Analysis of Bourgeois Theories*. No author for the work was listed.

For those in the United States who thought that the signing of SALT I had brought in a new era in U.S.-Soviet relations, the book would have made disturbing reading. Below are some excerpts:

> Today, the arms race launched by imperialism has assumed unprecedented proportions. Imperialism has placed the vast resources of the technological revolution in the service of militarism. The technological revolution has brought about a colossal increase in the destructive capacity of the instruments of war. The stock-piles of nuclear and thermonuclear weapons that already exist in the world are enough to threaten the very existence of human society, and the stock-piling and development of nuclear and other weapons of mass destruction continues. The arms race has become a major source of international tension, greatly increasing the danger of a world war. All this makes the problem of disarmament one of vital importance to mankind in our day and age ....[38]
>
> Is there a real possibility of achieving general disarmament? Marxist-Leninists have no hesitation in answering in the affirmative. The theory of scientific socialism from the outset connected the possibility of preventing wars and reducing armaments with action on the part of the masses and all progressive social forces. The founders of scientific socialism rejected the fatalistic approach to the assessment of the concrete processes of social development, and pointed to the need to conduct anti-militarist activities in the conditions of capitalism and the possibility of solving the practical questions of struggle against the burden of arms.
>
> Today, the Marxist demand for disarmament has been enriched with new concrete content and its importance is greater than ever. New possibilities have arisen for its solution. This can be deduced from the scientific analysis of the tendencies of the present age, taking careful account of the main trends of world development, the relationship of class forces in the world, and various other relevant material and moral factors. The possibility of achieving disarmament exists today because imperialism and the militarism engendered by it have lost their dominant role in international relations, while socialism has become the decisive factor of world development.
>
> For the first time in history powerful organized forces are demanding disarmament: the Soviet Union, which has taken the lead in decisive branches of science and technology; the other socialist countries, who have placed their economic and political might in the service of peace; the international labour movement and Communist parties throughout the world, who consider it their first duty to save mankind from the horrors of a new world war and put an end to war; the peoples of Asia, Africa, and Latin America, who are vitally interested in preserving peace; national liberation movements, throwing off the chains of imperialism and colonialism, and the world peace movement uniting in its ranks people of various social positions, political opinions and religious convictions. The growth and consolidation of these progressive social factors, their unity and solidarity, improves the prospects for progress in the question of disarmament.[39]
>
> The events of the last few years have confirmed the correctness of the Marxist-Leninist definition of the character of the present age, its content and major trends: namely, that the main course of mankind's development is determined by the world socialist system, the international working class and

all other revolutionary forces. The International Meeting of Communist and Workers' Parties held in Moscow in 1969 expressed the opinion that, in view of the changes that have taken place in the world during the last decade, stable peace is no longer a utopian dream but a perfectly attainable aim, and appealed to the peoples to struggle hard for general and complete disarmament.

On the basis of the theory of scientific socialism that international disarmament of states under international control is perfectly feasible, for years the Soviet Union, supported by the other socialist countries, has been waging a ceaseless struggle for the attainment of universal peace. . . .

Efforts to halt the race in all types of weapons and achieve disarmament occupied a prominent place among the basic tasks set forth in the programme for peace and international security passed by the 24th Congress of the CPSU. . . .

The solution of disarmament problems would be facilitated by the implementation of other proposals of the programme, designed to increase international security, namely: the elimination of hotbeds of war in South-East Asia and in the Middle East and a political settlement in these areas on the basis of the legitimate rights of states and peoples subjected to aggression; repudiation of the threat or use of force in settling outstanding issues and the conclusion of appropriate bilateral or regional treaties; the adoption of measures to ensure a radical turn towards detente and peace in Europe and the convocation and success of an all-European conference; the simultaneous annulment of the Warsaw Treaty and of the North Atlantic alliance or—as a first step—dismantling of their military organizations; full implementation of the UN decisions on the abolition of the remaining colonial regimes; the development of relations of mutually advantageous cooperation in every sphere, including such problems as the conservation of the environment, development of power and other natural resources, development of transport and communications, and so on.

Determined action in this direction would substantially facilitate the solution of the cardinal problem of universal, total disarmament, opening a new chapter in the history of human society.[40]

President Nixon traveled to Moscow in May 1972 to sign a treaty on the limitation of strategic arms. In the aftermath of the SALT I agreement, one U.S. proponent of the treaty wrote:

Defending people is the most troublesome of all strategic options, for stability demands that each of the two societies stand wholly exposed to the destructive power of the other. Acceptance of this severe and novel doctrine illustrates the growing sophistication of Soviet thinking.[41]

In contrast to this view, four years after the treaty was signed a prominent Soviet spokesman asserted:

Now victory or defeat in war will depend on how well the state will be able to reliably protect important objectives on their own territory from destruction by strikes from the air and out of space.[42]

FINAL OBSERVATIONS

Today, fifteen years after the signing of SALT I, the United States and the Soviet Union again are actively engaged in arms control negotiations. Many people in the United States hold great expectations that something worthwhile and permanent will be achieved.

Much of the hope is based on the belief that major changes have taken place in the Soviet leadership. But as discussed earlier, the men now in the Politburo do not represent a new slate, coming into high positions for the first time. Instead, they represent a continuum, and will modify policies only as technology and the world balance of forces change.

Rather than concentrating solely on arms control negotiations, as we in the West tend to do, it might be good to look at what has appeared basic in Soviet foreign policies over the past decades—to examine what has dropped out, and what has been added.

Since 1967, Soviet spokesmen have stressed four "mighty" forces capable of defending the peace: the world socialist system, the international workers' movement, the national liberation movement, and the antiwar and peace movement.[43] All are used to prevent the United States from building up its own defenses. The Soviet military buildup, in contrast, is portrayed as being in the interest of peace.

In arms control treaties we have signed with the Soviets, there are no provisions for remedial actions in the event of violations. The Soviet leadership, representing a system that considers itself infallible, *cannot admit to violations on its own part*. When a violation is clear, as it was in the case of the Soviet violation of the moratorium on nuclear testing in the early 1960s, the Soviet leadership must claim otherwise. And when a violation does occur, those in the United States supporting arms control as a concept become a party to the Soviet stand—they themselves cannot admit that the Soviets have violated an agreement, because they have no recommendation to make about what actions should be taken against the Soviets because of the violation.

Finally, a fundamental goal of Marxism-Leninism and of the Kremlin is the elimination of "capitalism"—meaning those nations not under the Kremlin's control—and the "victory of communism," which equates to the victory of the Soviet state. A careful reading of Soviet writings from the 1950s to the signing of SALT I and to the present day strongly suggests that Soviet participation in arms control activities simply is a tactic to contribute to the basic Soviet goal.

Soviet textbooks on Marxism-Leninism may be dull reading for most Americans, but they provide certain insights into Soviet actions and policies. As one Soviet spokesman asserted:

> The basic positions of the [political] strategy of the Communist party form

the political base for the military strategy of the Soviet Army. Let us examine these positions.

- Concentration of the main forces of the revolution at the decisive moment at the most vulnerable point for the enemy. . . .
- Selection of the moment for the decisive strike. . . .
- Unswerving conduct of the course already selected in spite of difficulties and complications on the way to the goal. . . .
- Maneuvering with the reserves which are meant for regular retreat, when the enemy is strong, when retreat is inevitable. . . in order to preserve them.[44]

In the Soviet Union, "military strategy is subordinate to and derives from political strategy." It is this political strategy, on which Soviet positions on arms control are based, that is so often overlooked in our own arms control negotiations with Communist party representatives.

NOTES

1. N.S. Khrushchev, *On Peaceful Co-Existence* (Moscow: Foreign Languages Publishing House, 1961), p. 10.
2. Ibid., p. 83.
3. Ibid., p. 88.
4. Ibid., p. 89.
5. Ibid., p. 135.
6. Ibid., p. 136.
7. Ibid., p. 137.
8. N.S. Khrushchev, *Communism—Peace and Happiness for the People* (Moscow: Foreign Languages Publishing House, 1963), pp. 421–422.
9. N.S. Khrushchev, *Prevent War, Safeguard Peace* (Moscow: Progress Publishers, 1962), p. 25.
10. Ibid., p. 29.
11. Ibid.
12. Ibid., p. 30.
13. Ibid., p. 31.
14. Ibid., pp. 40–41.
15. Ibid., p. 42.
16. Ibid., pp. 233–234.
17. Ibid., p. 234.
18. Ibid.
19. Ibid., pp. 241–242.
20. Ibid., pp. 258–259.
21. Ibid., pp. 280–281.
22. Ibid., pp. 281–282.
23. Alexander Dallin, editor, *The Soviet Union, Arms Control, and Disarmament* (New York: School of International Affairs, Columbia University, 1964), p. 23.

24. *23rd CPSU Congress: Results and Prospects* (Moscow: Novosti Press Agency Publishing House, n.d.), pp. 79–80.
25. Robert Strange McNamara, "Is Russia Slowing Down the Arms Race?," *U.S. News and World Report*, Vol. 58, No. 5, April 1965, pp. 52–61.
26. P.T. Astashenkov, *Soviet Rocket Troops* (Moscow: Voyenizdat, 1967), p. 225.
27. V.D. Sokolovskiy, *Soviet Military Strategy*, third edition, edited, with commentary and analysis by Harriet Fast Scott (New York: Crane, Russak and Company, 1976), p. 117.
28. A. Gromyko, "Report Delivered to the USSR Supreme Soviet," June 26, 1968, TASS International Service; reprinted in FBIS, *Soviet Union*, June 27, 1968, p. B-5.
29. Ibid., p. B-7.
30. A. Gromyko, "Questions of the International Situation and the Soviet Union's Foreign Policy," from a report by A. Gromyko to the session of the USSR Supreme Soviet on July 10, 1969; reprinted in FBIS, *Soviet Union*, July 11, 1969, pp. B-14–15.
31. L.I. Brezhnev, *24th Congress of the CPSU: Report of the Central Committee of the Communist Party of the Soviet Union* (Moscow: Novosti Press Agency Publishing House, 1971), p. 6.
32. Ibid., p. 8.
33. Ibid., p. 22.
34. Ibid., pp. 29–30.
35. Ibid., p. 44.
36. Ibid., p. 47.
37. Ibid., pp. 49–51.
38. *Problems of War and Peace: A Critical Analysis of Bourgeois Theories* (no author given) (Moscow: Progress Publishers, 1972), p. 359.
39. Ibid., p. 360.
40. Ibid., pp. 361–362.
41. John Newhouse, *Cold Dawn: The Story of SALT* (New York: Holt, Rinehart, Winston, 1973), p. 3.
42. G.V. Zimin, *The Development of Anti-Air Defense* (Moscow: Voyenizdat, 1976), p. 191.
43. V.G. Afanasyev, *Fundamentals of Scientific Communism* (Moscow: Progress Publishers, 3rd printing, 1982), p. 103. For a discussion of these movements, see chapters 3, 4, and 5.
44. P.A. Chuvikov, *Marxism-Leninism on War and Army* (Moscow: Voyenizdat, 1956), p. 138.

Bibliography

Afanasyev, V.G. *Marxist Philosophy*. Moscow: Progress Publishers, 1980.

Aleksandrov, V.S. *The Political Strategy and Tactics of the Communist Party*. Moscow, 1971.

Ambartsumov, Yevgeniy, and Adolf Dobieszewski. *Politics and Socialism*. Trans. JPRS–EPS–85–007–L, June 14, 1985.

Analyses of Activities of MoD under the Order of the Ministry of National Defense. April 13, 1965. Czech Top Secret.

Antonov-Ovseyenko, Anton. *The Time of Stalin*. New York: Harper & Row, 1981.

"Arbatov Views CPSU Conference Stand on Disarmament." *Komsomolskaya Pravda*. Translation: FBIS, USSR International Affairs, March 12, 1986.

Arzumanov, G. "The Armies and Military-Political Blocks of Imperialist States." *Communist of the Armed Forces*, January 1986. Translation: Harriet Fast Scott.

Baroch, Charles T. *Freedom Under Communist Siege: A Primer on Marxism-Leninism*. Republican Study Committee, October 28, 1985.

Beecher, William. "Brezhnev Termed Detente a Ruse, 1973 Report Said." *The Boston Globe*, February 11, 1977.

Beobyeb, E. *Voyennaya Vestnik*, No. 3, 1964.

Booth, Ken. *Strategy and Ethnocentrism*. New York: Holmes & Meier Publishers, Inc., 1979.

Churchill, Winston II. *Defending the West*. Westport, Conn.: Arlington House Publishers, 1981.

Codevilla, Angelo M. "How SDI Is Being Undone From Within." *Commentary*, May 1986.

Crozier, Brian. "Introduction." In Ion Ratiu. *Moscow Challenges the World*. London: The Sherwood Press, 1986.

———. *The Price of Peace*. Second, revised edition. Washington, D.C.: The National Center for Public Policy Research, 1983.

———. *Strategy of Survival*. Westport, Conn.: Arlington House Publishers, 1978.

———, Drew Middleton, and Jeremy Murray-Brown, *This War Called Peace*. New York: Universe Books, 1985.

Dailey, Brian, and Patrick Parker, editors. *Soviet Strategic Deception*. Lexington, Mass.: Lexington Books, 1968.

Department of Defense. *Soviet Military Power*. Washington, D.C.: U.S. Government Printing Office, March 1986.

Diplomaticus (John Ausland). "Stalinist Theory and Soviet Foreign Policy." *Review of Politics*, October 1952.

Douglass, Joseph D., Jr. "Chemical Weapons: An Imbalance of Terror." *Strategic Review*, Summer 1982.

———. "Soviet Strategic Deception." *Defense Science 2002+*, October 1984.

———, and Amoretta M. Hoeber. *Selected Readings From Military Thought 1963–1973, Studies in Communist Affairs*, Vol. 5, Part II. Washington, D.C.: U.S. Government Printing Office, 1982.

Dyadkin, Iosif G. *Unnatural Deaths in the USSR 1928–1954*. Translation: Tania Deruguine. New Brunswick, N.J.: Transaction Books, 1983.

Dziak, John J. "Soviet Deception: The Organizational and Operational Tradition." *Soviet Strategic Deception*. Lexington, Mass.: Lexington Books, 1986.

Epstein, Edward J. "Incorporating Analysis of Foreign Governments' Deception into the U.S. Analytical System." In Roy Godson, editor. *Intelligence Requirements for the 1980s: Analysis and Estimates*. Washington, D.C.: National Strategy Information Center, 1980.

Finder, Joseph. *Red Carpet*. New York: Holt, Rinehart and Winston, 1983.

Finney, John W. *New York Times*, September 17, 1973.

Ford, Robert A.D. "The Soviet Union: The Next Decade." *Foreign Affairs*, Summer 1984.

Fundamentals of Marxism-Leninism. Moscow: Foreign Languages Publishing House, 1961.

The Fundamentals of Marxist-Leninist Philosophy. Moscow: Progress Publishers, 1974.

Gareev, Makhmut Al. *M. V. Frunze—Military Theorist*. McLean, Va.: Pergamon-Brassey's International Defense Publishers, Inc., 1987.

Green, William C. *U.S. Interpretations of Soviet Publications on the Nuclear Weapons Policy of the USSR 1950–1980*. Ph.D. Thesis, University of Southern California, May 1986.

Golitsyn, Anatoliy. "From the Satellites to the Partners," unpublished manuscript, 1983.

———. *New Lies for Old*. New York: Dodd Mead & Co., 1985.

Gouré, Leon. "'Nuclear Winter' in Soviet Mirrors." *Strategic Review*, Summer 1985.

Haig, Alexander M., Jr. *Caveat.* New York: Macmillan Publishing Co., 1984.

Harris, William R. "Soviet Maskirovka and Arms Control Verification." In Brian Dailey and Patrick J. Parker, editors, *Soviet Strategic Deception.* Lexington, Mass.: Lexington Books, 1987.

Joshua, Wynfred. *Detente in Soviet Strategy.* Defense Intelligence Agency, September 1975.

Kapchenko, K. "The Leninist Theory and Practice of Socialist Foreign Policy." In *Principles of Lenin's Foreign Policy.* Moscow: Novosti Press Agency Publishing House, 1970.

Khrushchev, N.S. *Disarmament—The Way to Secure Peace and Friendship Between Nations.* Report to the Supreme Soviet of the USSR and the Appeal to the Governments and Parliaments of the World, January 14–15, 1960.

———. *Prevent War, Safeguard Peace.* Moscow: Progress Publishers, 1962.

Kirkpatrick, Jeane J. "The Myth of Moral Equivalence." *Imprimis.* Hillsdale, Mich.: Hillsdale College, January 1986.

Kissinger, Henry. *White House Years.* Boston: Little, Brown & Company, 1979.

———. *Years of Upheaval.* Boston: Little, Brown & Company, 1982.

Kohler, Phyllis Penn, editor and translator. *Journey for Our Time: The Journals of the Marquis de Custine.* London: Arther Barker, Ltd., 1951.

Larionov, V.V. "The Relaxation of Tension and the Principle of Equal Security." *Krasnaya Zvesda*, July 18, 1974. Translation: USAF, *Soviet Press Selected Translations*, No. 74–7, July 31, 1974.

Lenin, V.I. *One Step Forward, Two Steps Back.* Moscow: Progress Publishers, 1973.

———. *Works.* Vol. 22.

———. *Complete Works.* Third Edition. Vol. 23.

Leninist Strategy and Tactics. Moscow: Novosti Press Agency Publishing House, 1969.

Marxism-Leninism on War and Army. Moscow: Progress Publishers, 1972. Translation: U.S. Government Printing Office, *Soviet Military Thought*, No 5, 1974.

Mayagkov, Aleksei. *Inside the KGB.* London: Foreign Affairs Publishing Company, 1976.

Nitze, Paul H. "Living With The Soviets." *Foreign Affairs*, Winter 1984-1985.

Nixon, Richard. *The Memoirs of Richard Nixon.* New York: Grosset & Dunlap, 1978.

———. *U.S. Foreign Policy for the 1970's, A Report to the Congress by Richard Nixon.* Washington, D.C.: U.S. Government Printing Office, February 18, 1970.

———. *U.S. Foreign Policy for the 1970's, A Report to the Congress by Richard Nixon.* Washington, D.C.: U.S. Government Printing Office, February 9, 1972.

———. *U.S. Foreign Policy for the 1970's, A Report to the Congress by Richard Nixon.* Washington, D.C.: U.S. Government Printing Office, May 3, 1973.

Ogarkov, N.F. *History Teaches Vigilance.* Moscow: Voyenizdat. Translation: JPRS–UMA–85–021–L, August 30, 1985.

Parry, Albert. "Lenin's Rope." *Novoye Russkoye Slovo*, June 25, 1978. Translation: Harriet Fast Scott.

Party Congresses. Foreign Broadcast Information Service, February 26, 1985.

The Philosophical Heritage of V.I. Lenin and Problems of Contemporary War. Moscow: Voyenizdat, 1972.

Pincher, Chapman. *The Secret Offensive.* London: Sidgwick & Jackson, 1985.

Pipes, Richard. *Survival Is Not Enough.* New York: Simon & Schuster, 1984.

Ponomarev, Boris. "The Communists and Our Day's Pressing Issues." *World Marxist Review*, February 1985.

Present Day Bourgeois Theory About Capitalism and Socialism. Moscow: USSR Academy of Sciences, 1970.

Problems of the Party's Military Policy in Light of the 13th Congress of the Communist Party of Czechoslovakia. Czech Secret. Translation: DIA LN 048–79, January 1979.

Ra'anan, Uri, and Richard H. Schultz, Jr. "Methodologies for Assessing and Projecting Soviet Strategic Defense and Arms Control Policy." Paper presented at the Conference on Emerging Doctrines and Technologies: Implications for Global and Regional Political–Military Balances. Fletcher School of Law and Diplomacy, April 16–18, 1986.

Rose, Stephen, editor. *CBW: Chemical and Biological Warfare.* Boston: Beacon Press, 1968.

Sakharov, Andrei D. "Sakharov Urges Europeans to Join U.S. in Standing Up to Soviet Expansionism." *Washington Star*, June 9–11, 1980.

Scott, Harriet Fast, and William F. Scott, editors. *The Soviet Art of War.* Boulder, Colo.: Westview Press, 1982.

Sejna, Jan. *We Will Bury You.* London: Sidgwick & Jackson, 1982.

———, and Joseph D. Douglass, Jr. *Decision-Making in Communist Countries: An Inside View.* McLean, Va.: Pergamon-Brassey's, 1986.

Shapalin, N. "Ideological Work, Experience, Opinions." *Krasnaya Zvezda.* Translation: FBIS, USSR National Affairs, Military Developments, July 31, 1984.

Shevchenko, Arkady N. *Breaking With Moscow.* New York: Alfred A. Knopf, 1985.

Shtemenko, S.M. *The General Staff During the War.* Second Edition. Moscow, 1981.

Sleeper, Raymond S., editor. *A Lexicon of Marxist-Leninist Semantics.* Western Goals, 1983.

Smith, Hedrick. *The Russians.* New York: Quadrangle/The New York Times Book Company, 1976.

Sokolovskiy, V.D. *Soviet Military Strategy.* Harriet Fast Scott, editor. New York: Crane Russak, 1974.

Taubman, Philip. "Gorbachev's Gloomy America." *New York Times,* November 15, 1985.

Thorin, Duane. *The Pugwash Movement and U.S. Arms Policy.* Oakton, Va.: Monte Cristo Press, 1965.

Toth, Robert C. "U.S. Faces Arms Decision Amid Soviet Cheating." *Los Angeles Times,* April 16, 1986.

"Trickery on Chemical War." *Washington Star,* June 5, 1978.

Trukhanovsky, V. "Proletarian Internationalism and Peaceful Coexistence—Foundation of the Leninist Foreign Policy." *Principles of Lenin's Foreign Policy.* Moscow: Novosti Press Agency Publishing House, 1970.

U.S. Arms Control and Disarmament Agency. *Arms Control and Disarmament Agreements.* August 1980.

U.S. Congress, House. Permanent Select Committee on Intelligence. *Soviet Covert Action and Propaganda.* Central Intelligence Agency. 1980. Edited and reprinted in *Soviet Covert Action (The Forgery Offensive).* Hearings Before the Subcommittee on Oversight.

U.S. Congress, House. Permanent Select Committee on Intelligence. *Soviet Strategic Forces.* Hearings Before the Subcommittee on Oversight, February 7 and 20, 1980.

U.S. Congress, Senate. Committee on the Judiciary. Subcommittee to Investigate the Administration of the Internal Security Act and Internal Security Laws. *Analysis of the Khrushchev Speech of January 6, 1961.* 1961

U.S. Congress, Senate. Committee on the Judiciary. *Khrushchev's Strategy and Its Meaning for America: A Study Presented to the Subcommittee to Investigate the Administration of the Internal Security Act and Others.* 1956.

Volkogonov, D.A. editor, et al. *War and Army.* Moscow: Voyenizdat, 1977.

Voslensky, Michael. *Nomenklatura.* Garden City, N.Y.: Doubleday & Co. Inc., 1984.

———. *Nomenklatura: Anatomy of the Soviet Ruling Class.* Translated by Eric Mosbacher. London: The Bodley Head, 1984.

Vyshinsky, Andrei. *The Law of the Soviet State.* New York: Macmillan Company, 1948.

Weeks, Albert L. "The Kremlin's Russian Superiority Complex." *Military Intelligence,* January–March 1986. Citing Paul W. Blackstock and Bert F. Hoselitz, editors. *The Russian Menace to Europe by Karl Marx and Friedrich Engels.* Glencoe, Ill.: The Free Press, 1952.

Will, George F. "Abolishing the 20th Century." *Newsweek,* December 9, 1985.

World History in Facts: USSR and European Socialist States. Prague: Political Literature Publishing Company, 1964.

INDEX

ABM. *See* Antiballistic missiles (ABM).
Academicians. *See* "Learned Professionals."
Academy of Sciences, CSSR, 65, 66, 77
Academy of Sciences, USSR, 19, 25n, 51, 65, 76–79, 129; Commission on Disarmament, 78, 79
Academy of Social Sciences, USSR, 45
Accident Avoidance Measures, 161
Accidents Measures Agreement of 1971, 104
ACDA. *See* Arms Control and Disarmament Agency (ACDA).
"Active Measures," Soviet use of, 30, 42, 44, 60, 78, 87, 112, 114, 115–116; "Activist approach," 76
Administration Department, CSSR. *See* Administrative Organs Department, CSSR.
Administration Department, USSR. *See* Administrative Organs Department, USSR.
Administration for Foreign Relations, USSR, 127
Administrative Organs Department, CSSR, 73, 133
Administrative Organs Department, USSR, 42, 44, 46–47, 48, 50, 56, 57, 125, 126, 127
Administration for Special Propaganda, USSR, 127

Administration of Special State Interests, USSR, 47, 49, 127. *See also* Deception.
Aerial photography zone in Europe, 170
Afghanistan, 86, 92, 99, 115, 150, 154n, 159, 160. *See also* Chemical and biological weapons (CBW).
Agayantz, Ivan, 9
Agayantz, Nikolai, 9
Akhromeyev, Sergei, 100, 120n
Albania, 103
American Security Council, 37n
Andropov, Yuri, 15, 59, 100, 143
Angola, 37n
Antarctic Treaty (of 1959), 161; (of 1961), 23n
Antiballistic missiles (ADM), 155; ABM Treaty of 1972, 5, 81nn, 104, 112, 155; experiments, 72; Soviet national system, 85, 174; Soviet treaty violations, 89; US Safeguard system, 175
Antonov, Alexei I., 64
Arms Control and Disarmament Agency (ACDA), 172
Arms race: Nixon tries to avert CBW race, 68; and SALT II, 73; Soviet propaganda about, 32, 64, 90, 98, 105, 111, 174, 176, 178, 180; US feels it necessary to stop, 8; and US nuclear testing, 72, 166; USSR aware it could lose, 118

Atlantic Alliance. *See* North Atlantic Treaty Organization (NATO).
Ausland, John, 29

Balance of power, 117; Mao's secret speech on, 31; NEP and impact on, 34; Soviet military, 45, 79, 123, 124, 128, 129, 148; use of arms control in shift of, 44, 94; Western view, 30
Beecher, William, 9
Belgium, 30
Beria, Lavrenti P., 15
Berlin Wall, 66, 67, 83, 84, 92nn, 140, 152n
Bezmenov, Yuri. *See* Schuman, Tomas
Biological weapons. *See* Chemical and biological weapons.
Biological Weapons Convention (1972), 159
Brezhnev, Leonid, 4, 42, 58, 81nn, 125, 127, 131, 174; adoption of "peaceful coexistence," 44; "Brezhnev" Constitution of the USSR, 150; and CBWs, 68; Declaration of Basic Principles, 146; "revolutionary wars," 5; role in arms control, 46, 47; statements of, 176–179; view of detente, 9
Brezhnev Doctrine, 6, 150
Brezhnev-Kosygin-Podgorny troika, 100
Britain. *See* United Kingdom.
Bukharin, Nikolai, 141
Bulgaria, 84, 119n; Communist Party of, 32
Byelorussia, USSR, 99

Capitalism: and arms control, 124; coexistence with communism and socialism, 17, 18–20, 50, 54, 57, 97, 102, 106, 130, 151; conflict within capitalist countries, 147; destruction of, 1, 16, 23, 24, 29, 31, 32, 38, 41, 42, 98, 122, 123, 142; exploitation of by Soviet Union, 34, 35, 148; language of, 138, 139; Soviet fascination with, 108; Soviet recruiting of capitalists, 39; Soviet view of, 13, 15, 22, 56, 58, 134, 135; US distinguished from European, 144

Capitalists. *See* Capitalism.
Carter, James E., 58
Catholic People's Party, CSSR, 131
CBW. *See* Chemical/Biological weapons (CBW).
Central Committee of the Communist Party of Czechoslovakia, 56, 177
Central Committee of the Communist Party of the Soviet Union (CC): Administrative Organs Department of, 44, 77; apparat, 143; Brezhnev's report to, 176; departments of, 46; Institute of Marxism-Leninism of, 45; International Department of, 9, 42, 43, 46, 47, 48, 55, 56, 60, 64, 70, 78, 79, 126; leaders of, 162; Lenin's notes to, 60; Main Political Administration Department of, 71; objective of splitting the West, 42; responsibility to Soviet homeland, 72, 166; Secretariat of, 21
Central Europe, 179
Central Intelligence Agency (CIA), 52n, 86
Chalfont, Alun, 8
Chandra, Romesh, 78. *See also* World Peace Council
Chazov, Yevgeni I., 114
Cheating Doctrine, Soviet, 115–116; Soviet views on cheating, 112–115
Chebrikov, Viktor M., 71
Chemical and biological weapons (CBW): 1968 arms control conference on CBW, 77; 1972 Biological and Toxin Weapons Convention, 69, 86; Agent Orange, 67; binary weapons, 115; conventions on, 104, 114–115; conventional-CBW conflict, 118; "mutual restraint" in, 67, 68; nerve gas testing by United States, 67–68; Soviet cheating and deception in field of, 67–70, 85; Soviet R&D in, 67; Soviet substitute for nuclear weapons, 50, 125, 129; Soviet use of in Afghanistan, Laos and Kampuchea, 86, 114–115, 159; stored in space for future use, 65; technological advances in, 34, 69; Yellow Rain, 86, 115

Index

Chernenko, Konstantin, 58
Chernobyl, 119n
Chicherin, Georgi V., 5
Chief Intelligence Directorate of the Soviet General Staff (GRU), 46, 47, 59, 77, 101, 112, 127
China. *See* People's Republic of China (PRC).
Churchill, Winston, 80
CIA. *See* Central Intelligence Agency (CIA).
Class struggle, 6, 16, 18, 80, 149
Classifications, 66, 89; Secret, 66; Top Secret, 65, 66, 76; "State Importance," 66
Clifford, Clark, 37n
CMEA. *See* Council for Mutual Economic Assistance (CMEA/COMECON).
Cold War, 31, 33, 41, 57
Collectivization of agriculture, 33–35. *See also* New economic Plan (NEP), Lenin, Vladimir Ilyich
COMECON. *See* Council for Mutual Economic Assistance (CMEA/COMECON).
COMINFORM. *See* Communist Information Bureau (COMINFORM).
Comintern. *See* Communist International (Comintern).
Commission on Disarmament. *See* Academy of Sciences, USSR.
Committee on the Present Danger, 37n
Committee of State Security (Komitet Gosudarstvennoy Bezopasnosti—KGB), 65, 71, 92n; development of arms control strategy, 48, 125, 127; Disinformation Department D of the KGB, 9, 42; influence of, 100, 101; *New Times*, 54; relations with Main Operations Administration, 126; relationship to Administrative Organs Department, 44; reorganization and restructuring of, 42–43, 45–46, 50; Soviet civilian connections with, 55; US vulnerability to, 60; use of deception, 75–77, 79, 92n, 115; KGB–MVD subcomplex, 108

Communism, 70, 77; and anti-Western education, 57; and arms control negotiations, 183; Communist cause, 113; Communist ideology as a vital force today, 2, 13, 14, 28, 33, 35, 141, 143, 145, 167; CPSU, 121; disarmament and, 39; forces of in Southeast Asia, 177; in China, 14; in the world, 180; international, 4, 145, 177; international Communist movement, 177; Marxism-Leninism and, 3, 20, 29, 31, 34, 120n, 148; morality of, 22; press organs of, 46; spread of, 41; strategy, 182; tenets, 163; triumph of, 16, 28, 73, 133; use of disinformation in Communist societies, 115, 140–143; "victory of communism" goal, 182
Communist Information Bureau (COMINFORM), 43, 52n
Communist International (Comintern): 39, 42, 61, 78, 126; 3rd World Congress of, 39
Communist Party of Czechoslovakia, 132, 177; 13th Congress of, 66, 81n
Communist Party of the Soviet Union (CPSU): 20th Party Congress (1956), 31, 41, 163; 21st Party Congress (1959), 31, 45; 23rd Party Congress (1961), 173, 174, 177–179; 24th Party Congress (1971), 176, 181; 27th Party Congress (1986), 22, 40, 50, 51, 52, 54, 71, 129; and adherence to Marxism-Leninism, 7, 122; apparatus, 7, 15, 25n; and arms control, 64, 99, 101, 183; Central Committee meeting, July 4–12, 1955, 42; and Constitution of USSR, 28; as controller of Soviet policy, 1, 17, 20, 30, 121, 143, 150–152, 166, 182; and crisis of Communist regime, 15; daily, 143; and deception, 71, 72, 73; elite, 144; functionaries, 102, 115; and General Secretary of, 46; Khrushchev, 162; leaders, 132, 133; and Lenin, 60; line, 106, 120n; and military research, 77;

program of, 58; and propaganda, 125; workers, 150
Congress of Communist Parties (1960), 45
Convention for the Definition of Aggression (1933), 98
Convention on Environmental Modification of 1977, 161
Convention on the Physical Protection of Nuclear Material, 161
Conventional Weapons Convention, 1981, 160
Convergence theory, 18–19, 106, 109
Cosmos. *See* Space.
Council of Ministers, Poland, 100
Council of Ministers, USSR, 48, 171
Council for Mutual Economic Assistance (CMEA/COMECON), 50, 119n, 144
Cuba, 83, 87, 136; Cuban Constitution of 1976, 150; Cuban Missile Crisis, 84, 86, 107, 136, 173; offensive weapons in, 159; Soviet missiles in, 167, 168
Czechoslovak Socialist Republic (CSSR), 46, 49, 56, 58, 70, 73, 77, 83, 119, 125, 126, 131; Administration Department, 66; Administrative Organs Department, 73; Central Committee, 61; Defense Council, 49, 64, 65, 66, 73, 81n, 124; Department of Special Propaganda, 66; Foreign Department, 66; General Staff, 70; leadership, 41, 58, 59, 64, 66, 73, 124, 132, 134; military, 45, 49, 66; Ministry of Defense, 65, 66, 124; Ministry of Interior, 66; Secretariat, 66; Soviet occupation of, 132, 133, 136, 150, 154n, 176, 177; technical espionage by, 77; working people of, 177
Czechoslovakia. *See* Czechoslovak Socialist Republic (CSSR).

Deception: *Kitman*, 139–140; of Lenin's New Economic Policy (NEP), 35; Lenin's peaceful coexistence strategy is a, 41, 42, 43, 122; of Marxism-Leninism, 3,
6, 16, 19, 21, 25n, 35; "parity," 123; role of KGB in, 127; Soviet covert activities, 89; Soviet instructions on, 73–76, 77, 133–135; Soviet linguistic, 6, 79–80, 102, 131–133, 138–154, 175; Soviet strategic, 7, 21, 34, 39, 42, 43, 44, 47, 48, 50, 51, 52nn, 55, 57, 63, 64, 66, 67, 69, 70, 75, 76, 79, 85, 87, 91, 94, 96, 101, 107, 109, 112, 114, 115, 119n, 120n, 127, 130–135
Declaration of Basic Principles of Relations Between the United States and the USSR (1972), 9, 146, 147, 149, 150
Decree on Peace (1918), Lenin's. *See* Lenin, Vladimir Ilyich.
Defense budget: Polish, 100; Soviet, 111, US, 120n; of Western nations, 117
Defense Committee (KOK), Poland, 100
Defense Council, CSSR, 124, 133
Defense Council, Poland, 100
Defense Council, USSR, 47, 48, 126, 128, 131, 133
Defense Intelligence Agency (DIA), US, 10
De Gaulle, Charles, 92n, 169
Department of Defense, US, 90
Department of Ideology, USSR, 21
Detente, 57, 91; as Soviet strategy, 9, 10, 179, 181; US views of, 18, 32, 35, 36, 62n
Dialectical materialism, 18, 145. *See also* Historical materialism.
Dictatorship of the proletariat, 1, 4, 16, 18, 20, 22, 29, 30, 33, 122
"Disarmament process," Soviet strategic, 101, 102, 111
Disinformation Department D of the KGB. *See* Committee of State Security (KGB)
Dobrynin, Anatoliy F., 52n, 55, 107
Double agents, Soviet. *See* Union of Soviet Socialist Republics (USSR). *See also* Fedora, Top Hat.
"Dropshot," 105
Dubcek, Alexander, 132
Dugway Proving Grounds, 67, 68. *See also* Chemical/biological weapons: Nerve gas testing by United States.

Dulles, John Foster, 32
Dzherzinski, Felix Edmundovich, 34

East Germany. *See* German Democratic Republic (GDR).
Eastern Europe, 49, 51, 58, 83, 118; boundaries of, 179; Communist parties of, 9, 33; emigrees from, 143; Soviet "democratic camp," 144; Soviet aggression in, 99, 153n. *See also* Warsaw Treaty Organization.
Eisenhower, Dwight D., 58, 170
Electromagnetic pulse (EMP), 165, 166
England. *See* United Kingdom.
Estonia, 98
Ethiopia, 37n
Europe: aerial photography zone in, 170; Communist party workers in, 150; detente and peace in, 177, 181; territorial changes in after World War II, 179
Exporting "counter-revolution," by United States, 31

Far East, 71, 99, 117, 170
FBI. *See* Federal Bureau of Investigation (FBI).
Federal Bureau of Investigation (FBI), 68–69
Federal Republic of Germany (FRG): 92n; "militarism," 66, 67; intelligence, 140
Fedora, 68–69. *See also* Top Hat.
Fedoseyev, P.N., 24
Felfe, Heinz, 140, 152n
Finland, 85, 99
First strike, 106, 107, 109, 116, 118
Ford, Gerald, 58
Ford, Robert A.D., 6, 37n
Foreign Ministry, USSR, 47, 48, 52n, 127
France, 30, 58, 92n, 117, 118, 148; France-USSR Accidents Agreement (1976), 161
"Free Flow." *See* Convergence Theory.
Free World, 117
Frunze, Mikhail V., 24, 32

"Full and complete disarmament," 163. *See also* "General and complete disarmament."

Gagarin, Yuri, 72. *See also* Space.
Gareev, Makhmut, 32
"General and complete disarmament," 6, 38, 73, 166, 168–170, 172, 174–176, 178, 181
General disarmament, 171, 180
Geneva Disarmament Commission, 115
Geneva Protocol (of 1925), 67, 69, 86, 114–115, 159. *See also* Chemical and biological weapons (CBW).
German Democratic Republic (GDR), 92n, 119n, 142, 170
Germany (pre-World War II), 30
Gierek, Edward, 100
Giscard d'Estaing, Valéry, 106
GKES. *See* State Committee for Economical Co-operation, USSR.
Glasnost, 107
Gornov, Alexander, 9
Great Britain. *See* United Kingdom.
Greece, 169
Gromyko, Andrei, 65
GRU. *See* Chief Intelligence Directorate of the Soviet General Staff.
"Gunshot," 105
GVS. *See* Main Military Council, USSR.

Hajek, Jiri, 125
Headquarters of Peace and Socialism, USSR, 43
Helsinki Final Act of 1975, 133, 160, 179
Historical materialism, 16, 20. *See also* Dialectical materialism.
Holland. *See* Netherlands, Kingdom of the.
Hoover, J. Edgar, 68
Hot Line Agreement of 1963, 104
Hungary, 83, 136
Hyland, William, 7

IAEA. *See* International Atomic Energy Agency (IAEA).
ICBMs. *See* Intercontinental ballistic missiles (ICBMs).
India: 9, 33, 43, 59, 122; Soviet-Indian Agreement, 59
Intelligence Administration No. 2, CSSR, 77; technical espionage by, 77
Intercontinental ballistic missiles (ICBMs), 110, 112, 117, 156, 157, 174
Intermediate-Range Ballistic Missiles, SS-20 Moratorium, 160
International Atomic Energy Agency Guidelines for Nuclear Transfers, INFCIRC/209 of 1974, 161; INFCIRC/254 of 1978, 161
International Court of Justice (ICJ), 103
International law, 23, 98, 103, 115
International Meeting of Communist and Workers' Parties (1969), 181
"International solidarity," 144, 177
International working-class movement, 176–178, 180, 182
Iron Curtain, 108
Israel, 69
Italy, 99, 169

Japan, 23, 58, 71, 99
Johnson, Lyndon B, 58

KGB. *See* Committee of State Security, USSR.
Kampuchea, 86, 115
Karpov, Viktor, 117
Kellogg-Briand Pact (1929), 98
Kennedy, John F., 58, 84, 136, 171
Kirilenko, Andrei P., 46, 47, 125, 127
Kirkpatrick, Jeane, 138, 145
Kissinger, Henry, 4, 6, 7, 18, 36n, 55, 100
Kitman, 139–140
KOK. *See* Defense Committee (KOK), Poland.
Kolegium, of the Ministry of Defense, CSSR, 124
Kolegium, of the Ministry of Defense, Poland, 100

Korean Airlines flight 007, 71
Korean War, 138
Kvitsinski, Yuri, 117

Language. *See* Deception: Linguistic.
Laos, 86
Larionov, Valentin V., 38
Laser weapons, 65
Latin American Nuclear Free Zone. *See* Treaty of Tlatelolco, Protocol II.
Latvia, 98
Law of the Sea Convention (1982), 159
League of Nations, 85, 99
"Learned professionals," 52n, 76, 77, 114; Coopted civilians, Soviet use of, 101, 113
Lenin, Vladimir Ilyich: and arms control, 46, 60, 123; and Bolshevik leadership, 141; Decree on Peace, 147; and disarmament, 39; and NEP, 34–35; objectives of Soviet strategy, 31; philosophic background of, 142; and peaceful coexistence theory, 5, 41, 95, 147–149; precepts of, 163; and Soviet ideology, 122; "temporary alliance," 147–149; use of Marxism as a tool in political strategy by, 3, 19–22; view of the United States, 54
Lenin Peace Prize, 77
Leninism, 3, 6, 7, 20, 147, 148
"Liberation" (in Soviet terminology): of Third World countries, 144; theology, 145; national movements, 150, 180, 182; peoples' national struggles for, 176, 177
Libya, 169
Limited Test Ban Treaty (1963), 65, 158
Liquidation of private interests, 33
Litvinov, Maksim, 141
"Low-intensity operations," Soviet assistance for, 150

MAD. *See* Mutual Assured
  Destruction (MAD).
Main Administration for Material and
  Technical Supply, USSR, 47, 127
Main Military Council (GVS—*Glavniy
  Voyenniy Sovet*), USSR, 100, 101
Main Political Administration, USSR,
  59, 70, 71
Main Political Administration of the
  Army and Navy, USSR, 124
Malek, Ivan, 77
Malenkov, Georgi M., 142
Malinovskiy, Rodion Ya., 45, 123,
  124
Marx, Karl, 3, 20, 63, 140, 142
Marxism, 113, 142–145
Marxism-Leninism: and arms control,
  38; as a basis of Soviet policy, 1–6,
  27–31, 34; and deception, 63, 113,
  122, 135; and decisionmaking and
  risk assessment, 121; and
  disarmament, 180; goal to destroy
  capitalism, 182; and Khrushchev,
  25; and image of the United
  States, 55, 56, 58, 109; materialism
  of, 145; opponents of, 33, 102; as a
  political theory, 142, 143; and role
  of doctrine, 115; and role of Soviet
  society, 10, 13–24; and Russian
  language, 132–134; and Stalin, 41;
  theses, 163; and working class, 39
Maskirovka, 110, 120n; misleading the
  enemy, by Soviet Union, 7, 73, 75,
  133. *See also* Deception.
Matlock, Jack, 85
Media. *See* Press.
Military Industrial Commission
  (*Voyenno Promishlennaya
  Komisya*—VPK), USSR, 100
Military–industrial complex, of the
  West, 49, 51, 86, 89, 111, 128,
  130
Military–police complex, Soviet, 102,
  105, 106, 108, 109, 151. *See also
  Nomenklatura.*
Military procurement programs, Soviet,
  33, 77
Ministry of Interior, USSR, 56, 65, 66,
  77
Ministry of Internal Affairs
  (*Ministerstvo Vnutrenikh
  Del*—MVD), 101, 108, 115

Ministry of National Defense, Poland,
  100
Mironov, N.R., 42, 46, 47
Mirror imaging: of Soviet Union by
  United States, 7, 33, 34, 79, 94, 95,
  162; of United States by Soviet
  Union, 57, 94
MIRV. *See* Multiple
  Independently-Targetable
  Reentry Vehicle (MIRV).
Molotov, Vyacheslav, 141
Moment II, 105. *See also* Zvezda
  II.
Monitoring technology, US, 64
Montreux Convention (1936), 159
"Moral equivalence" theory, 151
Mozambique, 37n
Multiple Independently-Targetable
  Reentry Vehicle (MIRV): US
  development of MIRVed
  warheads, 174 anti-MIRV limits in
  SALT treaties, 157
Mutual Assured Destruction (MAD),
  79
MVD. *See* Ministry of Internal Affairs
  (MVD).
Myth of unanimity, 142

NATO. *See* North Atlantic Treaty
  Organization (NATO).
National Security Council, US, 85
"Negotiation," in Soviet terminology,
  146–147
Netherlands, Kingdom of the, 30
New Economic Plan (NEP), 33, 34–35,
  60
Neyev, Valery, 9
Nicaragua, 141, 145
Nitze, Paul, 27
Nixon, Richard M., 2, 4, 6, 7, 9, 18, 35,
  37n, 55, 58, 68, 100, 146, 179, 181
Nobel Prize, 114
Nomenklatura, 14; *nomenklaturist*, 14,
  143; *nomklats*, 143
Nonproliferation Treaty of 1968, 161
North Atlantic Treaty Organization
  (NATO): and arms control, 10,
  39, 48, 49, 66, 74, 94, 106, 111,
  118, 129, 181; border with
  Czechoslovakia, 136;
  developments in military

technology, 128; forces, 124; France out of military integrated command structure, 92n; military buildup of, 134; military headquarters, 176; parity with Warsaw Pact, 128; and Soviet military superiority over, 123; and Soviet risk assessment of, 83; as target of Soviet deceptive operations, 134; treaties with Warsaw Pact countries, 147; Non-aggression Pact (1929), 98, 170

Novosti Press Agency, 9, 39, 42–43, 51

Nuclear blackmail, by USSR, 89, 124

Nuclear disarmament, 40, 42, 175

Nuclear Non-Proliferation Treaty (1970), 23n

Nuclear test ban, 64, 72, 166, 167, 171, 175

Nuclear Test Moratorium (1958–1961), 71, 158, 164, 165, 171, 177, 182

Nuclear war, threatened by Soviet propaganda, 6, 8, 23, 24, 41–42, 51, 67, 88, 106, 109, 117, 118, 130, 170; protests against, 175; Soviet fear of, 88

Nuclear weapons tests, 167, 170, 171, 177

"Nuclear winter," 79

Obligations, Soviet view of treaty, 102–104, 109, 110, 112–114

Offensive denial, 71, 73, 90, 115, 133–135

Ogarkov, Nikolai V., 71, 100, 115, 120, 147–149

On-site inspection, 110, 166. *See also* Verification.

Operations Main Administration, USSR, 46, 47, 49, 63; "special state interests," 63

Operations Plan, CSSR, 124

Operations Plan, USSR, 47, 77, 126

"Opportunistic," 4–5, 35

Outer Space Treaty: of 1967, 119n, 161

Pakistan, 59

Parity, rough strategic, 107, 109, 118, 123, 128

Party. *See* Communist Party of the Soviet Union (CPSU).

Peace: and achievement of communism, 31; and arms control, 38–40; in Bolshevik slogan, 141, 153n; cause of, 165; communism brings, 167, 168; and end of political differences between East and West, 18; in Europe, 175; and KGB, 77; and linguistics, 141; movements, 77, 130, 182; and peaceful coexistence, 5, 6, 8, 61, 80, 129; "peace-loving" image of Soviet Union, 64, 88, 90, 94, 95, 97, 110, 111, 118, 164, 177; proposals, 123; Soviet "battle" for, 163, 164; Soviet definition of, 147, 149; and Soviet image of US as opponent of, 51, 54, 57, 104, 107; Soviet propaganda, 168, 170, 175; and success of, 114; as tactic of revolution, 20; and treaty making, 23; and underlying Soviet philosophy of aggressiveness, 24, 32. *See also* Peaceful coexistence.

Peaceful coexistence (*mirnoe sosushchestvovanie*): and arms control, 38, 49, 88, 96, 147–149, 168; and disarmament, 40–44, 178; and discussions between Kennedy and Khrushchev, 83, 84; and ideological warfare, 106; as intelligence objective, 46; and Khrushchev, 76; Lenin's concept of, 41, 95; and Marxism-Leninism, 17; and peace as Soviet propaganda, 5–6, 8, 61, 80, 129; and Soviet policy, 136, 176, 177; and Soviet superiority, 31; use in deceiving the West, 164; and use of trade and economic assistance, 90, 91, 122

Pegov, N.M., 9

People's Republic of China (PRC), 4, 14, 103, 117, 118

Pepich, Egit, 125, 127

Pipes, Richard, 7, 36n

Poland, 70, 77, 78, 92, 98–101, 113, 119nn, 120n, 170; armed forces, 78, 113; Communist Party, 23; "Lesson of 1980," 108; martial law in, 92; Military Intelligence

Directorate (ZII), 70, 77, 101, 119n; secret police, 78
Politburo, CSSR, 65, 81n
Politburo, Poland, 100
Politburo, USSR, 27, 47, 48, 56, 64, 68, 133, 162, 182
Politico-strategic objectives, of USSR, 99, 102
Ponomarev, Boris, 40, 55
Portugal, 30
Press: "antisocialist," 132; communist, 43, 45, 46, 72, 105, 115, 142, 146, 165, 172; conference, 140; freedom of the, 130; "neutral," 46; Third World, 46, 86; Western, 40, 45, 46, 56, 59, 67, 68, 72, 77, 87, 95, 96, 103, 172; worldwide, 86, 135
Prevention of Nuclear War, Agreement on (of 1973), 104
Proletarian internationalism, 3, 20, 30, 122, 128
Proletarian revolution, 16. See also Dictatorship of the proletariat.
Proletariat, 15, 17, 18, 24, 31, 39
Protocol of Moscow (1929), 98
Pugwash Conferences, 76–79, 113
Purges, in USSR, 33–35, 141, 145, 162, 164. See also Stalin, Josef.

R&D Plan. See Research and Development Plan, USSR.
Reagan, Ronald, 13, 54, 58, 71–73, 87, 90, 104, 107, 131
Reagan–Gorbachev summit, 13
"Reconnaissance by negotiation," 101
"Red Revolution," 133; "Red Army," 145
Research and Development Plan, USSR, 126
Revolution: 1917 Russian, 103, 147, 152n; forces, 183; world, 143; Sandinista, 145; process of, 150; forces of counter-, 177
Revolutionary war movement, 5, 30, 32, 43, 124, 135. See also Wars of national liberation.
Reykjavik, 108, 111
Ribbentrop–Molotov Pact, 98, 99

Romania, 84, 98, 119n
Rumania. See Romania.
Rurarz, Zdzislaw, 23, 48, 50, 55, 59, 70, 76, 77, 79
Russian tradition in Soviet policy, 2, 22, 63, 84, 97, 104, 112

SALT. See Strategic Arms Limitation Talks (SALT).
Satellites of USSR. See Soviet bloc nations.
Savinkin, N.I., 126
Schuman, Tomas (formerly Yuri Bezmenov), 42, 76, 78, 80, 81n.
SDI. See Strategic Defense Initiative (SDI).
Seabed Treaty of 1971, 161
Seabed Arms Control Treaty of 1972, 23n
Secret police, 30, 113. See also KGB; Poland, ZII.
Security Council. See United Nations.
Sejna, Jan, 8, 15–16, 31, 35, 41, 42, 44, 47, 48, 49, 56, 57, 61, 64, 65–66, 70, 76, 77, 84
Semantics, See Deception.
Shelepin, Alexander, 42, 76
Shevchenko, Arkadiy, 52n, 69–70, 79
Smirnov, Leonid V., 100
"Social progress," 17, 23, 24, 58
Socialist internationalism, 57, 177
Sokolov, Sergei L., 105
Sokolovskiy, Vasiliy D., 115, 175
Sonnenfeldt, Hal, 7
"Sovereignty," in Soviet terminology, 149–150; applied to Czechoslovakia, 154n; consolidation of, 174
Soviet bloc countries, 31, 45, 81n; and COMECON, 50; and Pugwash strategy, 78; and Soviet political strategy, 8, 129; Czechoslovakia, 66; influence on Third World, 49; military buildup of, 128; Non-Aggression Pact (1929), 98, 170; restraint of trade and economic assistance to, 87; role in exploiting the West, 41; Western influence in, 83, 109. See also Warsaw Pact Treaty Organization, and Eastern European satellites.

Soviet Union. *See* Union of Soviet Socialist Republics (USSR).
Space, 40, 50, 55, 64–66; Czechoslovakia directed by USSR to do research on weapons for use in, 65, 66; military applications of, 65, 66, 105, 116; nuclear weapons in, 170–172, 178; US blamed for "militarizing," 171; "Space Strike Arms," 55, 105; strikes from, 181; USSR first in, 72, 172; USSR plans to control, 89, 125, 129; USSR refusal to adhere to 1967 Outer Space Treaty, 65, 89; weapons in, 64–66. *See also* Outer Space Treaty of 1967.
Spain, 30
Stalin, Josef, 15, 29, 80, 99; and Bolshevik leadership, 141; collectivization of agriculture under, 34; Comintern abolished under, 42–43; death of, 40–41; and Khrushchev, 164; Khrushchev's "secret speech" denouncing, 52n; and linguistics, 138–139, 142; and military leadership, 116; and the *nomenklatura*, 162–163; strategy after death of, 46; post-Stalin USSR, 122; "Stalin" Constitution of the USSR, 150
State Committee for Economical Co-operation (GKES), USSR, 59
State Department, US, 10, 91
State terrorism, US accused of by USSR, 71, 135
Strategic Arms Limitation Talks (SALT), 5, 52n, 79; SALT I, 80, 100, 104, 163, 176, 179–182; SALT I Interim Agreement, 156; 1974 Protocol to the SALT I ABM Treaty, 104, 156; SALT II, 73, 85, 104, 112, 157; dismantling procedures, 156; Soviet objectives in, 79; US adherence to unratified SALT II, 85
Strategic Deception War Board (*Voyennoye Upravleniye Strategicheskovo Obmana*), 112. *See also* Deception.
Strategic Defense Initiative (SDI), 55, 79, 89–90, 105, 107, 111, 114, 116, 118, 120n

Strauss, Franz Josef, 67
Sun Tzu, 10
Supreme Soviet, USSR, 45, 151, 164, 175, 176
Suslov, Mikhail, 42, 44, 46

T-2. *See* Yellow Rain.
"Tactical flexibility," 51, 130
Technological revolution, 180
Terrorism, Soviet-sponsored, 71
Thailand, 169
Think tanks. *See* Moment II, and Zvezda II.
Third World: adoption of policies favorable to Soviet bloc, 49; arms sales to, 127; and disarmament, 40; and emerging countries, 145; "liberation" of, 144; and press institutions, 46; and propaganda, 75; and revolutionary process, 31, 41, 45; and Soviet deception of, 90, 135; and Soviet risk assessment, 84; and support for Soviet arms control policies, 51, 128
Threshold Test Ban Treaty of 1974 & 1976 Protocol, 104, 158
"Top Hat," 68–69. *See also* "Fedora."
Toxin weapons. *See* Chemical and biological weapons (CBW).
Trade and economic assistance, from the West to the USSR, 31, 35, 61, 87, 90, 91, 92, 95, 122
Treaty of Riga (1912), 98
Treaty of Tlatelolco, Protocol II, 161
Treaty on Principles Governing the Activities of States in the Exploration and Use of Outer Space, Including the Moon and Other Celestial Bodies, 65, 66, 89
Trotsky, Leon, 141
Turkey, 169; Turkish Straits, 159

Ukraine, USSR, 98, 99, 141
UN. *See* United Nations (UN).
Union of Soviet Socialist Republics (USSR)
 atmospheric test series, 72; Constitution of, 15, 28, 121;

Index

counterintelligence, military, 49, 65, 75, 127;
decisionmakers, 99–102, 103;
double agents, 68–69;
elite, 152n;
"empire," 118, 168;
espionage, 77, 87, 90, 135;
Foreign Ministry, 79;
General Staff, 46–48, 50, 56, 59, 66, 71, 89, 101, 127;
image of United States, 13, 51, 55–57
military: Air Force, 59; and arms control, 48, 49, 52n, 176;
  and knowledge of, 55; armed forces, 58, 78, 120n; Army, 32, 99, 110, 145, 172;
  "bourgeois" officers, 131; buildup, 74, 182; Chief of the General Staff, 47, 56, 100–101, 120, 126; complex, 105; conventional/chemical forces, 114–115; doctrine, 45, 88, 115; exercises, 160; experts of, 59; nuclear forces, 54, 64, 105; objectives of the, 44, 117; officials/leadership, 77, 105, 106, 116; peace, 147; posture, 101; power guarantees programs, 94; research and development (R&D), 77, 89; security, 96; specializations in, 113; Strategic Rocket Troops/Forces, 45, 55; strategies, 45, 74, 183; use of deception in, 73, 74; and VPK, 100;
policy influenced by Marxism-Leninism:
  and risk assessment, 83–86, 87–90, 121, 136; morality associated with, 71; strategic goals of, 1–3, 5, 8, 22–23, 28, 29, 31, 32, 74, 76, 104;
  Western perspectives of, 7
Propaganda: apparatus for, 23, 41, 67, 70, 86, 95;
  and arms control, 8, 30, 44, 48, 49, 66, 67, 70, 124–127;
  belief in own, 105, 107;
  "bourgeois," 32, 131;

communist, 145;
counterpropaganda, 90; on detente, 9; Department, 46, 48, 56, 125; and disarmament, 40; hostile intent toward US, 55, 59; image of the US, 57; and linguistics, 151; and long-range planning, 129; and Marxism-Leninism, 13, 14, 15; money spent on, 86, 90; occupation of Czechoslovakia, 132; and offensive weapons, 86, 90; role of satellite nations in, 126; sheep operation, 81n; and success of, 86, 90; use of scientists, 77; of war, 41, 164, 170; "white," "gray," and "black," 144; and World Peace Organization, 78;
United Kingdom, 8, 58, 118, 167, 170, 173; nuclear weapons plans, 117; US military bases in, 169; United Kingdom–USSR Accidents Agreement (1976), 161
United Nations (UN), 68, 79, 103; General Assembly of, 65, 99; resolutions, 65, 89; Security Council, 99
United States
  Congress, 2, 9, 69, 91, 115, 120, 151;
  Economic sanctions, 92;
  Intelligence organizations, 9, 68, 71, 88, 89, 105.
    See also Central Intelligence Agency (CIA), and Federal Bureau of Investigation—FBI).
  Military, 72, 90; Army, 58, 67, 68;
    defense planning, 94; doctrine, 117; intelligence, 69; nuclear weapons, 117; programs, 44, 48; strategy, 117;
  Weapons development programs, 89;
  US–USSR Accidents Agreement (1971), 161;
  US–USSR Direct

Communications Link Agreement, 161
"Unjust wars," 38
Ushakov, Aleksandr, 19, 21
Ustinov, Dmitri F., 100

Velikhov, Yevgeny, 114
Verification, 79, 85, 110, 145, 162, 166–168. *See also* On-site inspection.
Vietnam, 67, 86, 159
Vocabulary. *See* Deception.
Voslensky, Michael, 14, 76, 78–79, 143, 147
VPK. *See* Military Industrial Commission (*Voyenno Promishlennaya Komisya*—VPR).

Wars of national liberation, 30, 43, 45. *See also* Revolutionary war movement.
Warsaw Pact. *See* Warsaw Treaty Organization.
Warsaw Treaty Organization: annulment of, 181; and arms buildup, 105; and arms control, 49, 74–75, 128, 129, 132–136; and COMECON, 50; Commander-in-Chief of, 49; communist countries, 103; defenses, 134; and disinformation, 112; forces, 64, 67, 74, 75, 83, 136, 181; "fraternal assistance by," 144; leaders, 84, 132, 136; and military research, 70; strategy, 124; treaties, 65, 123, 128, 147
West Germany. *See* Federal Republic of Germany (FRG).

Western alliance. *See* North Atlantic Treaty Organization (NATO).
Western Europe, 49, 50, 51, 60, 84, 90, 95, 128, 130; US nuclear weapons deployment in, 112, 117
Western scientific community, 113, 114
Workers' revolution, 3
Working class, 1, 3, 16, 22, 24, 29, 30, 39, 120n. *See also* Communism.
World Communist Conference (1960), 6
World communist movement, 42, 43, 45, 126. *See also* World revolutionary process.
World communist revolution, 126
World Congress for General Disarmament and Peace, 168, 171
World Peace Council, 78, 113
World revolutionary process, 6, 30, 31, 32, 34, 78, 126. *See also* World communist movement.

Yalta Accords, 99
Yashin, Yu., 55, 105,
Yasyukov, M., 98, 101
Yellow Rain, 86, 115. *See also* Chemical and biological weapons (CBW).
Yepishev, Alexei A., 59
Yom Kippur War, 69
Yugoslavia, 103

Zakharov, Matvei V., 58, 66
Zamyatin, Leonid, 118–119
Zhivkov, Todor, 32
ZII. *See* Poland: Military intelligence.
Zinoviev, Gregory, 141
Zvezda II, 105. *See also* Moment II.

About the Author

Joseph D. Douglass, Jr. is a leading U.S. national security affairs consultant. He is the author of *The Soviet Theater Nuclear Offensive* (1976) and *Soviet Military Strategy in Europe* (1980); co-author of *Soviet Strategy for Nuclear War* (1979), *Conventional War and Escalation* (1981), *CBW: The Poor Man's Atomic Bomb* (1984), *Decision-Making in Communist Countries* (1986), and *America the Vulnerable: The Threat of Biological Warfare* (1987); co-editor of *Selected Readings from Military Thought (1963–1973)* (1982) and of *Ending a Nuclear War: Are the Superpowers Prepared?* (forthcoming).